## OPERATION: SADDLEBAGS

Report of Proceedings

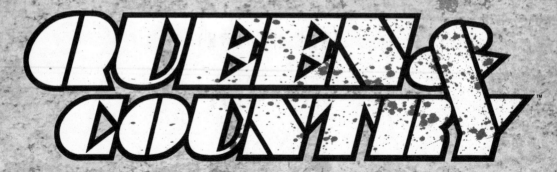

## OPERATION: SADDLEBAGS

### Report of Proceedings

compiled by
# GREG RUCKA

illustrated by
# MIKE NORTON & STEVE ROLSTON

# INTRODUCTION
## by GAIL SIMONE

As a long-time and semi-pathetic Rucka admirer, I've been devoutly following this book since the beginning. And I've come to believe that what makes it not just good, but the best espionage series ever done in comics, (more about that later), is what Greg's excised from the book—what he's snipped out— sometimes surgically, with a scalpel, sometimes brutally,  with a cleaver. He's formed an anti-recipe, where what makes the book special is what you take away from the stew.

First, the glamour.

All the elements of the cliché-ridden kiss kiss bang bang are here; the exotic settings, the betrayals, the gun battles, the steamy and slightly desperate couplings of people who know they'll never meet again. The average Q&C plot could well be the springboard for a thousand Bond-wannabes, as the agents of our side find themselves outnumbered by traitors and terrorists, or protecting classified documents in between ski runs at St. Moritz.

But here's where the pinking shears come out, and SNIP SNIP SNIP, suddenly the spy world is de-mythologized completely.

Suddenly, the Swiss Alps are just another setting, no more awe-inspiring than a back alley or an office building. Suddenly, an orgy isn't an excuse for swimsuit model eye-candy, but rather evokes a feeling of sadness and impatience.  A head office that smells of coffee and desperation replaces MI-6 and the flame-thrower underwear of Q Division.

And thank God, Tara Chace replaces any number of infallible, wisecracking super-agents. Tara, who limps after a fight, who has sweaty, unphotogenic sex, and who prefers her liquor not in a shaken martini, but straight from the bottle while in the shower, as a way to dull the moment.

Tara, who smokes and drinks too much, and carries a grudge a long, long time. Tara, who'll kick your ass if you betray her, but won't let you see a single tear. No Aston Martin and designer gowns for Ms. T. Chace.

I think she might have ruined me for other spies.

Next, the idealism.

Sometimes, reading Queen and Country, it appears that the only true believers are terrorists and fanatics. The agents in these stories don't pause to make speeches.  Greg's been at them again, SNIP SNIP SNIP. They hide their feelings, and more than one mission seems to be motored not by patriotism or a desire to protect the innocent, but by a simple 'we can't let the opponent win,' mentality.

It's thrilling, but a little bit sad, to see Tara and the other Minders risking their lives and peace of mind over tasks so esoteric.  Because we care about her, we want her life to be worth more than this, her loyalty to be sold more dearly, but in Tara's world (and Greg's),  an agent can easily be sent to their death over faulty information on a meaningless mission by an uncaring government.

That might tend to sap the gung ho right out of a body.

When things go ill for the Minders, as they often do, there's a world-worn resignation on their part, as though they expect to be pissed on in their chosen careers. They know full well that in the real world, politics is motivated by the rich and powerful exchanging favors and petty thefts, rather than a mad scientist with a plan to blot out the sun.

No one on Tara's team is getting a medal for risking their lives, let alone a submersible Lotus automobile. They're simply doing their job.

Finally, most importantly, the bullshit.

The last and most essential bit of fat-trimming Greg does is the blood-spattered hacking away of all the nonsense, the trivia, the flashy, and the unessential. Words aren't wasted in this series, and actions have consequences. A single issue may jump from the (fascinating) tedium of the Special Section head office, to the raw, exposed nerve of Tara's personal life, and back again with whipcrack speed. It's the rhythm of real life, not the latest Fleming imitator.

Rucka doesn't insult the reader with easy morality, clumsy exposition, bad guys who can't shoot and heroes who can't miss, bombs that get defused with two seconds on the clock, or other such action movie nonsense. He gives us instead a work environment not that different from that which we've all experienced, with the ambitions, loyalties, kindnesses, and lack thereof that we've all been part of in our own lives. And he gives us a lead character we alternately want to comfort and yell at, in Tara Chace, possibly the most complex and fascinating heroine in comics. Charlie's Angels is fine for what it is, but Rucka's not playing that game with THIS dame.

So, yeah, I love this book for what's NOT in it.

And that's no bullshit.

It's unfair of me to speak only of the writing on *Q&C*, so a word about the art, and I hope the many artists who have slaved over the book will forgive me for focusing on the bit I'm a little more knowledge-able about.

I was actually a Rolston skeptic when I first heard of the book's debut issue. I wasn't familiar with Steve's style, and the preview pieces I'd seen seemed far too light for a dark espionage book.

Happily, I can admit that I was an idiot, and Oni's original choice is well-made, and even more happily, he's joined by another favorite of mine, Mike Norton. All due respect to the other artists who have worked on *Queen & Country*, these two guys really know how to make the book sing, with the same kind of understatement and integrity that Greg brings to the writing. The lean panel arrangements and sparse (but textbook-perfect) composition are the perfect compliment to Greg's tight script, and have made me a complete devotee.

Like the author, Norton and Rolston don't have time for nonsense.

Bless them all for their restraint.

Gail Simone
February 2006

---

*Gail Simone is the smart and funny writer of about a bazillion* Simpsons *comics for Bongo,* Birds of Prey, Action Comics, *and more for DC Comics, and the co-creator of* Killer Princesses *with artist Lea Hernandez and published by Oni Press. She does have time for nonsense and comic readers worldwide are quite better off for it.*

# PROLOGUE

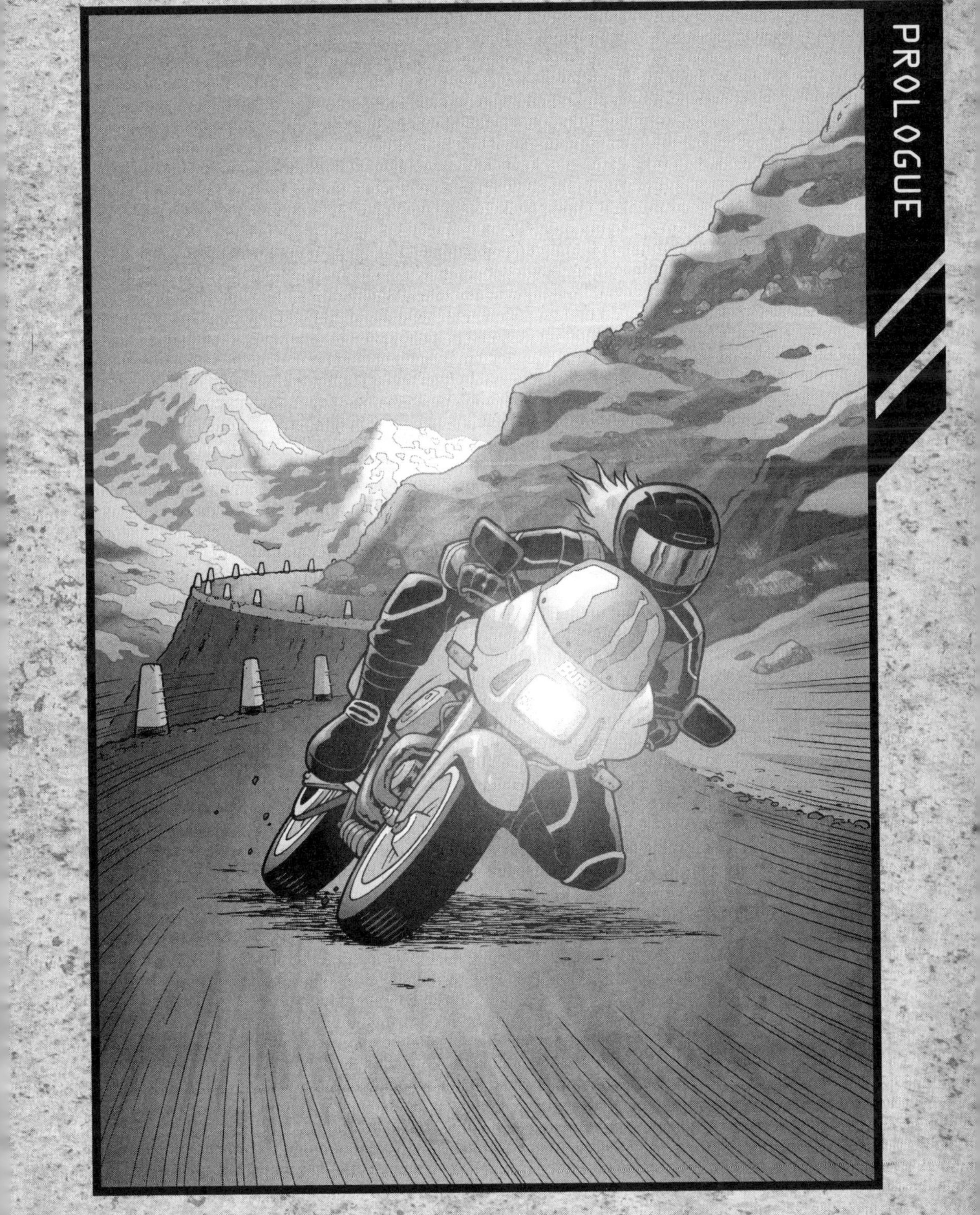

# ROSTER

### TARA CHACE

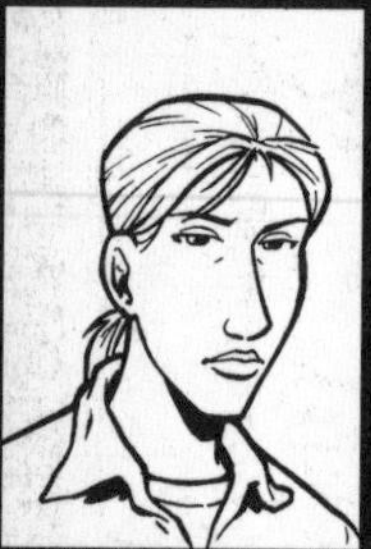

Special Operations Officer, designated Minder Two. Entering her third year as Minder.

### FRANCES BARCLAY

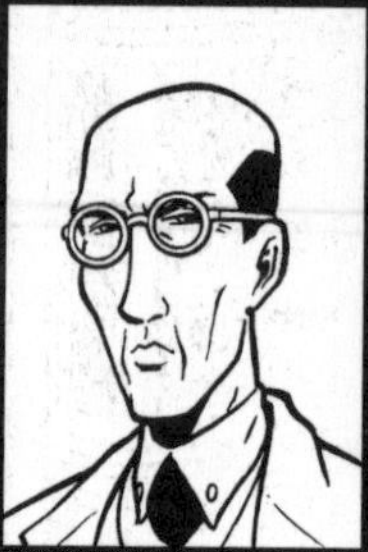

Chief of Service, also known as 'C.' Distinguished service as CIA-Liaison, Chairman of the Joint Intelligence Committee, and as Head of Station Prague (85-88), Saigon (89-91), and Paris (91-94).

### TOM WALLACE

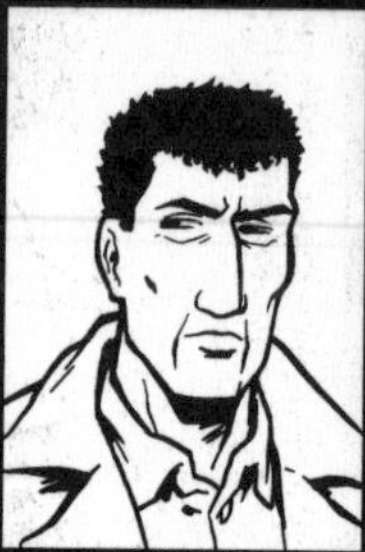

Head of the Special Section, a Special Operations Officer with the designation Minder One. Responsible for the training and continued well-being of his unit, both at home and in the field. Six year veteran of the Minders.

### PAUL CROCKER

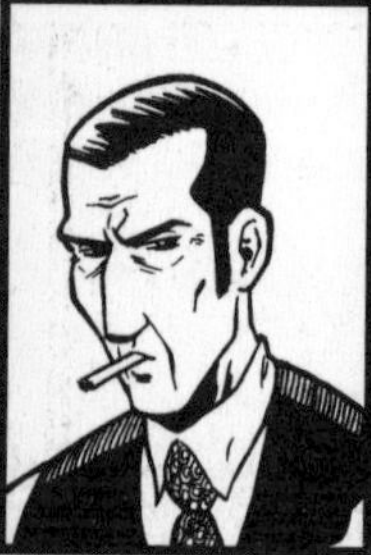

Director of Operations, encompassing all field work in all theaters of operations.

In addition to commanding individual stations, has direct command of the Special Section—sometimes referred to as Minders—used for special operations.

### Nick Poole

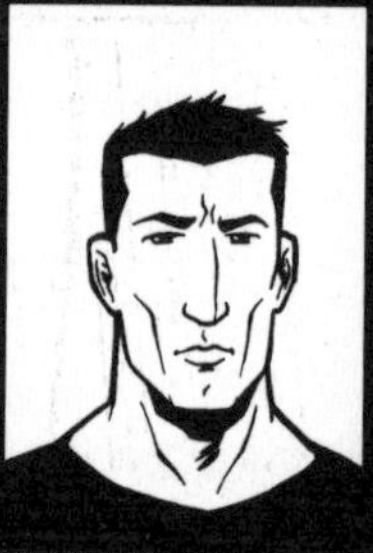

Former Sergeant in the S.A.S. and the third man to occupy the position of Minder Three in less than a year.

### DONALD WELDON

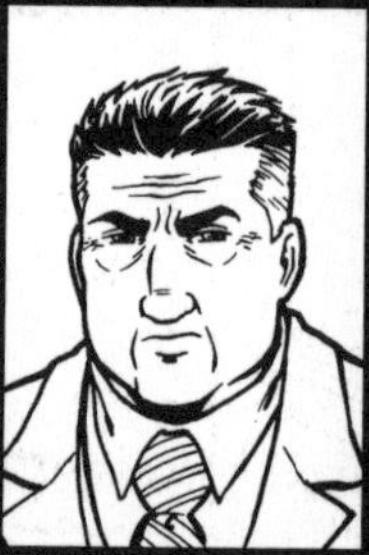

Deputy Chief of Service, has oversight of all aspects of Intelligence gathering and operations. Immediate superior to Crocker.

# OPS ROOM STAFF:

### KATE

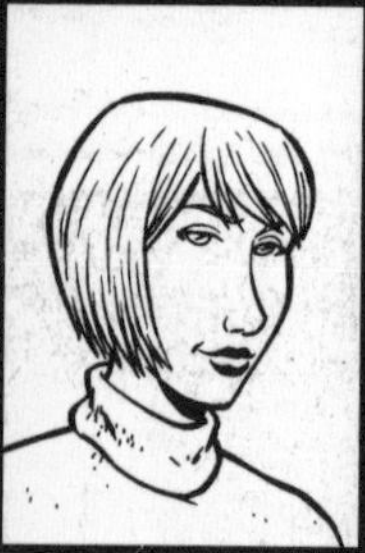

Personal Assistant to Paul Crocker, termed P.A. to D-Ops. Possibly the hardest and most important job in the Service.

### RON

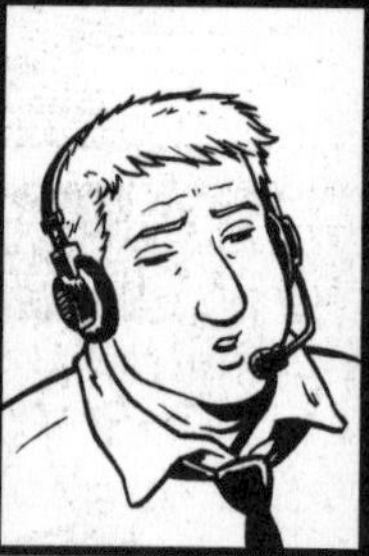

Duty Operations Officer, responsible for monitoring the status and importance of all incoming intelligence, both from foreign stations and other sources.

### ALEXIS

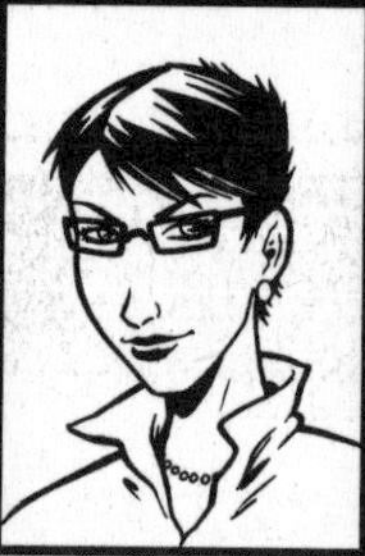

Mission Control Officer (also called Main Communications Officer)-responsible for maintaining communications between the Operations Room and the agents in the field.

# OTHERS:

### WALTER SECCOMBE

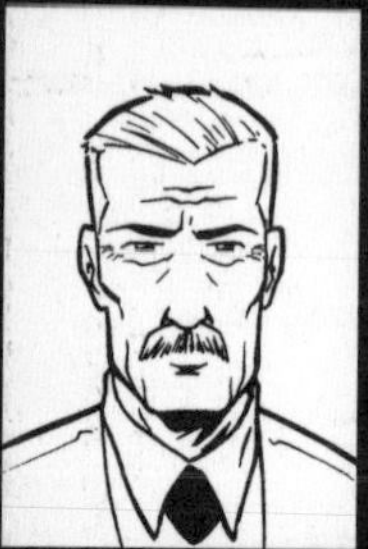

Permanent Under Secretary to the Foreign Office, a career civil servant with intimate knowledge of the inner workings of all levels of Government, and with the savvy to negotiate the corridors of power to achieve his own ends.

### EDWARD KITTERING

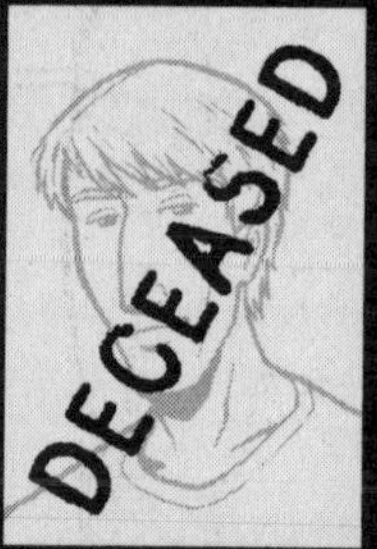
DECEASED

Special Operations Officer, designated Minder Three. Has been with the Special Section for less than a year.

### BRIAN BUTLER

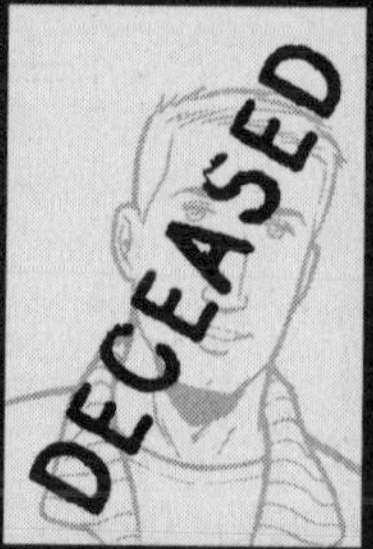
DECEASED

A former sergeant in one of the British Army's oldest and most respected regimens. An unique individual who actually requested assignment with special section.

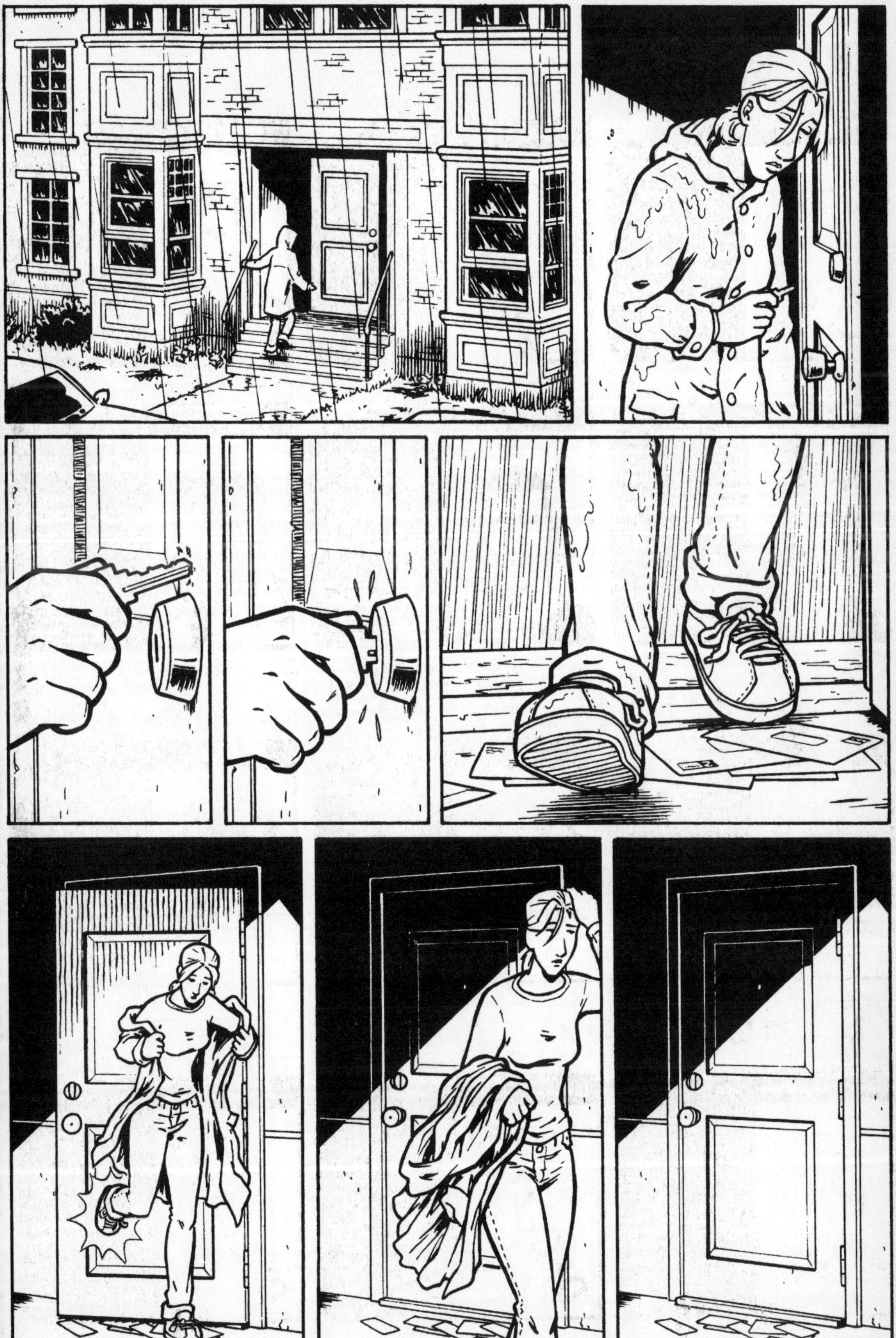

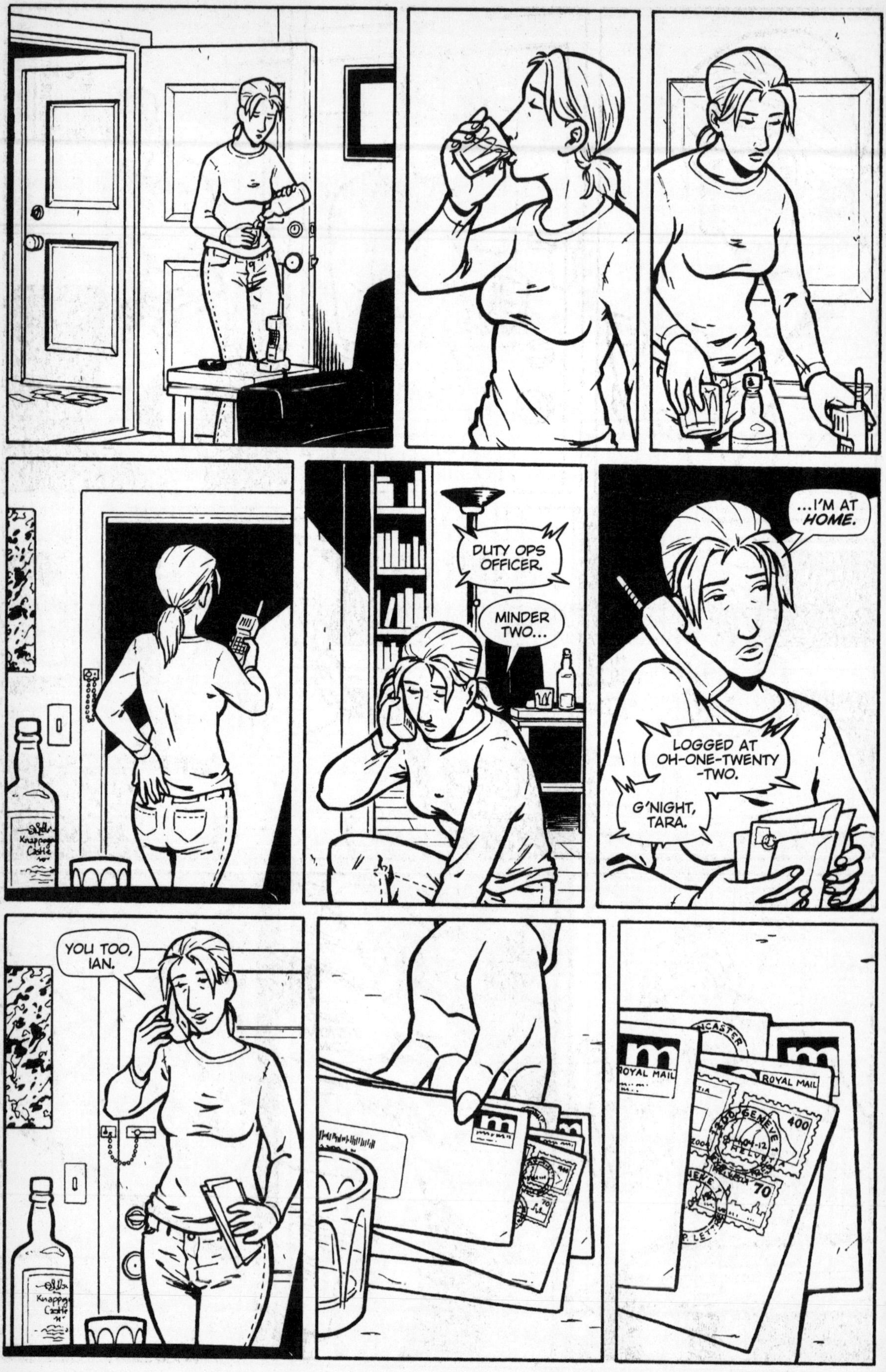
DUTY OPS OFFICER.
MINDER TWO...
...I'M AT *HOME.*
LOGGED AT OH-ONE-TWENTY -TWO.
G'NIGHT, TARA.
YOU TOO, IAN.
ROYAL MAIL
ROYAL MAIL

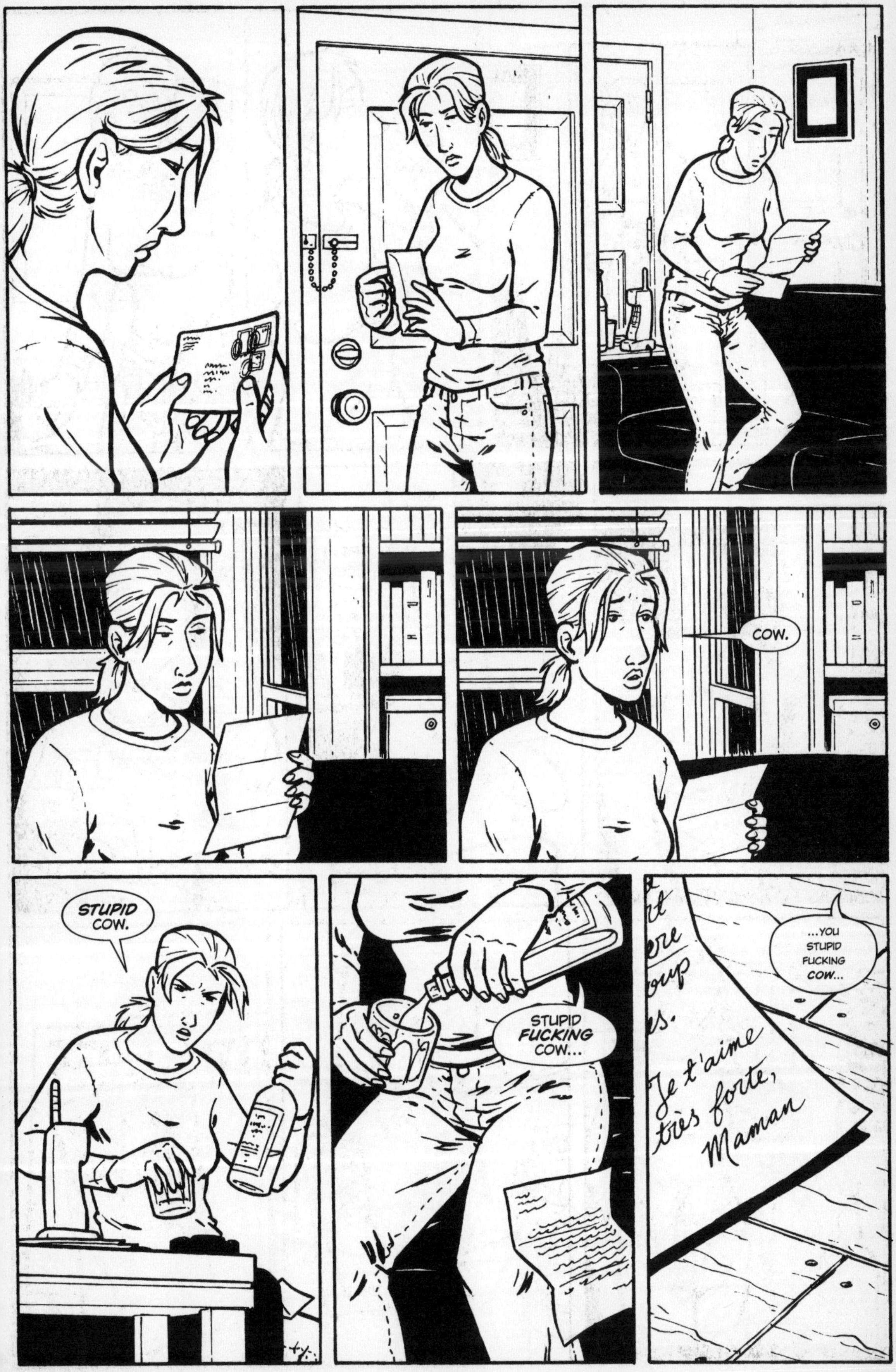
COW.
STUPID COW.
STUPID FUCKING COW...
...YOU STUPID FUCKING COW...
Je t'aime très forte, Maman

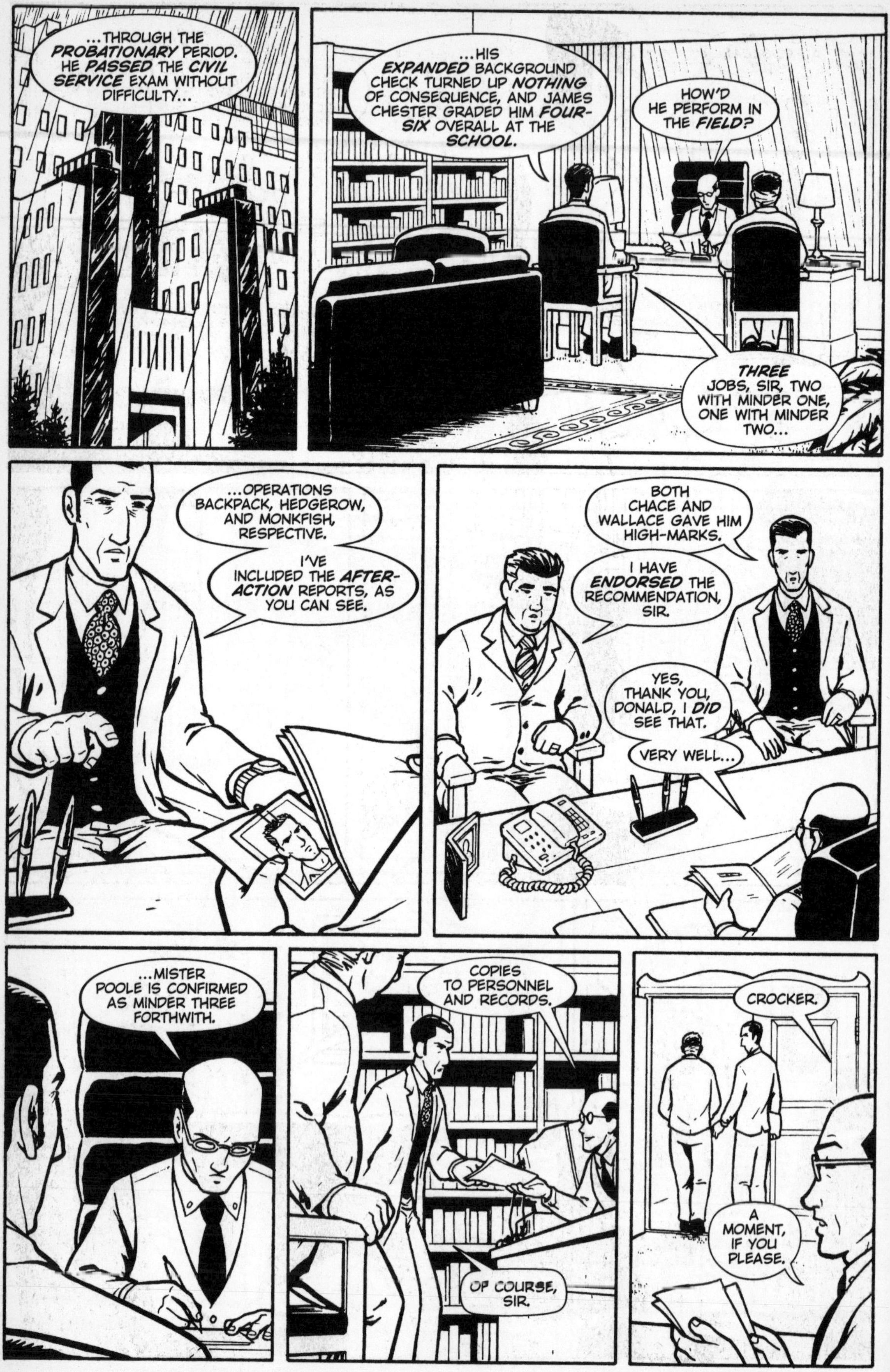
...THROUGH THE PROBATIONARY PERIOD. HE PASSED THE CIVIL SERVICE EXAM WITHOUT DIFFICULTY...
...HIS EXPANDED BACKGROUND CHECK TURNED UP NOTHING OF CONSEQUENCE, AND JAMES CHESTER GRADED HIM FOUR-SIX OVERALL AT THE SCHOOL.
HOW'D HE PERFORM IN THE FIELD?
THREE JOBS, SIR, TWO WITH MINDER ONE, ONE WITH MINDER TWO...
...OPERATIONS BACKPACK, HEDGEROW, AND MONKFISH, RESPECTIVE.
I'VE INCLUDED THE AFTER-ACTION REPORTS, AS YOU CAN SEE.
BOTH CHACE AND WALLACE GAVE HIM HIGH-MARKS.
I HAVE ENDORSED THE RECOMMENDATION, SIR.
YES, THANK YOU, DONALD, I DID SEE THAT.
VERY WELL...
...MISTER POOLE IS CONFIRMED AS MINDER THREE FORTHWITH.
COPIES TO PERSONNEL AND RECORDS.
OF COURSE, SIR.
CROCKER.
A MOMENT, IF YOU PLEASE.

lettering by
**JOHN DRANSKI**

introduction by
**GAIL SIMONE**

cover art by
**MIKE NORTON**

cover colors by
**GUY MAJOR**

chapter break tones by
**DAVE STEWART** and **GUY MAJOR**

book design by
**KEITH WOOD**

edited by
**JAMES LUCAS JONES**

Published by Oni Press, Inc.
**JOE NOZEMACK**, publisher
**JAMES LUCAS JONES**, senior editor
**RANDAL C. JARRELL**, managing editor

Original Queen & Country logo designed by
**STEVEN BIRCH** @ Servo

This collects issues 25-28 of the Oni Press comics series *Queen & Country*™.

ONI PRESS, INC.
1305 SE Martin Luther King Jr. Blvd
Suite A
Portland, OR 97214
USA

www.onipress.com • www.gregrucka.com
www.ihatemike.com • www.steverolston.com

First edition: March 2005
ISBN 1-932664-14-9

1 3 5 7 9 10 8 6 4 2

PRINTED IN CANADA.

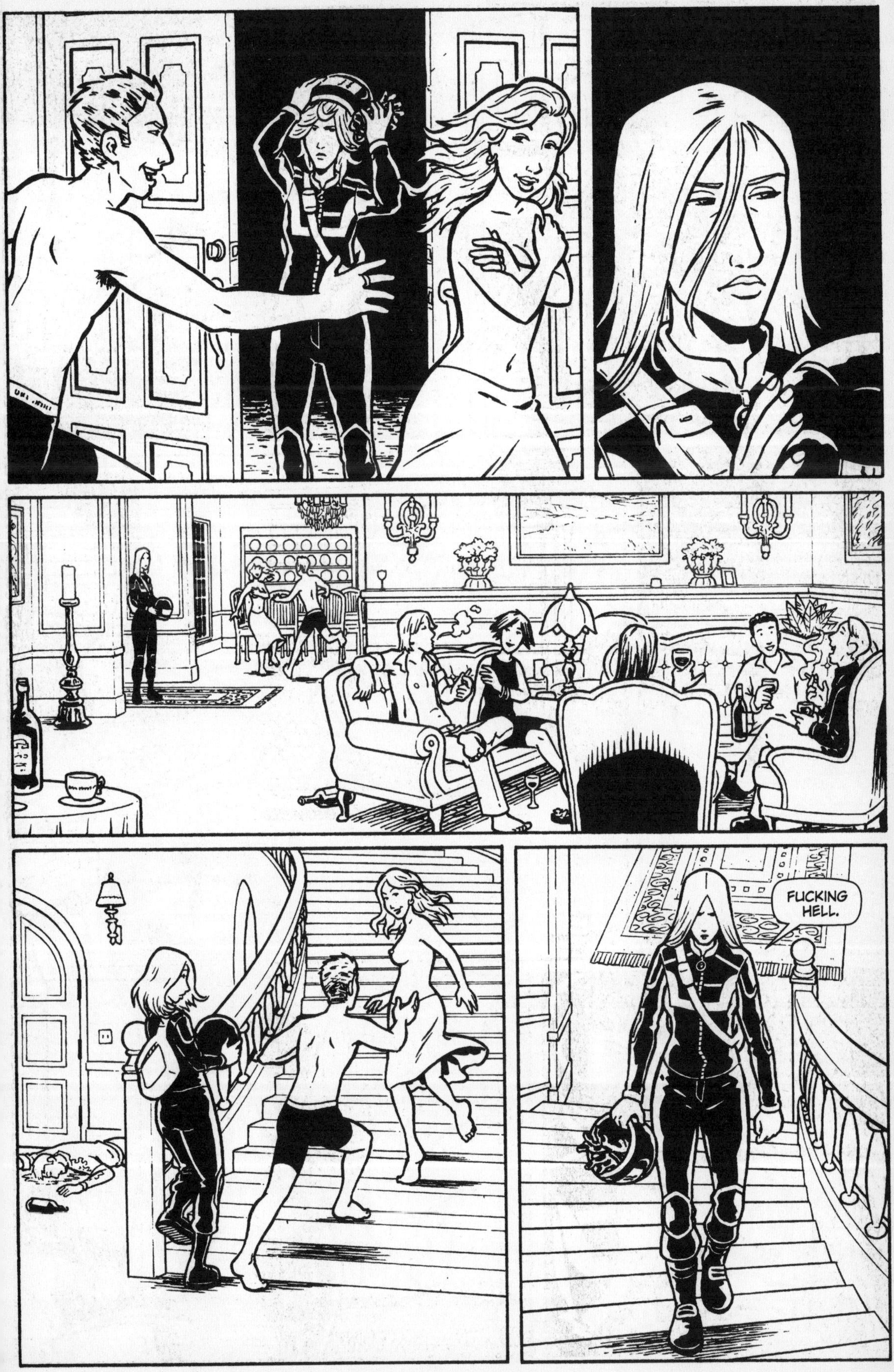
FUCKING HELL.

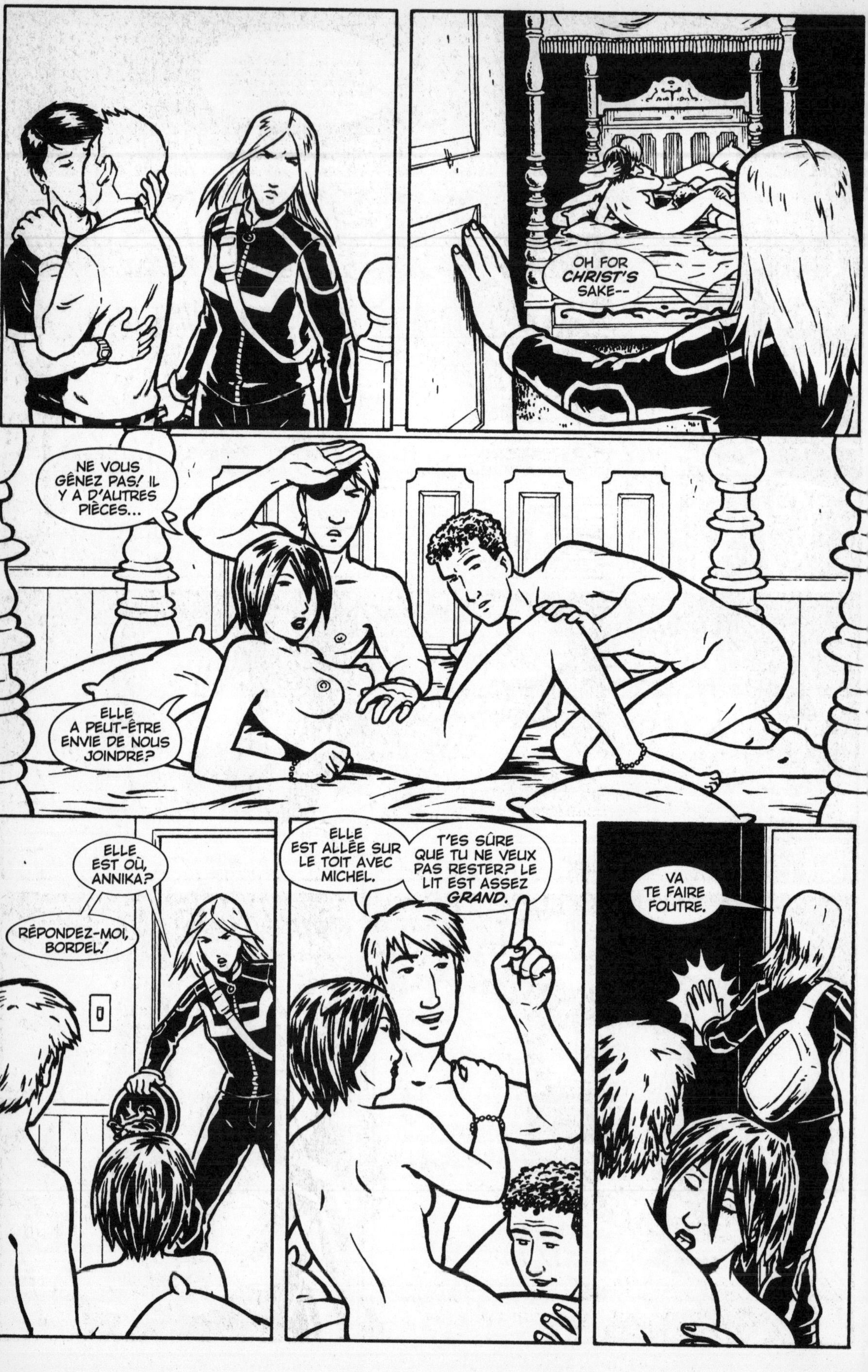
OH FOR CHRIST'S SAKE--
NE VOUS GÊNEZ PAS! IL Y A D'AUTRES PIÈCES...
ELLE A PEUT-ÊTRE ENVIE DE NOUS JOINDRE?
ELLE EST OÙ, ANNIKA?
RÉPONDEZ-MOI, BORDEL!
ELLE EST ALLÉE SUR LE TOIT AVEC MICHEL.
T'ES SÛRE QUE TU NE VEUX PAS RESTER? LE LIT EST ASSEZ GRAND.
VA TE FAIRE FOUTRE.

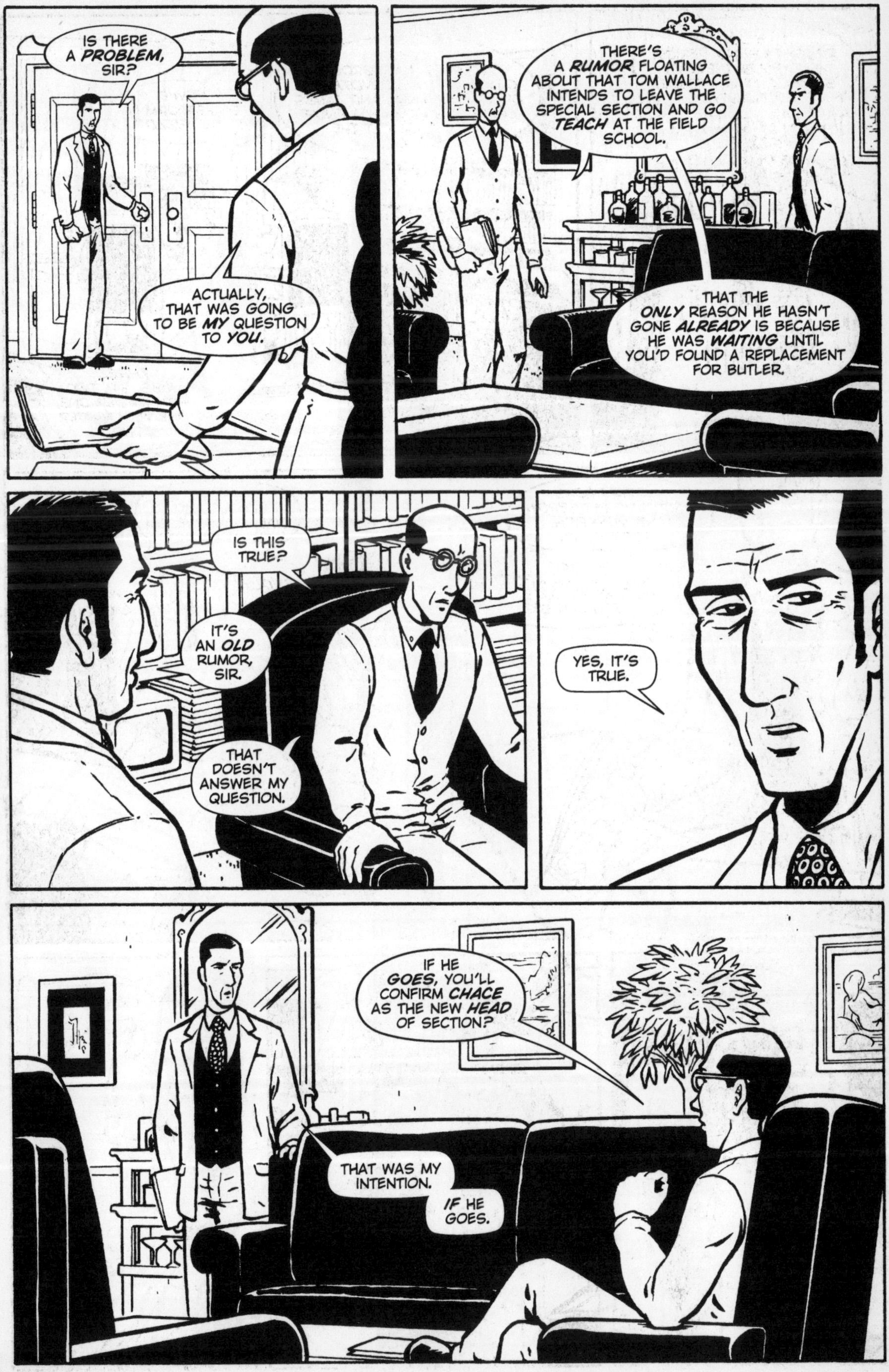
IS THERE A *PROBLEM*, SIR?
ACTUALLY, THAT WAS GOING TO BE *MY* QUESTION TO *YOU*.
THERE'S A *RUMOR* FLOATING ABOUT THAT TOM WALLACE INTENDS TO LEAVE THE SPECIAL SECTION AND GO *TEACH* AT THE FIELD SCHOOL.
THAT THE *ONLY* REASON HE HASN'T GONE *ALREADY* IS BECAUSE HE WAS *WAITING* UNTIL YOU'D FOUND A REPLACEMENT FOR BUTLER.
IS THIS TRUE?
IT'S AN *OLD* RUMOR, SIR.
THAT DOESN'T ANSWER MY QUESTION.
YES, IT'S TRUE.
IF HE *GOES*, YOU'LL CONFIRM *CHACE* AS THE NEW *HEAD* OF SECTION?
THAT WAS MY INTENTION.
*IF* HE GOES.

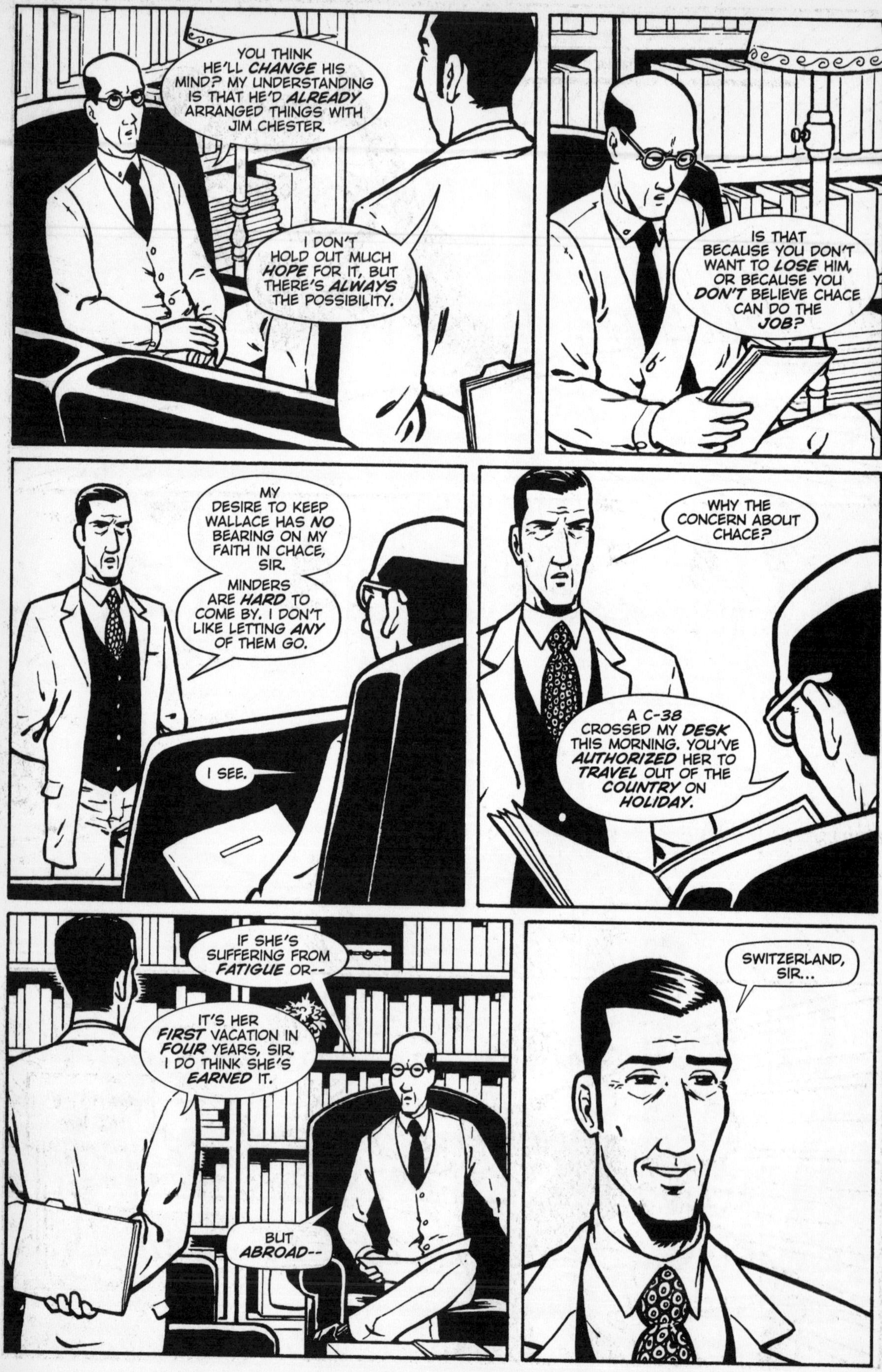
YOU THINK HE'LL CHANGE HIS MIND? MY UNDERSTANDING IS THAT HE'D ALREADY ARRANGED THINGS WITH JIM CHESTER.
I DON'T HOLD OUT MUCH HOPE FOR IT, BUT THERE'S ALWAYS THE POSSIBILITY.
IS THAT BECAUSE YOU DON'T WANT TO LOSE HIM, OR BECAUSE YOU DON'T BELIEVE CHACE CAN DO THE JOB?
MY DESIRE TO KEEP WALLACE HAS NO BEARING ON MY FAITH IN CHACE, SIR.
MINDERS ARE HARD TO COME BY. I DON'T LIKE LETTING ANY OF THEM GO.
I SEE.
WHY THE CONCERN ABOUT CHACE?
A C-38 CROSSED MY DESK THIS MORNING. YOU'VE AUTHORIZED HER TO TRAVEL OUT OF THE COUNTRY ON HOLIDAY.
IF SHE'S SUFFERING FROM FATIGUE OR--
IT'S HER FIRST VACATION IN FOUR YEARS, SIR. I DO THINK SHE'S EARNED IT.
BUT ABROAD--
SWITZERLAND, SIR...

...JE N'Y AVAIS PAS ENCORE TROP RÉFLÉCHI. ON POURRAIT ALLER À ST MORITZ DEMAIN ET FAIRE UN PEU DE SKI AVANT LA FIN DE LA SAISON.

CE SERAIT MERVEILLEUX, ANNIKA.

AM I INTERRUPTING?

TARA! THIS *IS* A SURPRISE, THIS IS *WONDERFUL!*

HELLO, MOTHER.

WOULD YOU LOOK AT YOU? YOU'RE A *SIGHT*, DEAR.

YOU *SMELL* LIKE *DIESEL* AND *DEAD BUGS!*

IT WAS A *LONG* DRIVE.

YOU *DROVE?* DARLING, GOD CREATED *PLANES* FOR A *REASON!*

MICHEL, VIENS ICI, VEUX-TU? JE VOUDRAIS TE PRÉSENTER MA FILLE...

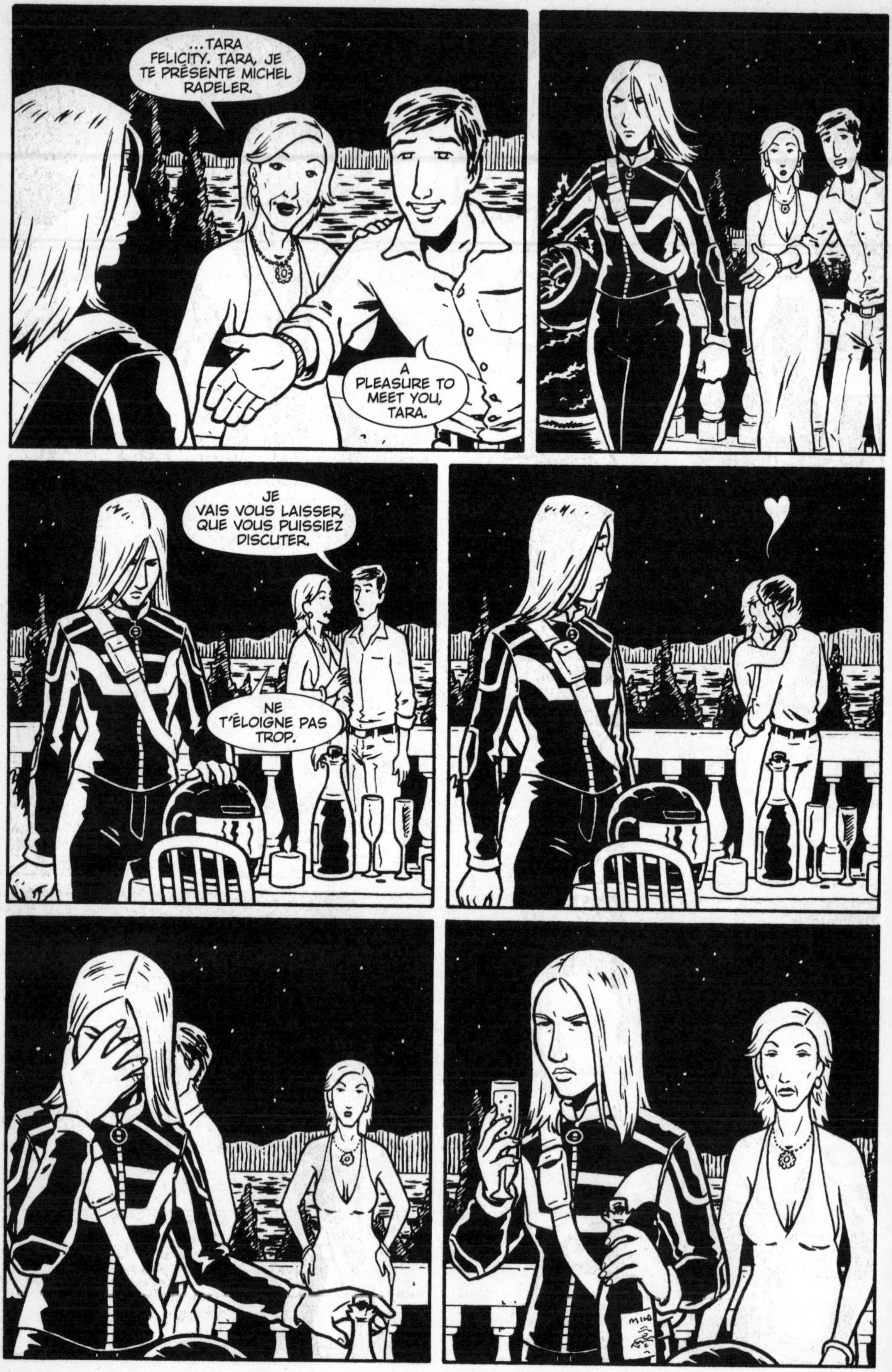
...TARA FELICITY. TARA, JE TE PRÉSENTE MICHEL RADELER.
A PLEASURE TO MEET YOU, TARA.
JE VAIS VOUS LAISSER, QUE VOUS PUISSIEZ DISCUTER.
NE T'ÉLOIGNE PAS TROP.
MIKO

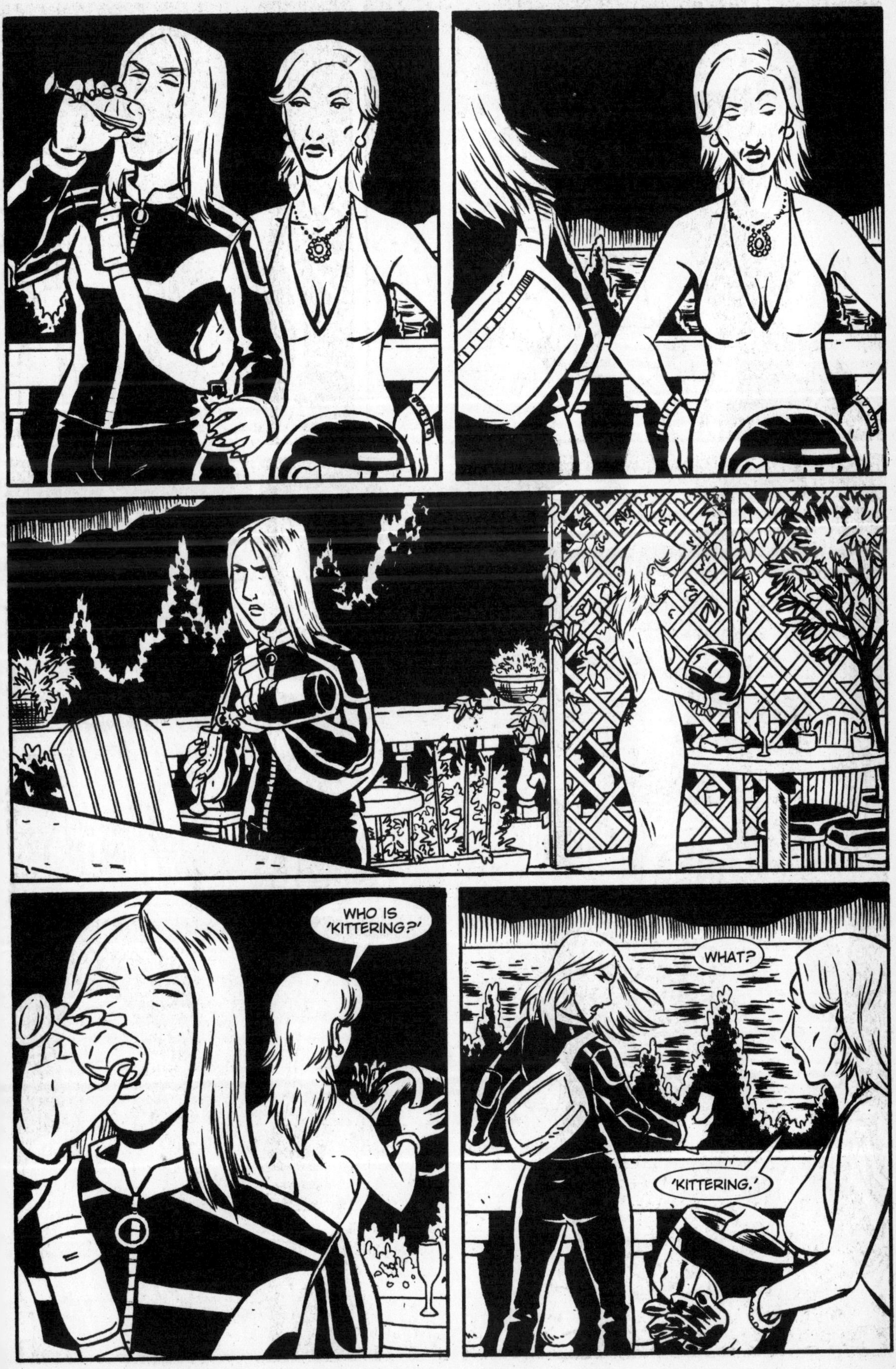
WHO IS 'KITTERING?'
WHAT?
'KITTERING.'

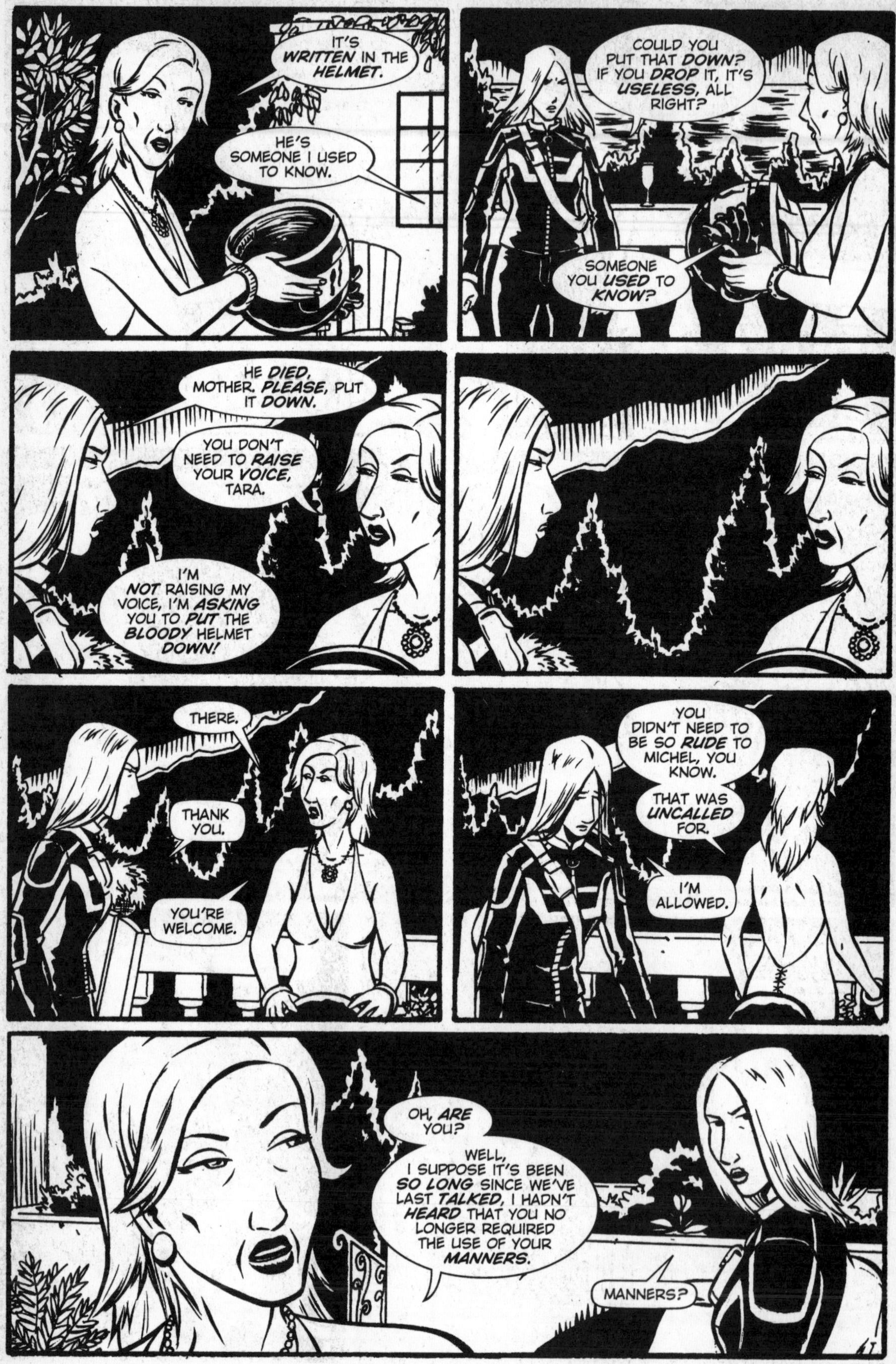
IT'S WRITTEN IN THE HELMET.
HE'S SOMEONE I USED TO KNOW.
COULD YOU PUT THAT DOWN? IF YOU DROP IT, IT'S USELESS, ALL RIGHT?
SOMEONE YOU USED TO KNOW?
HE DIED, MOTHER. PLEASE, PUT IT DOWN.
YOU DON'T NEED TO RAISE YOUR VOICE, TARA.
I'M NOT RAISING MY VOICE, I'M ASKING YOU TO PUT THE BLOODY HELMET DOWN!
THERE.
THANK YOU.
YOU'RE WELCOME.
YOU DIDN'T NEED TO BE SO RUDE TO MICHEL, YOU KNOW.
THAT WAS UNCALLED FOR.
I'M ALLOWED.
OH, ARE YOU?
WELL, I SUPPOSE IT'S BEEN SO LONG SINCE WE'VE LAST TALKED, I HADN'T HEARD THAT YOU NO LONGER REQUIRED THE USE OF YOUR MANNERS.
MANNERS?

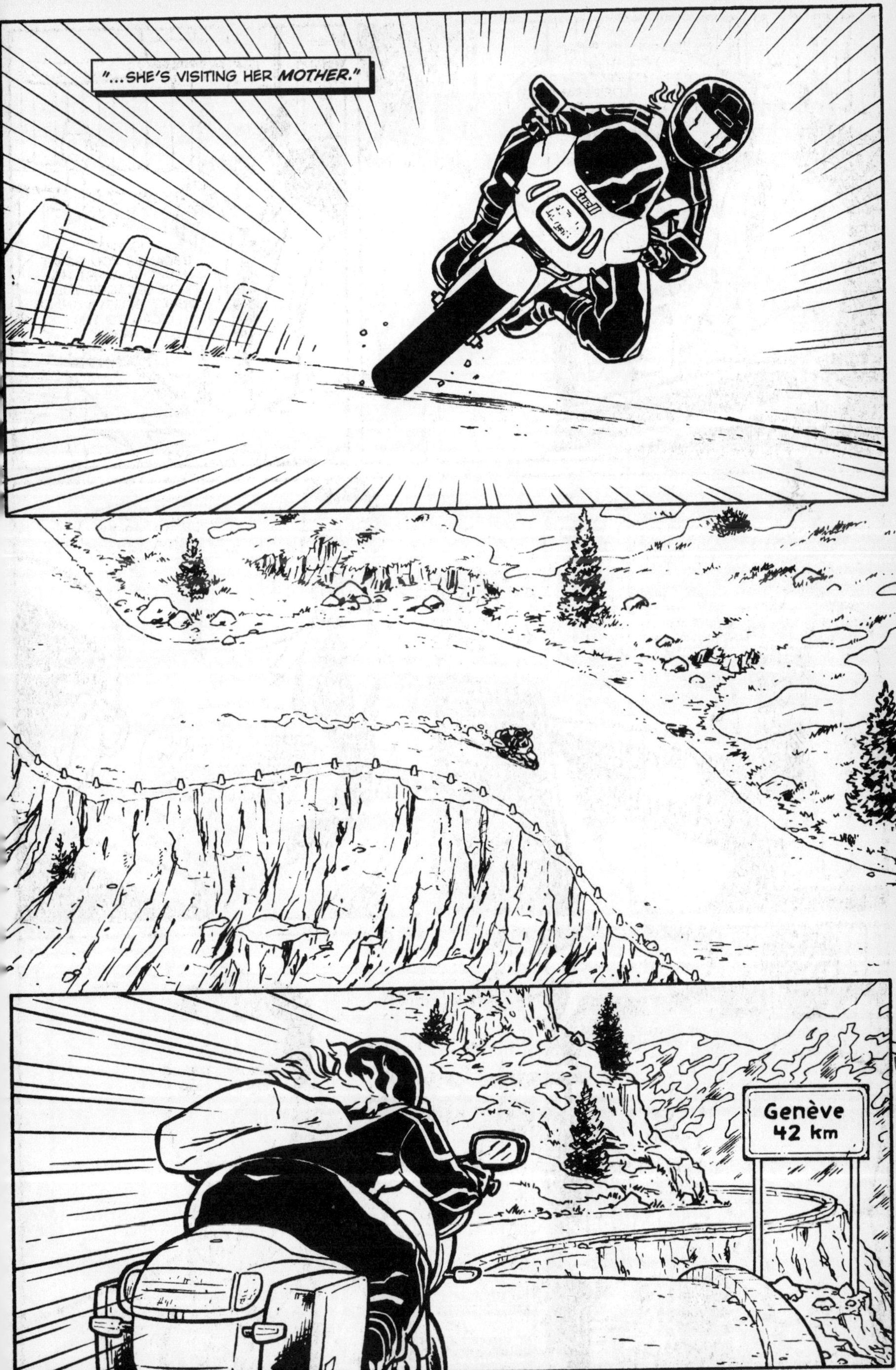
"...SHE'S VISITING HER *MOTHER*."
Buell
Genève
42 km

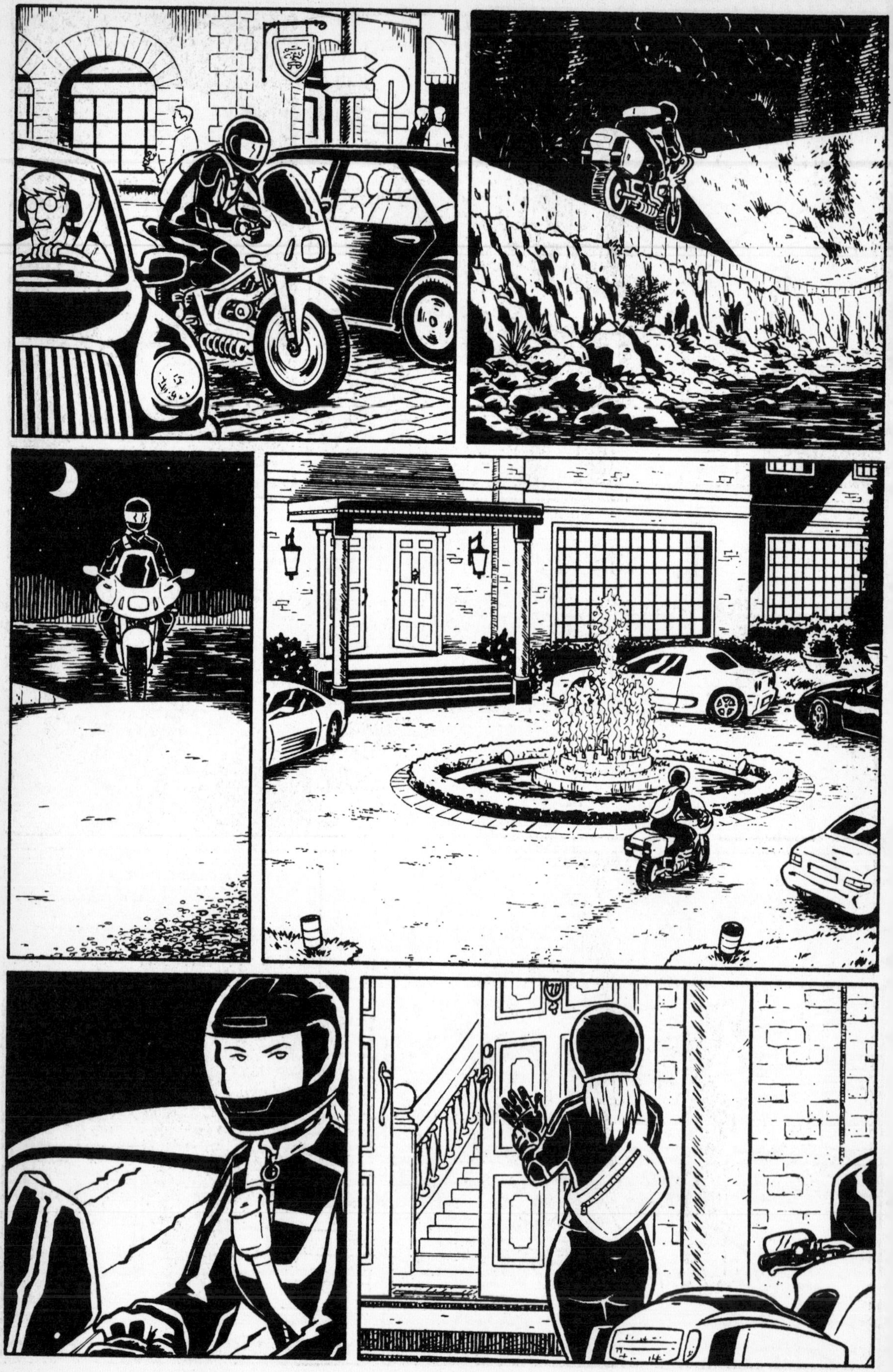

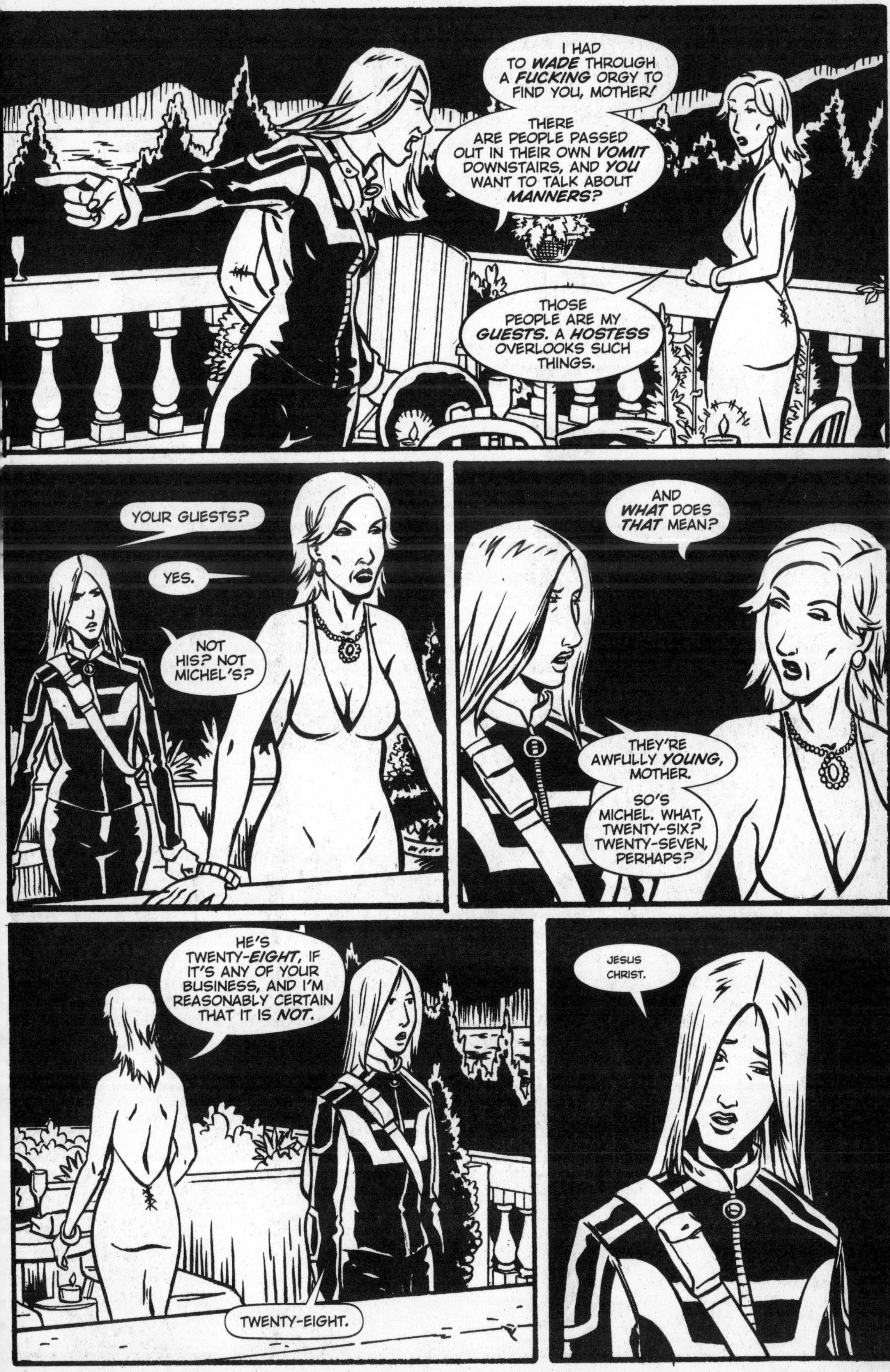
I HAD TO WADE THROUGH A FUCKING ORGY TO FIND YOU, MOTHER!
THERE ARE PEOPLE PASSED OUT IN THEIR OWN VOMIT DOWNSTAIRS, AND YOU WANT TO TALK ABOUT MANNERS?
THOSE PEOPLE ARE MY GUESTS. A HOSTESS OVERLOOKS SUCH THINGS.
YOUR GUESTS?
YES.
NOT HIS? NOT MICHEL'S?
AND WHAT DOES THAT MEAN?
THEY'RE AWFULLY YOUNG, MOTHER.
SO'S MICHEL. WHAT, TWENTY-SIX? TWENTY-SEVEN, PERHAPS?
HE'S TWENTY-EIGHT, IF IT'S ANY OF YOUR BUSINESS, AND I'M REASONABLY CERTAIN THAT IT IS NOT.
TWENTY-EIGHT.
JESUS CHRIST.

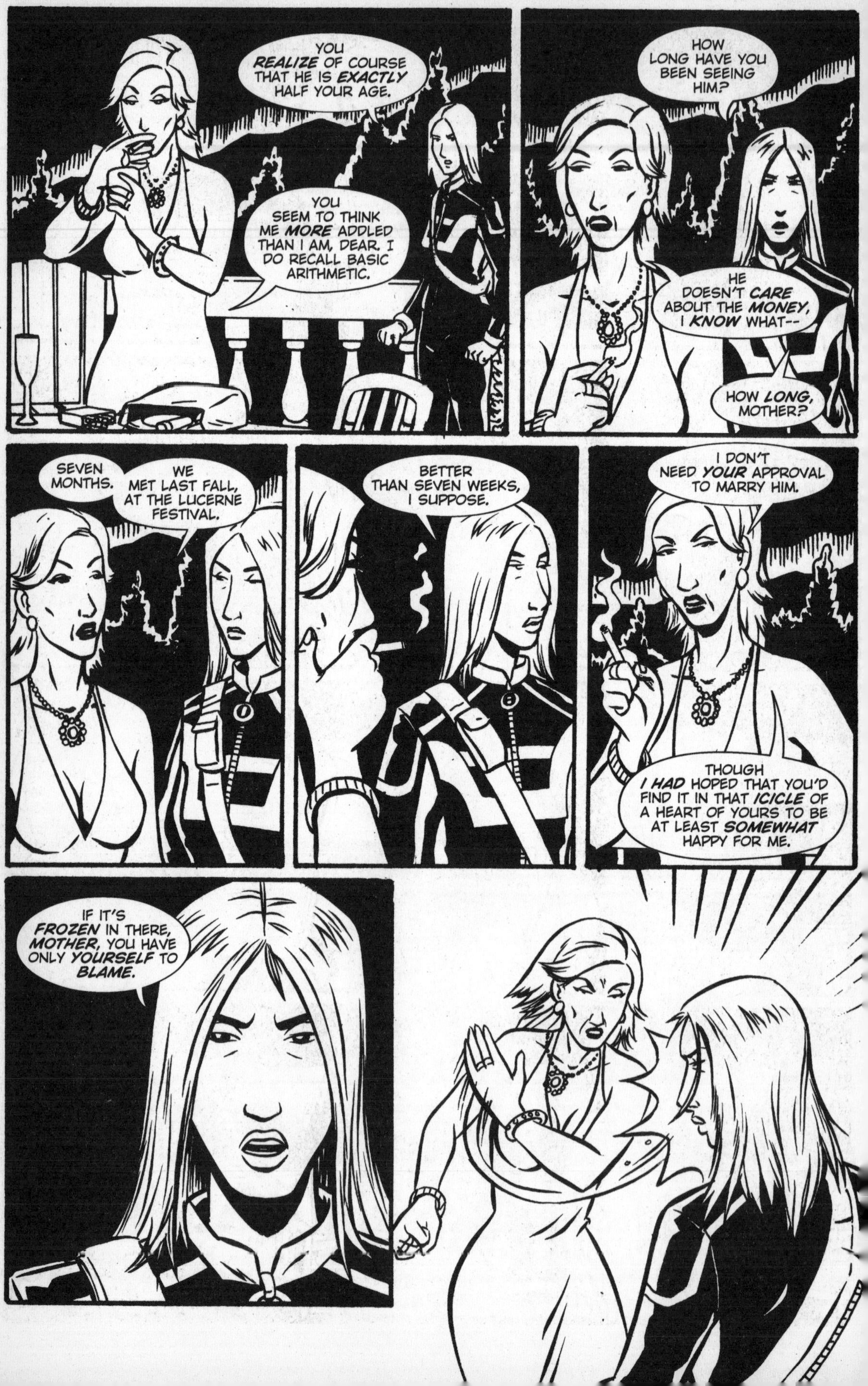
YOU REALIZE OF COURSE THAT HE IS EXACTLY HALF YOUR AGE.
YOU SEEM TO THINK ME MORE ADDLED THAN I AM, DEAR. I DO RECALL BASIC ARITHMETIC.
HOW LONG HAVE YOU BEEN SEEING HIM?
HE DOESN'T CARE ABOUT THE MONEY, I KNOW WHAT--
HOW LONG, MOTHER?
SEVEN MONTHS.
WE MET LAST FALL, AT THE LUCERNE FESTIVAL.
BETTER THAN SEVEN WEEKS, I SUPPOSE.
I DON'T NEED YOUR APPROVAL TO MARRY HIM.
THOUGH I HAD HOPED THAT YOU'D FIND IT IN THAT ICICLE OF A HEART OF YOURS TO BE AT LEAST SOMEWHAT HAPPY FOR ME.
IF IT'S FROZEN IN THERE, MOTHER, YOU HAVE ONLY YOURSELF TO BLAME.

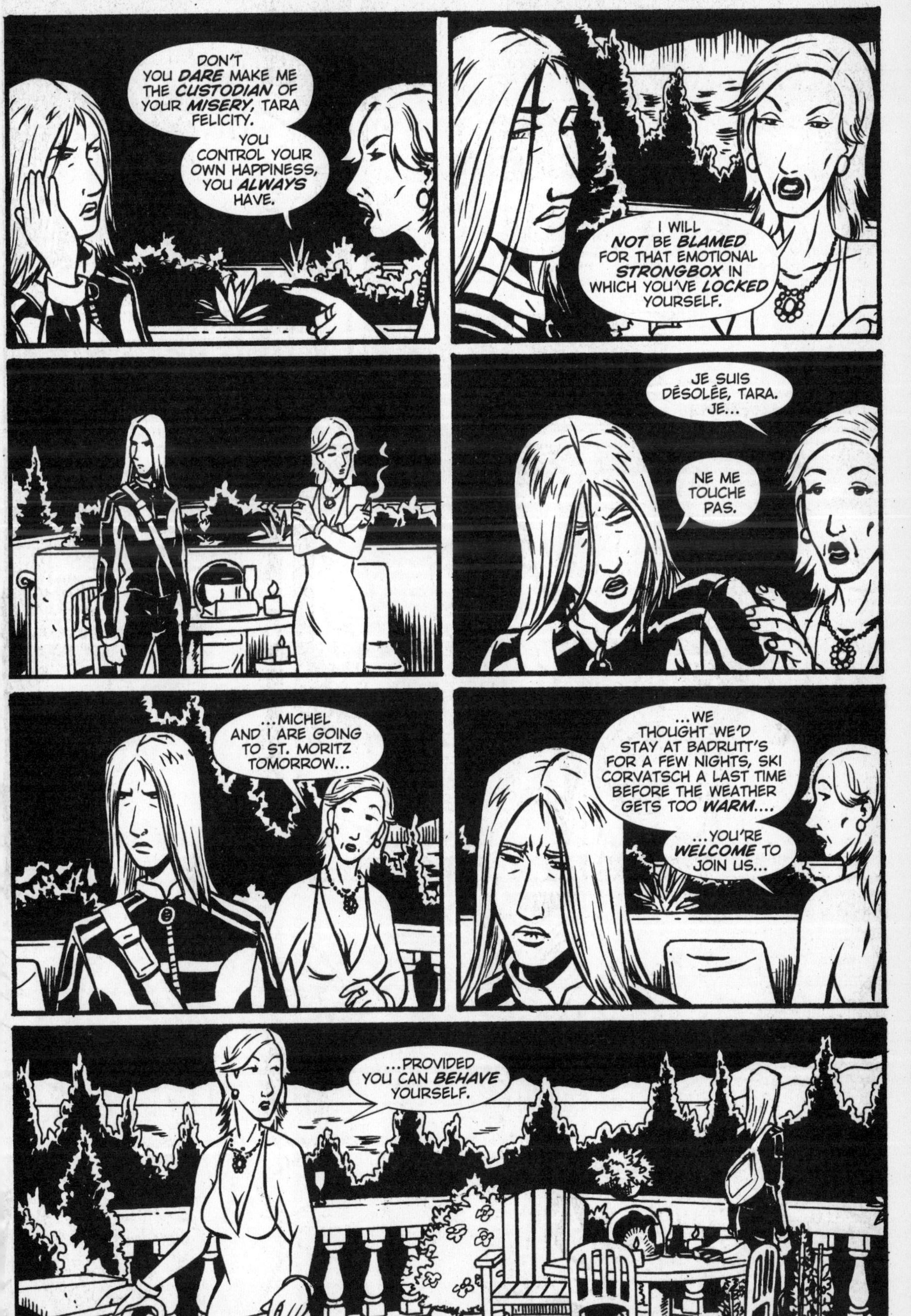
DON'T YOU DARE MAKE ME THE CUSTODIAN OF YOUR MISERY, TARA FELICITY.
YOU CONTROL YOUR OWN HAPPINESS, YOU ALWAYS HAVE.
I WILL NOT BE BLAMED FOR THAT EMOTIONAL STRONGBOX IN WHICH YOU'VE LOCKED YOURSELF.
JE SUIS DÉSOLÉE, TARA. JE...
NE ME TOUCHE PAS.
...MICHEL AND I ARE GOING TO ST. MORITZ TOMORROW...
...WE THOUGHT WE'D STAY AT BADRUTT'S FOR A FEW NIGHTS, SKI CORVATSCH A LAST TIME BEFORE THE WEATHER GETS TOO WARM....
...YOU'RE WELCOME TO JOIN US...
...PROVIDED YOU CAN BEHAVE YOURSELF.

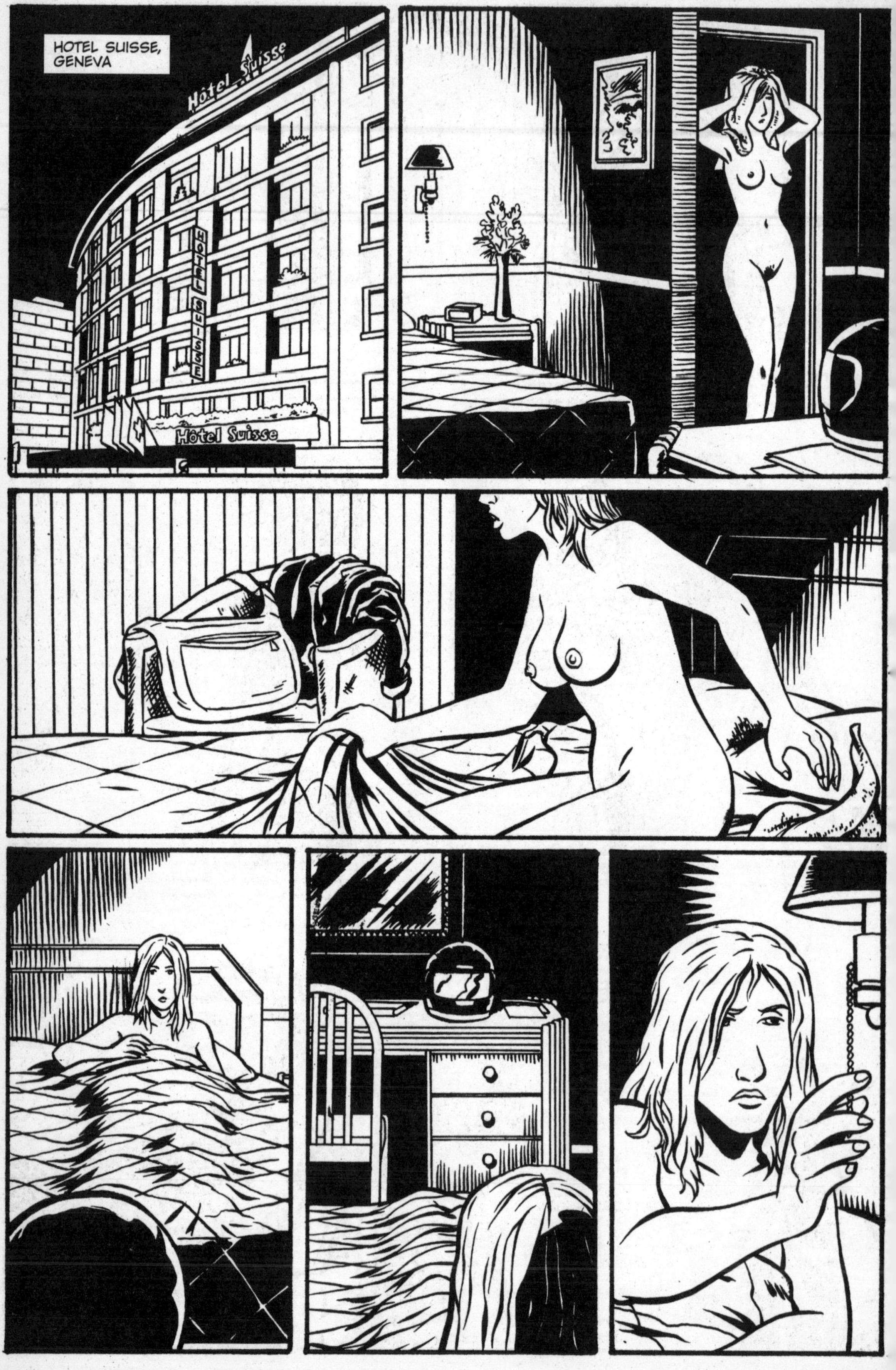
HOTEL SUISSE,
GENEVA
Hôtel Suisse
HOTEL SUISSE
Hôtel Suisse

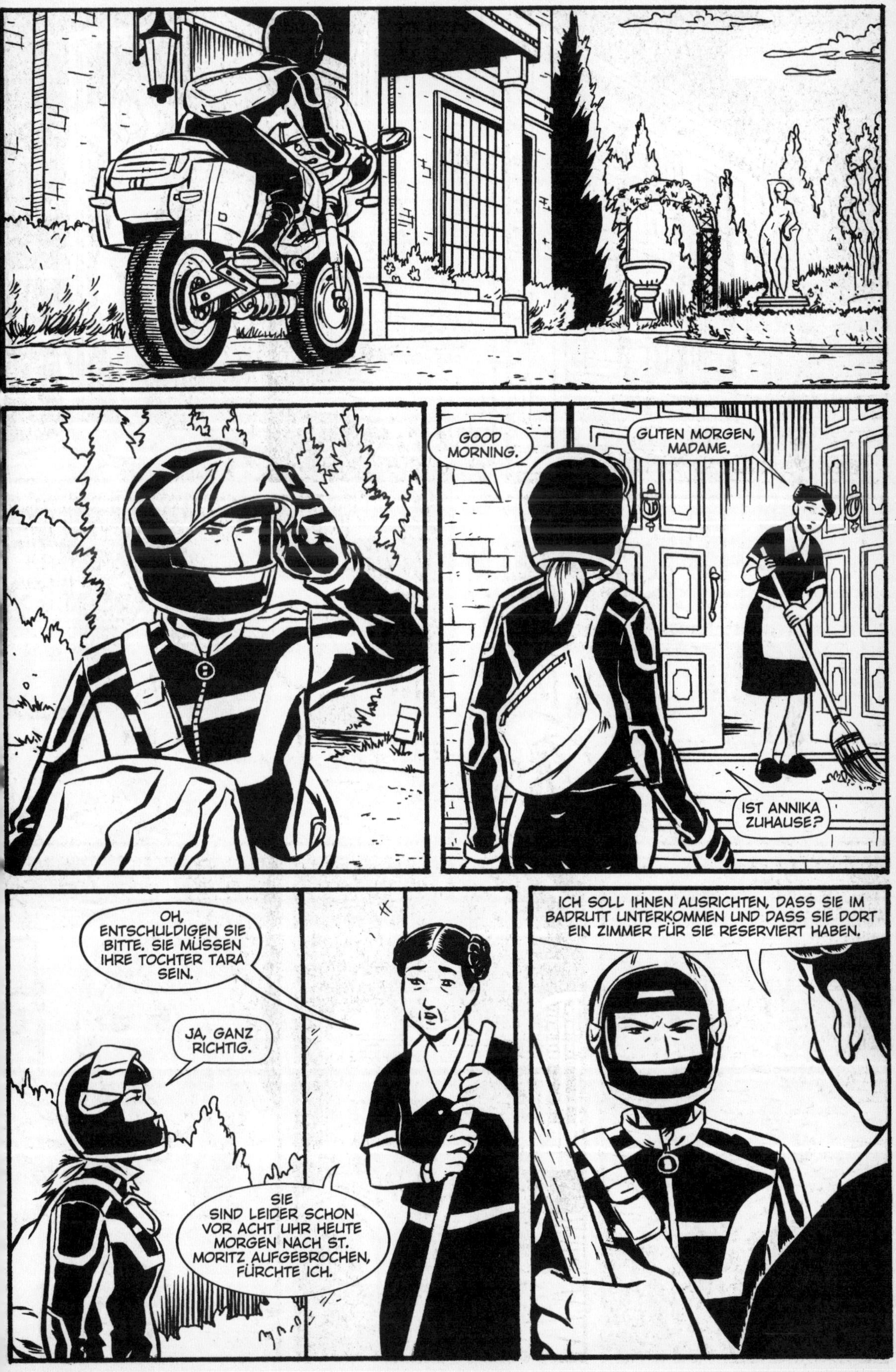
GOOD MORNING.
GUTEN MORGEN, MADAME.
IST ANNIKA ZUHAUSE?
OH, ENTSCHULDIGEN SIE BITTE. SIE MÜSSEN IHRE TOCHTER TARA SEIN.
JA, GANZ RICHTIG.
SIE SIND LEIDER SCHON VOR ACHT UHR HEUTE MORGEN NACH ST. MORITZ AUFGEBROCHEN, FÜRCHTE ICH.
ICH SOLL IHNEN AUSRICHTEN, DASS SIE IM BADRUTT UNTERKOMMEN UND DASS SIE DORT EIN ZIMMER FÜR SIE RESERVIERT HABEN.

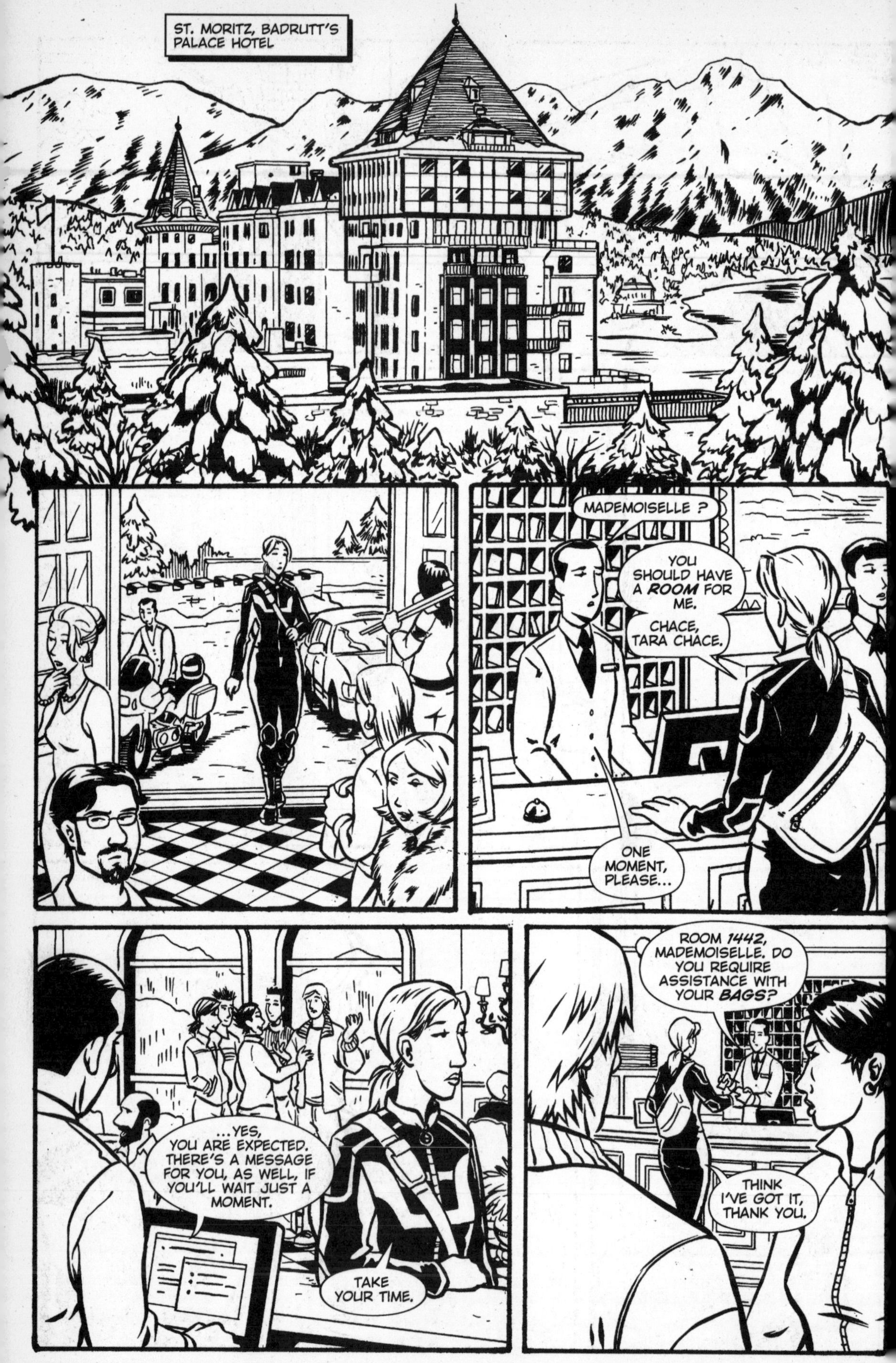
ST. MORITZ, BADRUTT'S PALACE HOTEL
MADEMOISELLE ?
YOU SHOULD HAVE A *ROOM* FOR ME.
CHACE, TARA CHACE.
ONE MOMENT, PLEASE...
...YES, YOU ARE EXPECTED. THERE'S A MESSAGE FOR YOU, AS WELL, IF YOU'LL WAIT JUST A MOMENT.
TAKE YOUR TIME.
ROOM *1442*, MADEMOISELLE. DO YOU REQUIRE ASSISTANCE WITH YOUR *BAGS?*
THINK I'VE GOT IT, THANK YOU.

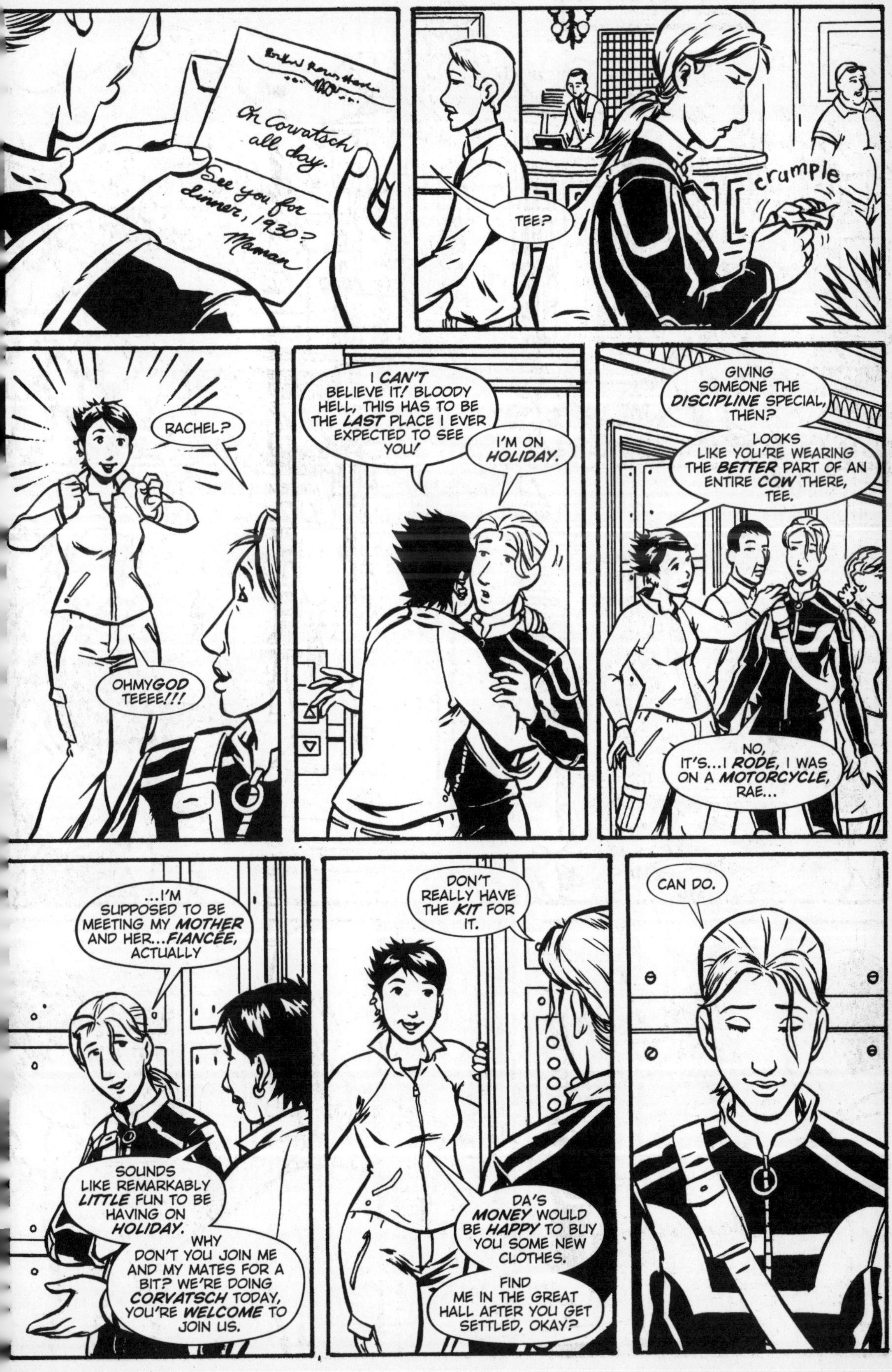
On Corvatsch all day.
See you for dinner, 1930?
Maman
TEE?
crumple
RACHEL?
OHMYGOD TEEEE!!!
I CAN'T BELIEVE IT! BLOODY HELL, THIS HAS TO BE THE LAST PLACE I EVER EXPECTED TO SEE YOU!
I'M ON HOLIDAY.
GIVING SOMEONE THE DISCIPLINE SPECIAL, THEN?
LOOKS LIKE YOU'RE WEARING THE BETTER PART OF AN ENTIRE COW THERE, TEE.
NO, IT'S...I RODE, I WAS ON A MOTORCYCLE, RAE...
...I'M SUPPOSED TO BE MEETING MY MOTHER AND HER...FIANCÉE, ACTUALLY
SOUNDS LIKE REMARKABLY LITTLE FUN TO BE HAVING ON HOLIDAY.
WHY DON'T YOU JOIN ME AND MY MATES FOR A BIT? WE'RE DOING CORVATSCH TODAY, YOU'RE WELCOME TO JOIN US.
DON'T REALLY HAVE THE KIT FOR IT.
DA'S MONEY WOULD BE HAPPY TO BUY YOU SOME NEW CLOTHES.
FIND ME IN THE GREAT HALL AFTER YOU GET SETTLED, OKAY?
CAN DO.

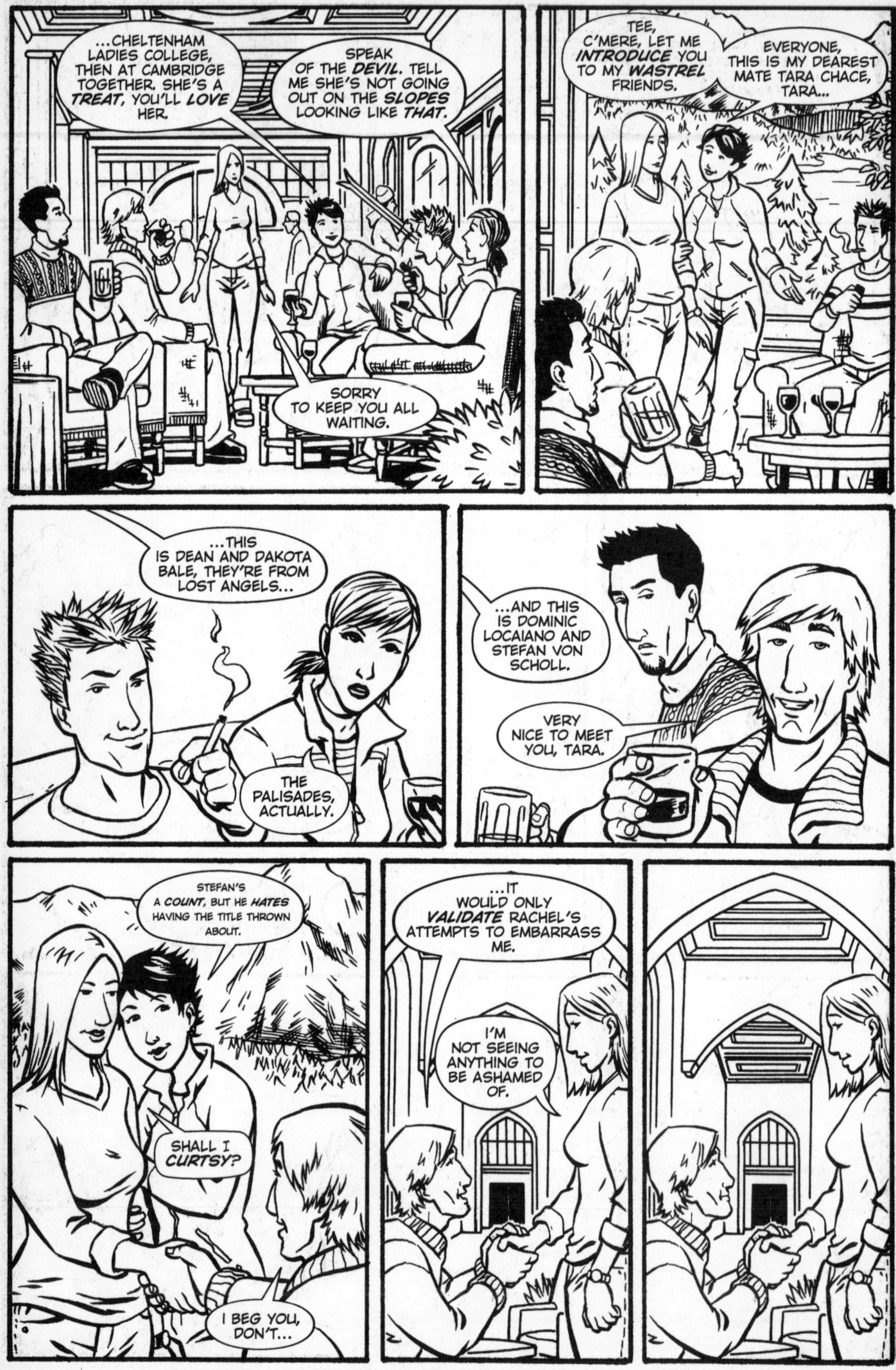
...CHELTENHAM LADIES COLLEGE, THEN AT CAMBRIDGE TOGETHER. SHE'S A TREAT, YOU'LL LOVE HER.
SPEAK OF THE DEVIL. TELL ME SHE'S NOT GOING OUT ON THE SLOPES LOOKING LIKE THAT.
SORRY TO KEEP YOU ALL WAITING.
TEE, C'MERE, LET ME INTRODUCE YOU TO MY WASTREL FRIENDS.
EVERYONE, THIS IS MY DEAREST MATE TARA CHACE, TARA...
...THIS IS DEAN AND DAKOTA BALE, THEY'RE FROM LOST ANGELS...
THE PALISADES, ACTUALLY.
...AND THIS IS DOMINIC LOCAIANO AND STEFAN VON SCHOLL.
VERY NICE TO MEET YOU, TARA.
STEFAN'S A COUNT, BUT HE HATES HAVING THE TITLE THROWN ABOUT.
SHALL I CURTSY?
I BEG YOU, DON'T...
...IT WOULD ONLY VALIDATE RACHEL'S ATTEMPTS TO EMBARRASS ME.
I'M NOT SEEING ANYTHING TO BE ASHAMED OF.

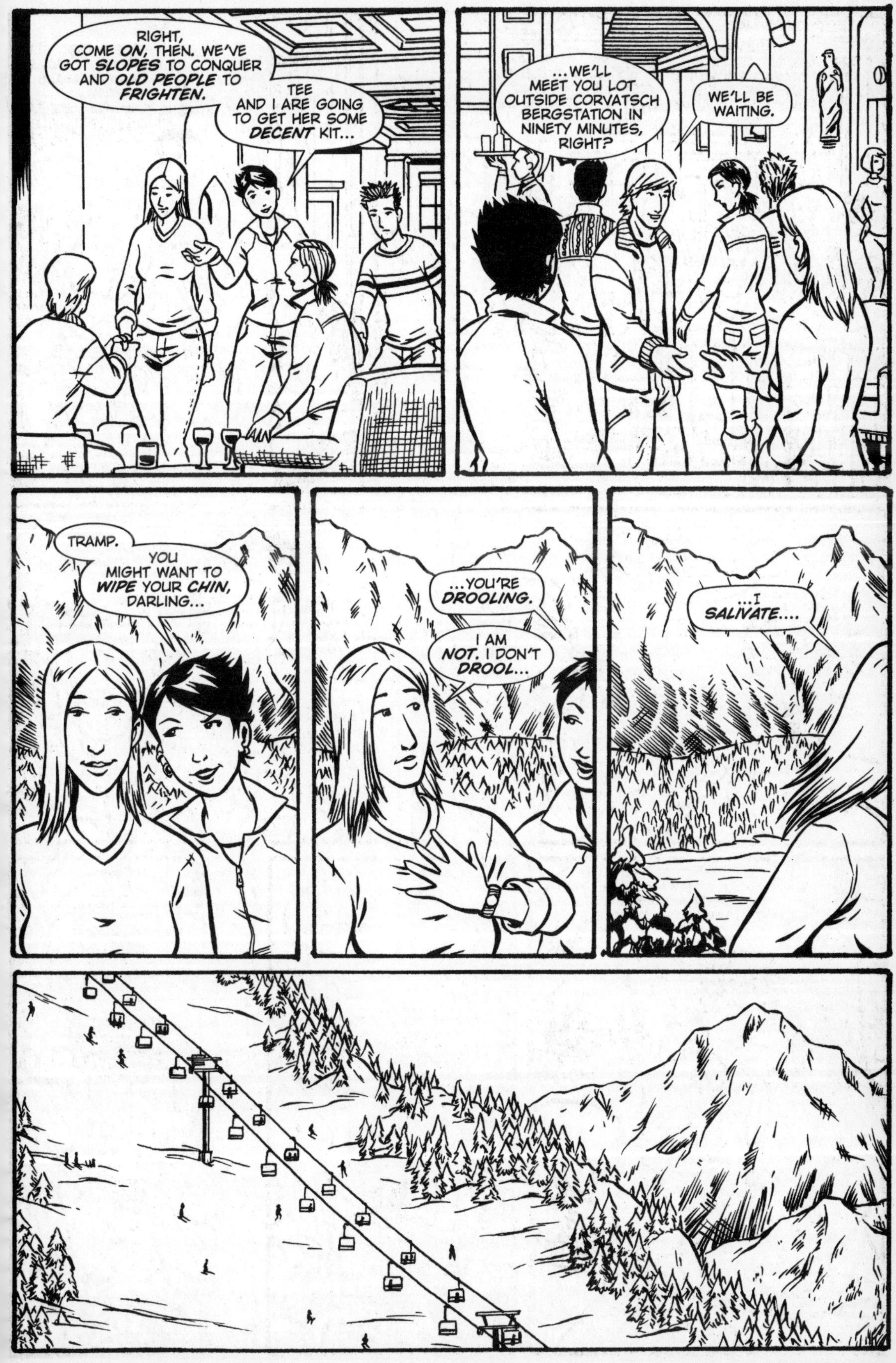
RIGHT, COME ON, THEN. WE'VE GOT SLOPES TO CONQUER AND OLD PEOPLE TO FRIGHTEN.
TEE AND I ARE GOING TO GET HER SOME DECENT KIT...
...WE'LL MEET YOU LOT OUTSIDE CORVATSCH BERGSTATION IN NINETY MINUTES, RIGHT?
WE'LL BE WAITING.
TRAMP.
YOU MIGHT WANT TO WIPE YOUR CHIN, DARLING...
...YOU'RE DROOLING.
I AM NOT. I DON'T DROOL...
...I SALIVATE....

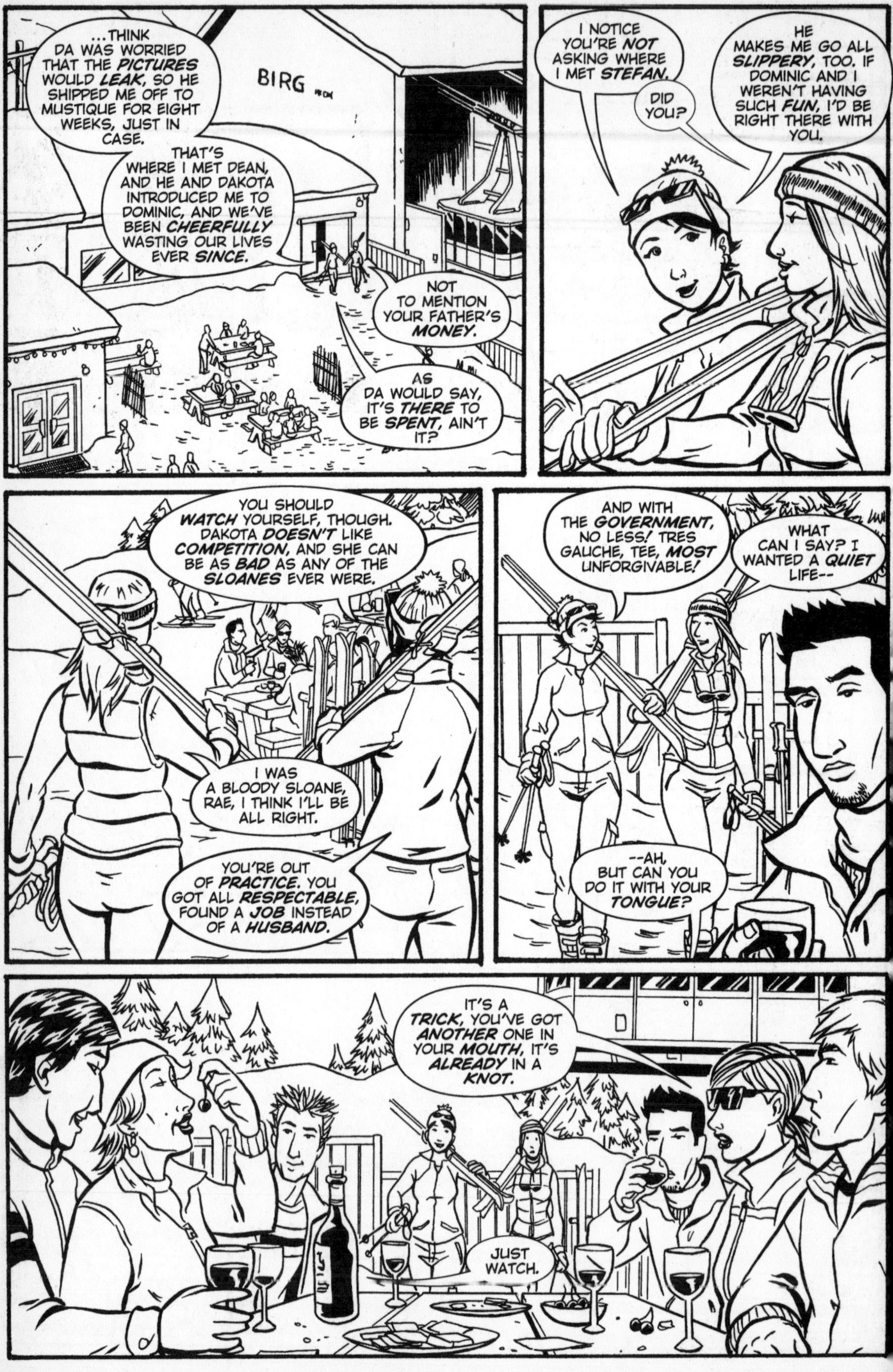
...THINK DA WAS WORRIED THAT THE PICTURES WOULD LEAK, SO HE SHIPPED ME OFF TO MUSTIQUE FOR EIGHT WEEKS, JUST IN CASE.
THAT'S WHERE I MET DEAN, AND HE AND DAKOTA INTRODUCED ME TO DOMINIC, AND WE'VE BEEN CHEERFULLY WASTING OUR LIVES EVER SINCE.
BIRG
NOT TO MENTION YOUR FATHER'S MONEY.
AS DA WOULD SAY, IT'S THERE TO BE SPENT, AIN'T IT?
I NOTICE YOU'RE NOT ASKING WHERE I MET STEFAN.
DID YOU?
HE MAKES ME GO ALL SLIPPERY, TOO. IF DOMINIC AND I WEREN'T HAVING SUCH FUN, I'D BE RIGHT THERE WITH YOU.
YOU SHOULD WATCH YOURSELF, THOUGH. DAKOTA DOESN'T LIKE COMPETITION, AND SHE CAN BE AS BAD AS ANY OF THE SLOANES EVER WERE.
I WAS A BLOODY SLOANE, RAE, I THINK I'LL BE ALL RIGHT.
YOU'RE OUT OF PRACTICE. YOU GOT ALL RESPECTABLE, FOUND A JOB INSTEAD OF A HUSBAND.
AND WITH THE GOVERNMENT, NO LESS! TRES GAUCHE, TEE, MOST UNFORGIVABLE!
WHAT CAN I SAY? I WANTED A QUIET LIFE--
--AH, BUT CAN YOU DO IT WITH YOUR TONGUE?
IT'S A TRICK, YOU'VE GOT ANOTHER ONE IN YOUR MOUTH, IT'S ALREADY IN A KNOT.
JUST WATCH.

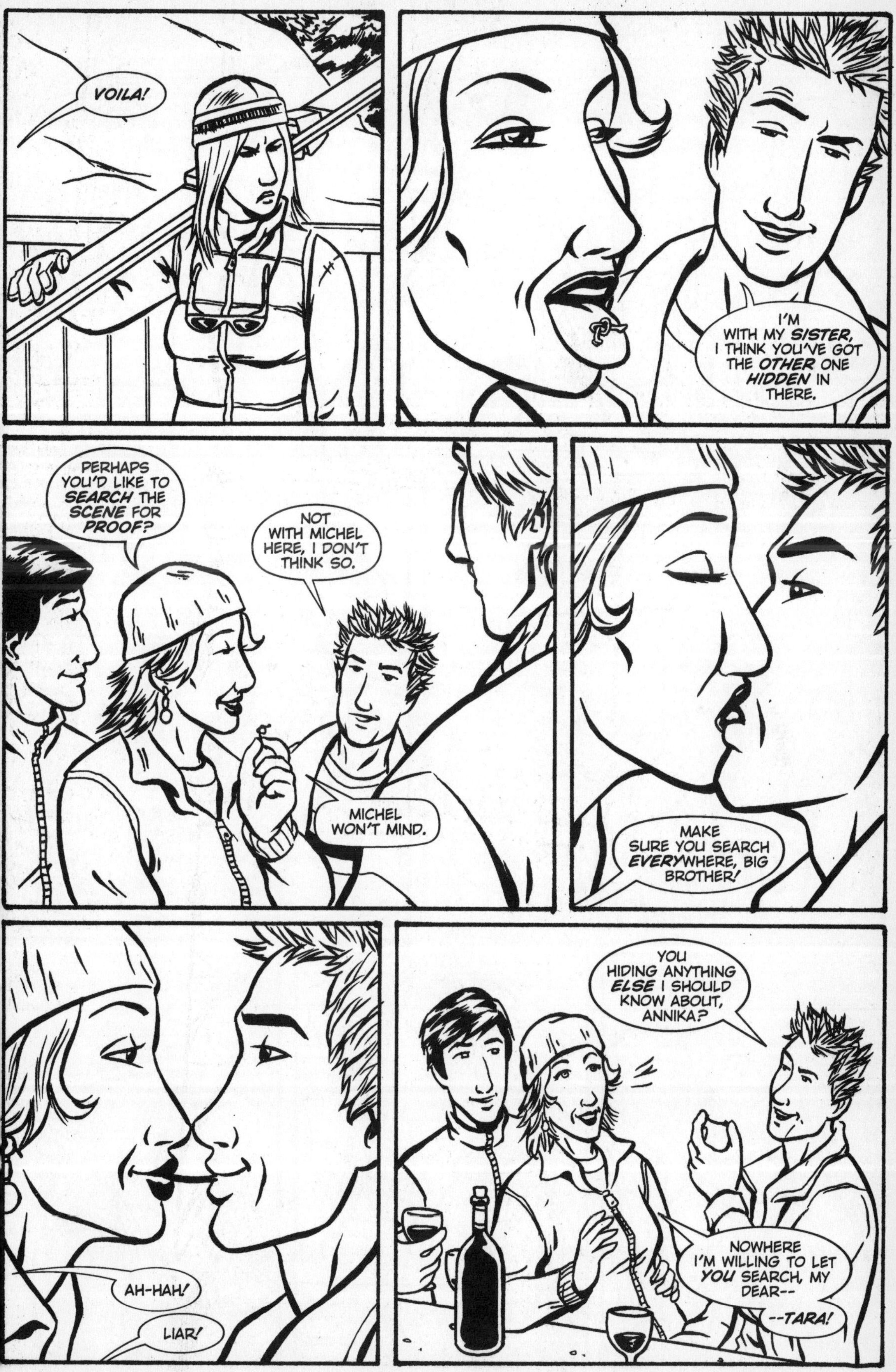
VOILA!
I'M WITH MY SISTER, I THINK YOU'VE GOT THE OTHER ONE HIDDEN IN THERE.
PERHAPS YOU'D LIKE TO SEARCH THE SCENE FOR PROOF?
NOT WITH MICHEL HERE, I DON'T THINK SO.
MICHEL WON'T MIND.
MAKE SURE YOU SEARCH EVERYWHERE, BIG BROTHER!
AH-HAH!
LIAR!
YOU HIDING ANYTHING ELSE I SHOULD KNOW ABOUT, ANNIKA?
NOWHERE I'M WILLING TO LET YOU SEARCH, MY DEAR--
--TARA!

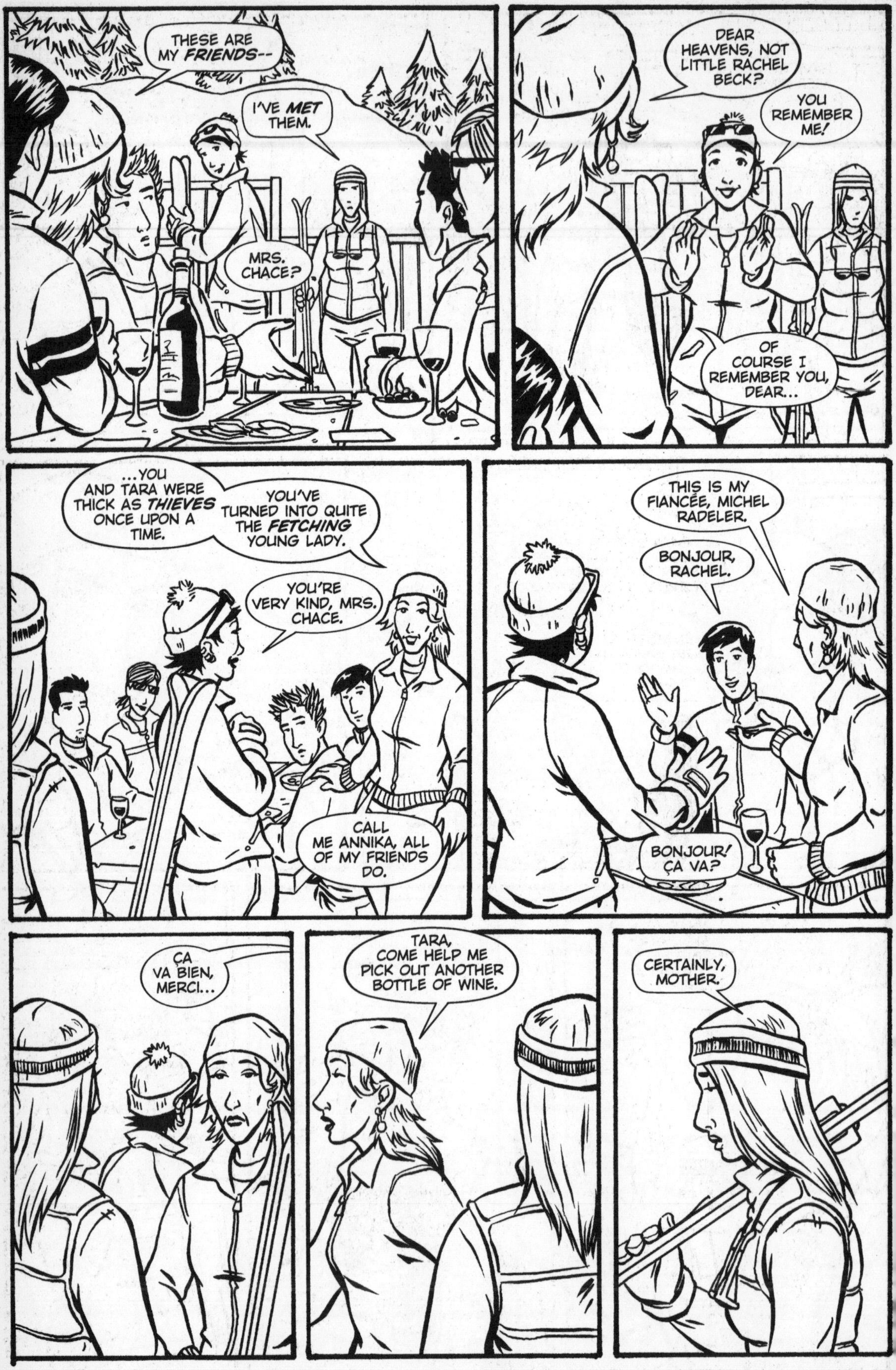
THESE ARE MY FRIENDS--
I'VE MET THEM.
MRS. CHACE?
DEAR HEAVENS, NOT LITTLE RACHEL BECK?
YOU REMEMBER ME!
OF COURSE I REMEMBER YOU, DEAR...
...YOU AND TARA WERE THICK AS THIEVES ONCE UPON A TIME.
YOU'VE TURNED INTO QUITE THE FETCHING YOUNG LADY.
YOU'RE VERY KIND, MRS. CHACE.
CALL ME ANNIKA, ALL OF MY FRIENDS DO.
THIS IS MY FIANCÉE, MICHEL RADELER.
BONJOUR, RACHEL.
BONJOUR! ÇA VA?
ÇA VA BIEN, MERCI...
TARA, COME HELP ME PICK OUT ANOTHER BOTTLE OF WINE.
CERTAINLY, MOTHER.

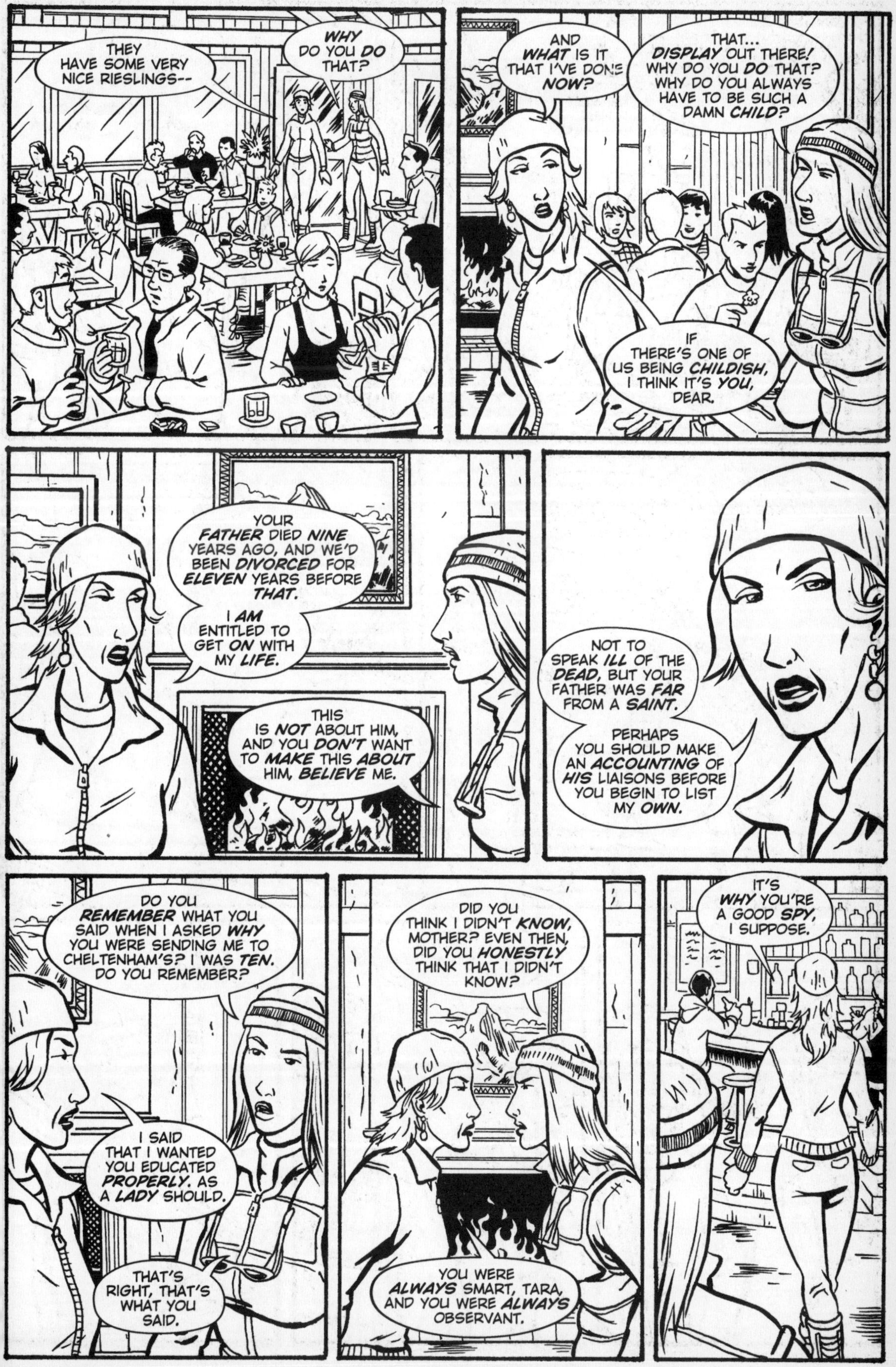
THEY HAVE SOME VERY NICE RIESLINGS--
WHY DO YOU DO THAT?
AND WHAT IS IT THAT I'VE DONE NOW?
THAT... DISPLAY OUT THERE! WHY DO YOU DO THAT? WHY DO YOU ALWAYS HAVE TO BE SUCH A DAMN CHILD?
IF THERE'S ONE OF US BEING CHILDISH, I THINK IT'S YOU, DEAR.
YOUR FATHER DIED NINE YEARS AGO, AND WE'D BEEN DIVORCED FOR ELEVEN YEARS BEFORE THAT.
I AM ENTITLED TO GET ON WITH MY LIFE.
THIS IS NOT ABOUT HIM, AND YOU DON'T WANT TO MAKE THIS ABOUT HIM, BELIEVE ME.
NOT TO SPEAK ILL OF THE DEAD, BUT YOUR FATHER WAS FAR FROM A SAINT.
PERHAPS YOU SHOULD MAKE AN ACCOUNTING OF HIS LIAISONS BEFORE YOU BEGIN TO LIST MY OWN.
DO YOU REMEMBER WHAT YOU SAID WHEN I ASKED WHY YOU WERE SENDING ME TO CHELTENHAM'S? I WAS TEN. DO YOU REMEMBER?
I SAID THAT I WANTED YOU EDUCATED PROPERLY. AS A LADY SHOULD.
THAT'S RIGHT, THAT'S WHAT YOU SAID.
DID YOU THINK I DIDN'T KNOW, MOTHER? EVEN THEN, DID YOU HONESTLY THINK THAT I DIDN'T KNOW?
YOU WERE ALWAYS SMART, TARA, AND YOU WERE ALWAYS OBSERVANT.
IT'S WHY YOU'RE A GOOD SPY, I SUPPOSE.

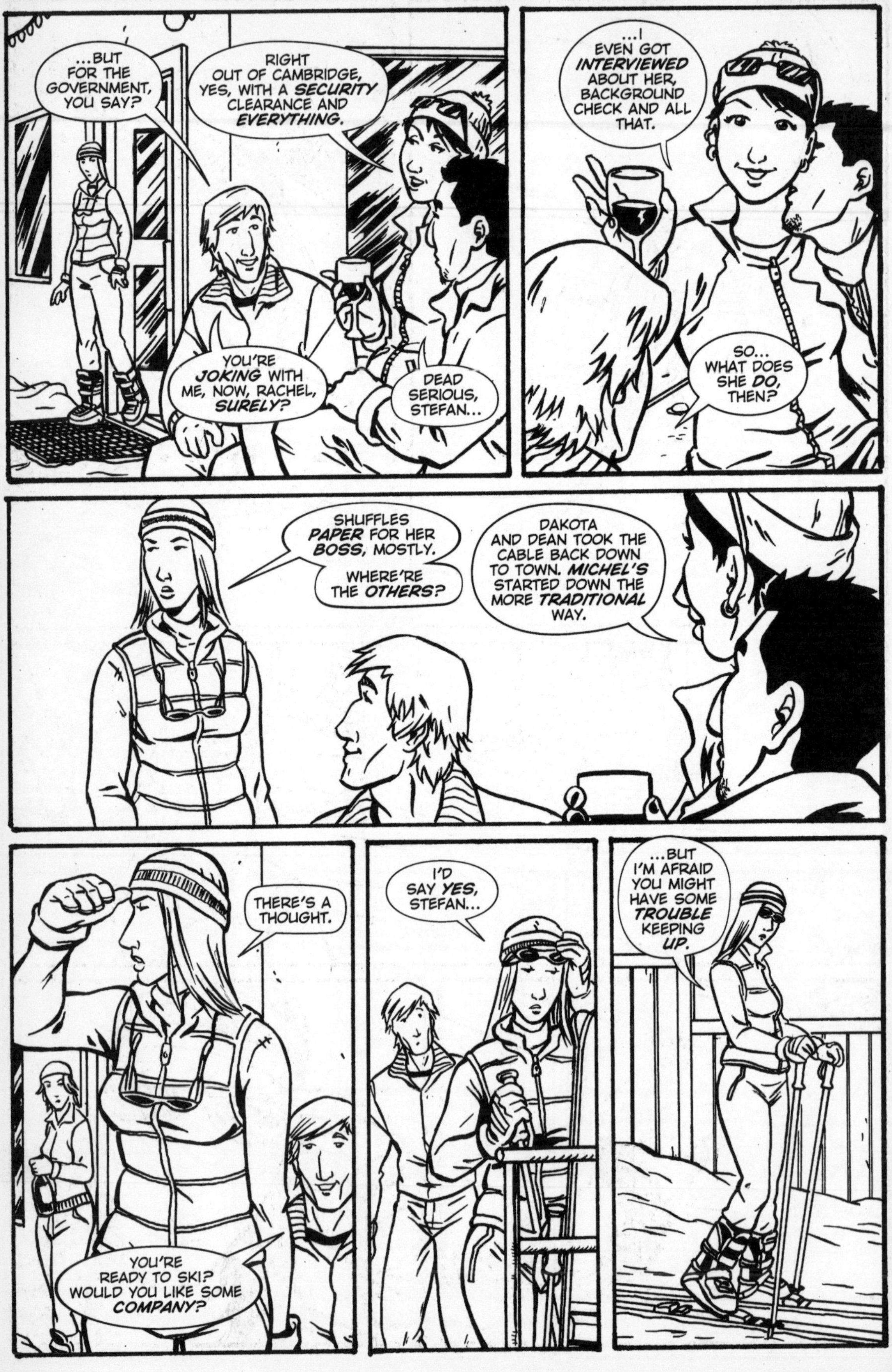
...BUT FOR THE GOVERNMENT, YOU SAY?
RIGHT OUT OF CAMBRIDGE, YES, WITH A SECURITY CLEARANCE AND EVERYTHING.
YOU'RE JOKING WITH ME, NOW, RACHEL, SURELY?
DEAD SERIOUS, STEFAN...
...I EVEN GOT INTERVIEWED ABOUT HER, BACKGROUND CHECK AND ALL THAT.
SO... WHAT DOES SHE DO, THEN?
SHUFFLES PAPER FOR HER BOSS, MOSTLY.
WHERE'RE THE OTHERS?
DAKOTA AND DEAN TOOK THE CABLE BACK DOWN TO TOWN. MICHEL'S STARTED DOWN THE MORE TRADITIONAL WAY.
THERE'S A THOUGHT.
YOU'RE READY TO SKI? WOULD YOU LIKE SOME COMPANY?
I'D SAY YES, STEFAN...
...BUT I'M AFRAID YOU MIGHT HAVE SOME TROUBLE KEEPING UP.

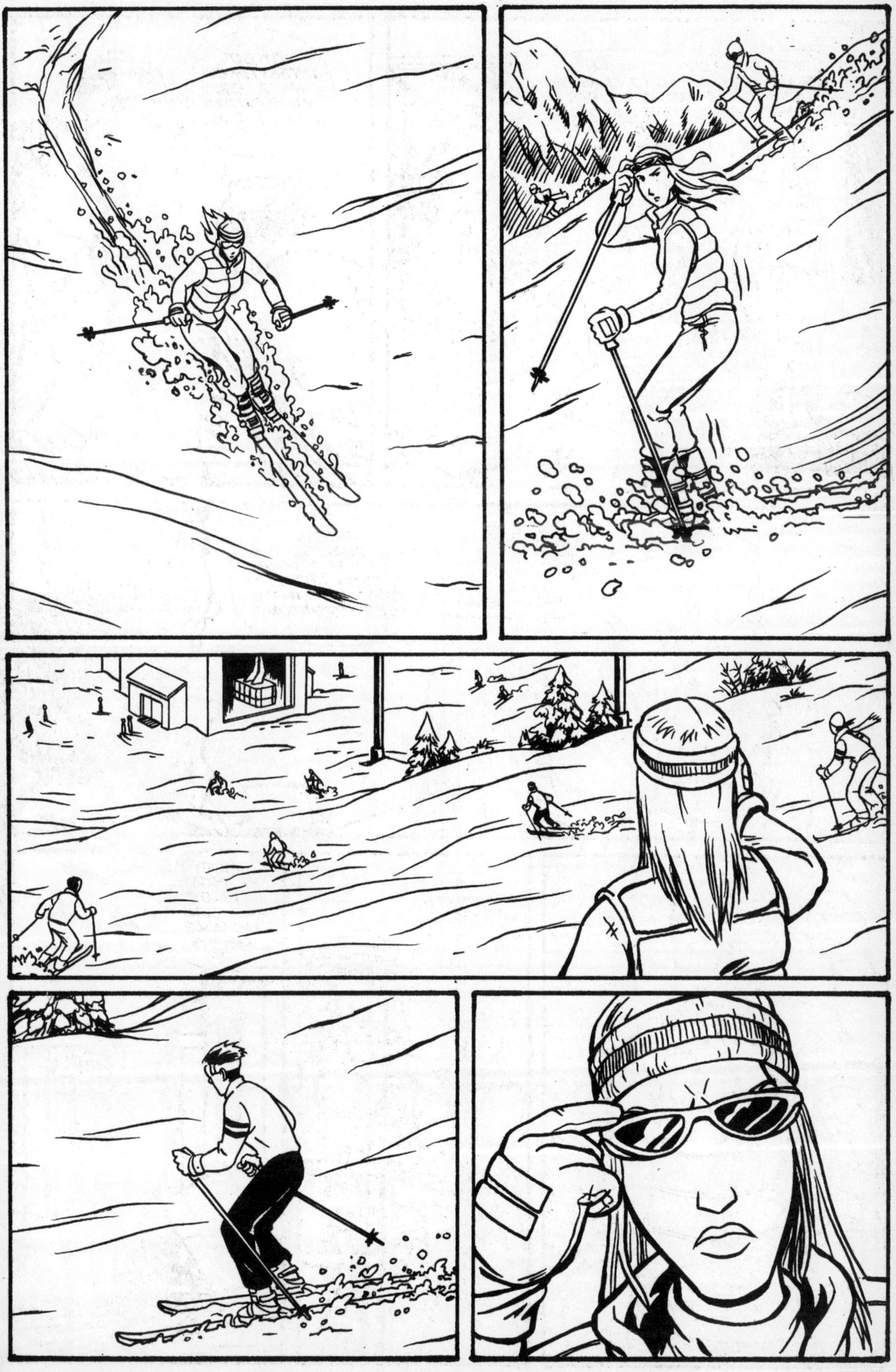

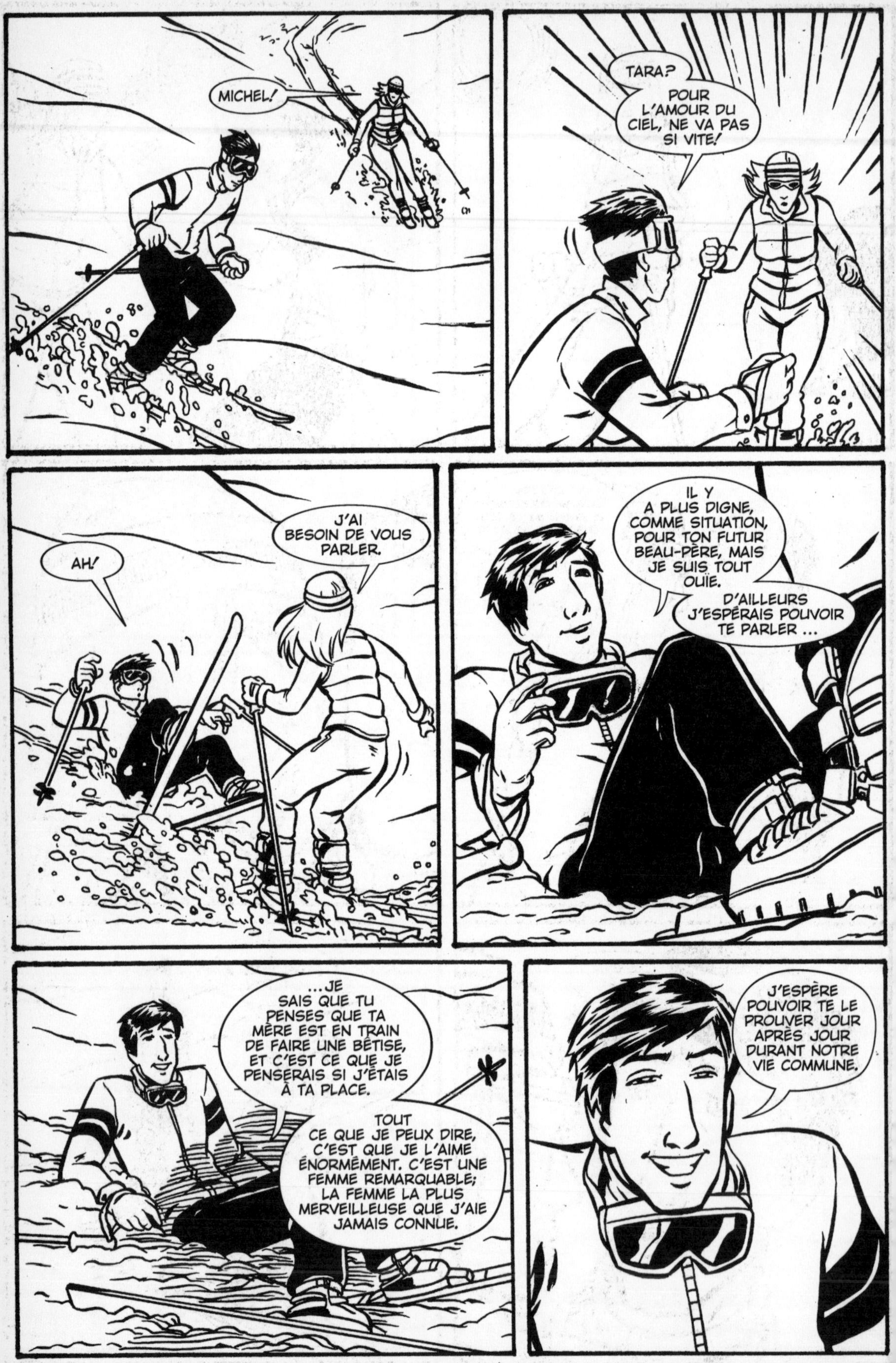
MICHEL!
TARA?
POUR L'AMOUR DU CIEL, NE VA PAS SI VITE!
AH!
J'AI BESOIN DE VOUS PARLER.
IL Y A PLUS DIGNE, COMME SITUATION, POUR TON FUTUR BEAU-PÈRE, MAIS JE SUIS TOUT OUÏE.
D'AILLEURS J'ESPÉRAIS POUVOIR TE PARLER ...
...JE SAIS QUE TU PENSES QUE TA MÈRE EST EN TRAIN DE FAIRE UNE BÊTISE, ET C'EST CE QUE JE PENSERAIS SI J'ÉTAIS À TA PLACE.
TOUT CE QUE JE PEUX DIRE, C'EST QUE JE L'AIME ÉNORMÉMENT. C'EST UNE FEMME REMARQUABLE; LA FEMME LA PLUS MERVEILLEUSE QUE J'AIE JAMAIS CONNUE.
J'ESPÈRE POUVOIR TE LE PROUVER JOUR APRÈS JOUR DURANT NOTRE VIE COMMUNE.

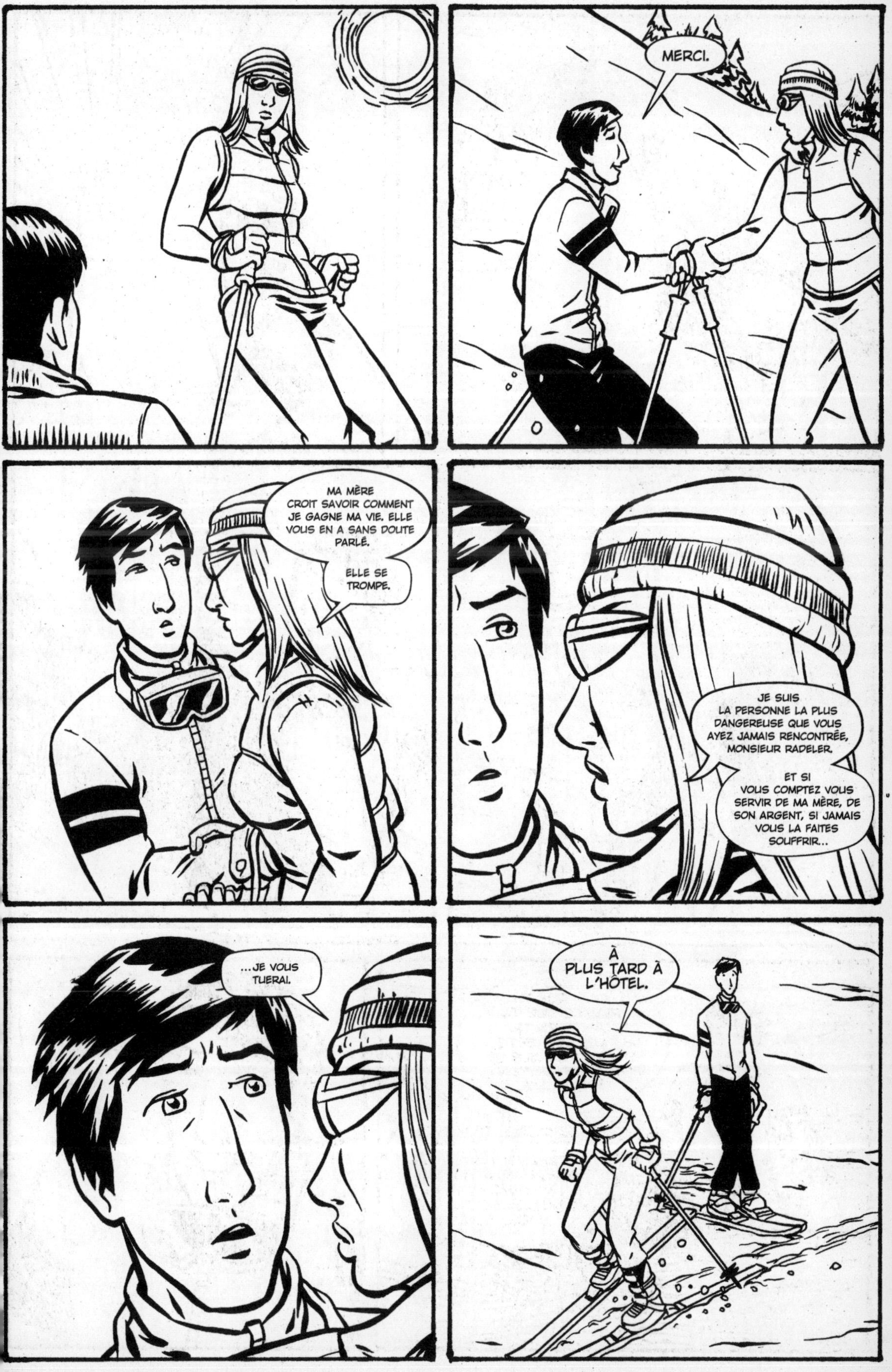
MERCI.
MA MÈRE CROIT SAVOIR COMMENT JE GAGNE MA VIE. ELLE VOUS EN A SANS DOUTE PARLÉ.
ELLE SE TROMPE.
JE SUIS LA PERSONNE LA PLUS DANGEREUSE QUE VOUS AYEZ JAMAIS RENCONTRÉE, MONSIEUR RADELER.
ET SI VOUS COMPTEZ VOUS SERVIR DE MA MÈRE, DE SON ARGENT, SI JAMAIS VOUS LA FAITES SOUFFRIR...
...JE VOUS TUERAI.
À PLUS TARD À L'HÔTEL.

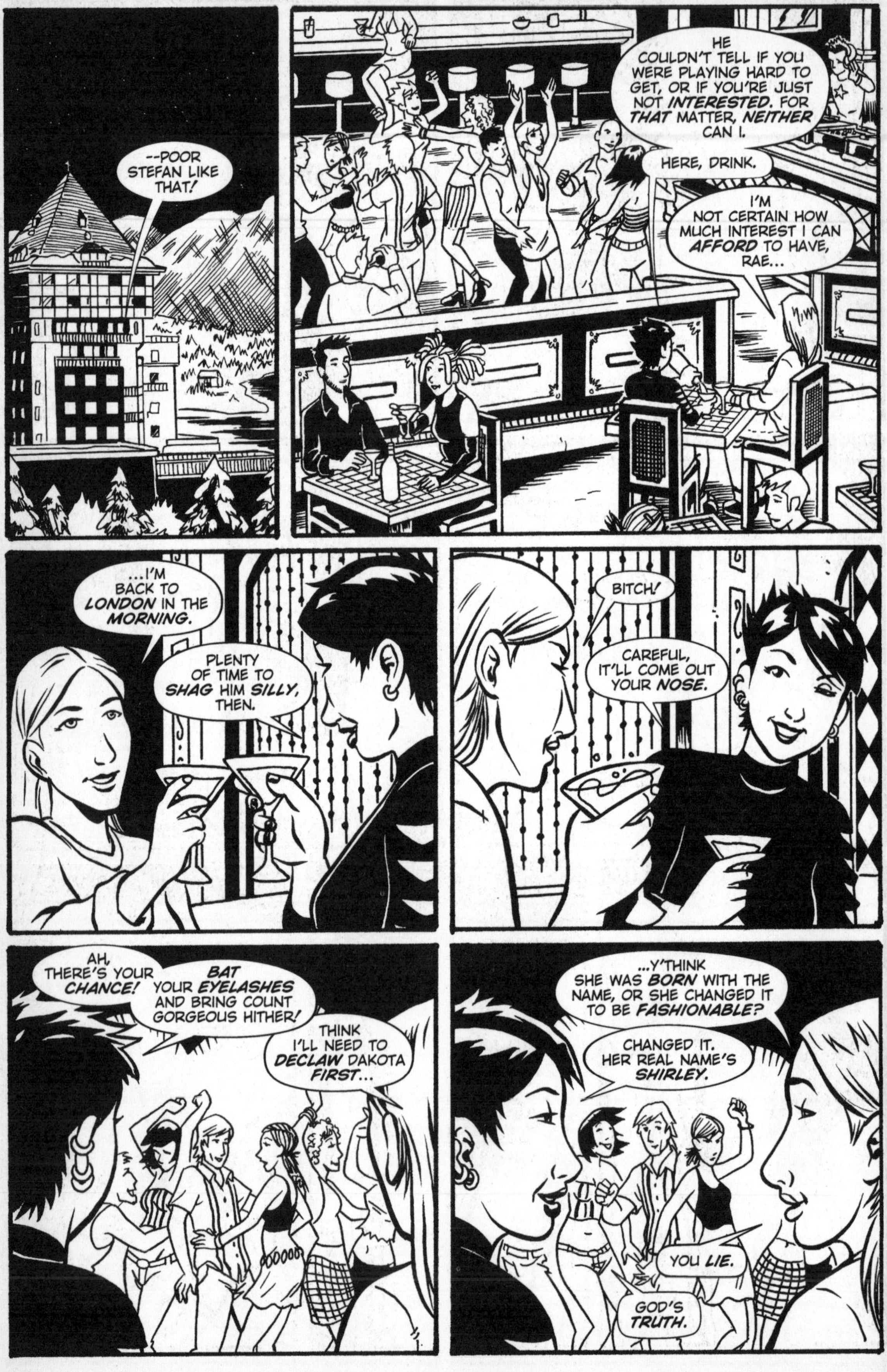
--POOR STEFAN LIKE THAT!
HE COULDN'T TELL IF YOU WERE PLAYING HARD TO GET, OR IF YOU'RE JUST NOT INTERESTED. FOR THAT MATTER, NEITHER CAN I.
HERE, DRINK.
I'M NOT CERTAIN HOW MUCH INTEREST I CAN AFFORD TO HAVE, RAE...
...I'M BACK TO LONDON IN THE MORNING.
PLENTY OF TIME TO SHAG HIM SILLY, THEN.
BITCH!
CAREFUL, IT'LL COME OUT YOUR NOSE.
AH, THERE'S YOUR CHANCE!
BAT YOUR EYELASHES AND BRING COUNT GORGEOUS HITHER!
THINK I'LL NEED TO DECLAW DAKOTA FIRST...
...Y'THINK SHE WAS BORN WITH THE NAME, OR SHE CHANGED IT TO BE FASHIONABLE?
CHANGED IT. HER REAL NAME'S SHIRLEY.
YOU LIE.
GOD'S TRUTH.

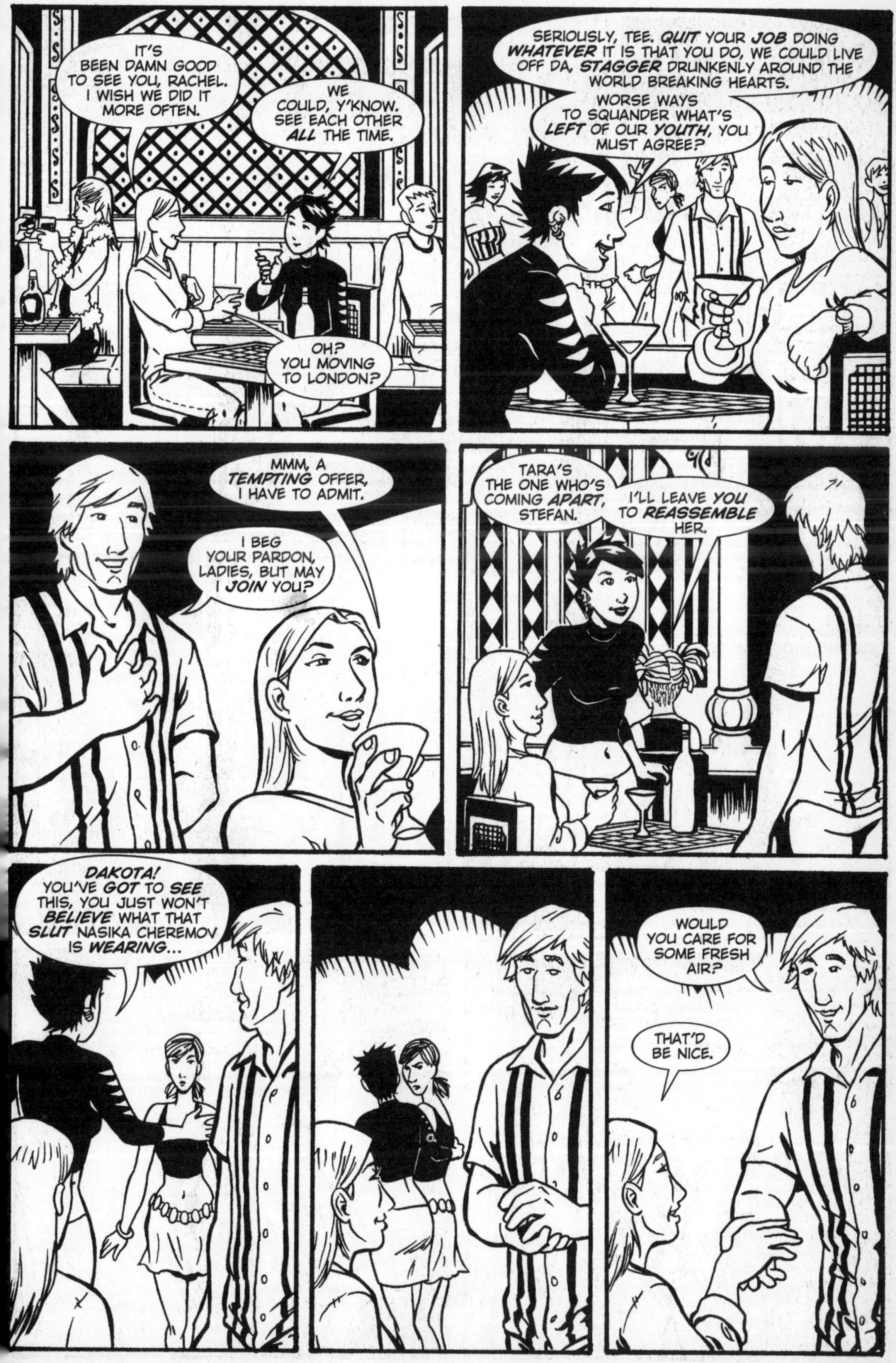
IT'S BEEN DAMN GOOD TO SEE YOU, RACHEL. I WISH WE DID IT MORE OFTEN.
WE COULD, Y'KNOW. SEE EACH OTHER ALL THE TIME.
OH? YOU MOVING TO LONDON?
SERIOUSLY, TEE. QUIT YOUR JOB DOING WHATEVER IT IS THAT YOU DO, WE COULD LIVE OFF DA, STAGGER DRUNKENLY AROUND THE WORLD BREAKING HEARTS.
WORSE WAYS TO SQUANDER WHAT'S LEFT OF OUR YOUTH, YOU MUST AGREE?
MMM, A TEMPTING OFFER, I HAVE TO ADMIT.
I BEG YOUR PARDON, LADIES, BUT MAY I JOIN YOU?
TARA'S THE ONE WHO'S COMING APART, STEFAN.
I'LL LEAVE YOU TO REASSEMBLE HER.
DAKOTA! YOU'VE GOT TO SEE THIS, YOU JUST WON'T BELIEVE WHAT THAT SLUT NASIKA CHEREMOV IS WEARING...
WOULD YOU CARE FOR SOME FRESH AIR?
THAT'D BE NICE.

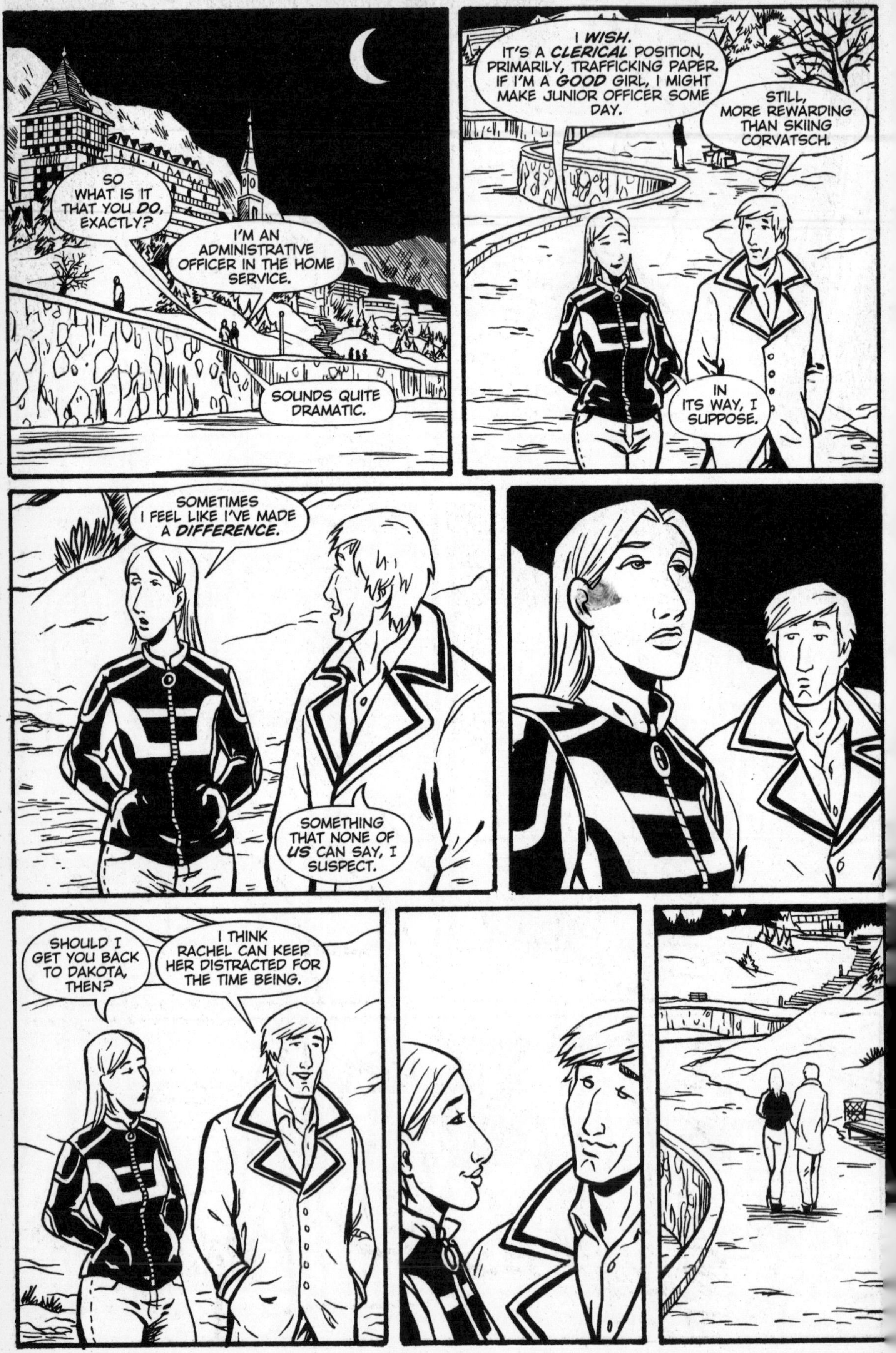
SO WHAT IS IT THAT YOU *DO*, EXACTLY?
I'M AN ADMINISTRATIVE OFFICER IN THE HOME SERVICE.
SOUNDS QUITE DRAMATIC.
I *WISH*. IT'S A *CLERICAL* POSITION, PRIMARILY, TRAFFICKING PAPER. IF I'M A *GOOD* GIRL, I MIGHT MAKE JUNIOR OFFICER SOME DAY.
STILL, MORE REWARDING THAN SKIING CORVATSCH.
IN ITS WAY, I SUPPOSE.
SOMETIMES I FEEL LIKE I'VE MADE A *DIFFERENCE*.
SOMETHING THAT NONE OF *US* CAN SAY, I SUSPECT.
SHOULD I GET YOU BACK TO DAKOTA, THEN?
I THINK RACHEL CAN KEEP HER DISTRACTED FOR THE TIME BEING.

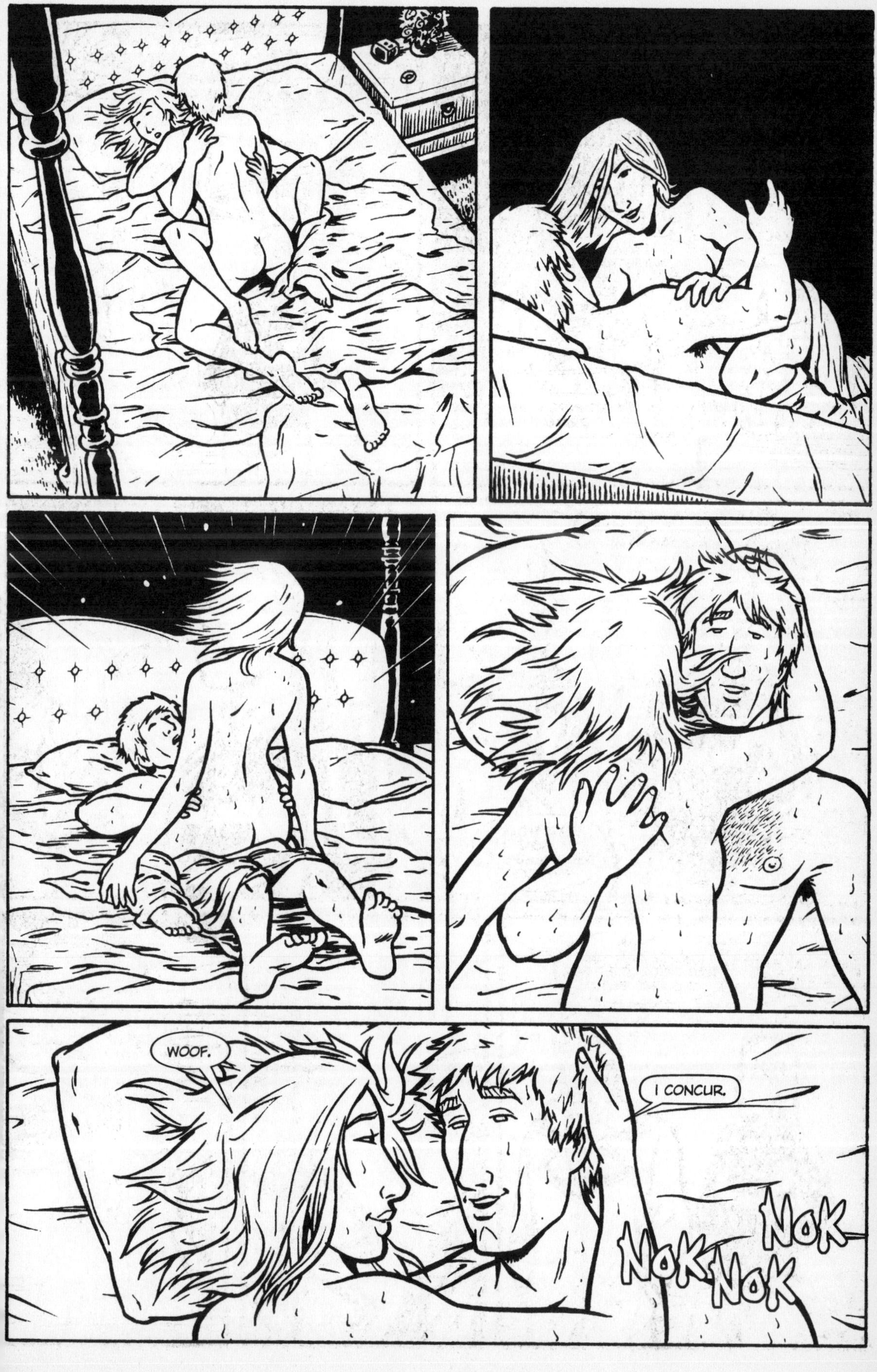
WOOF.
I CONCUR.
NOK NOK NOK

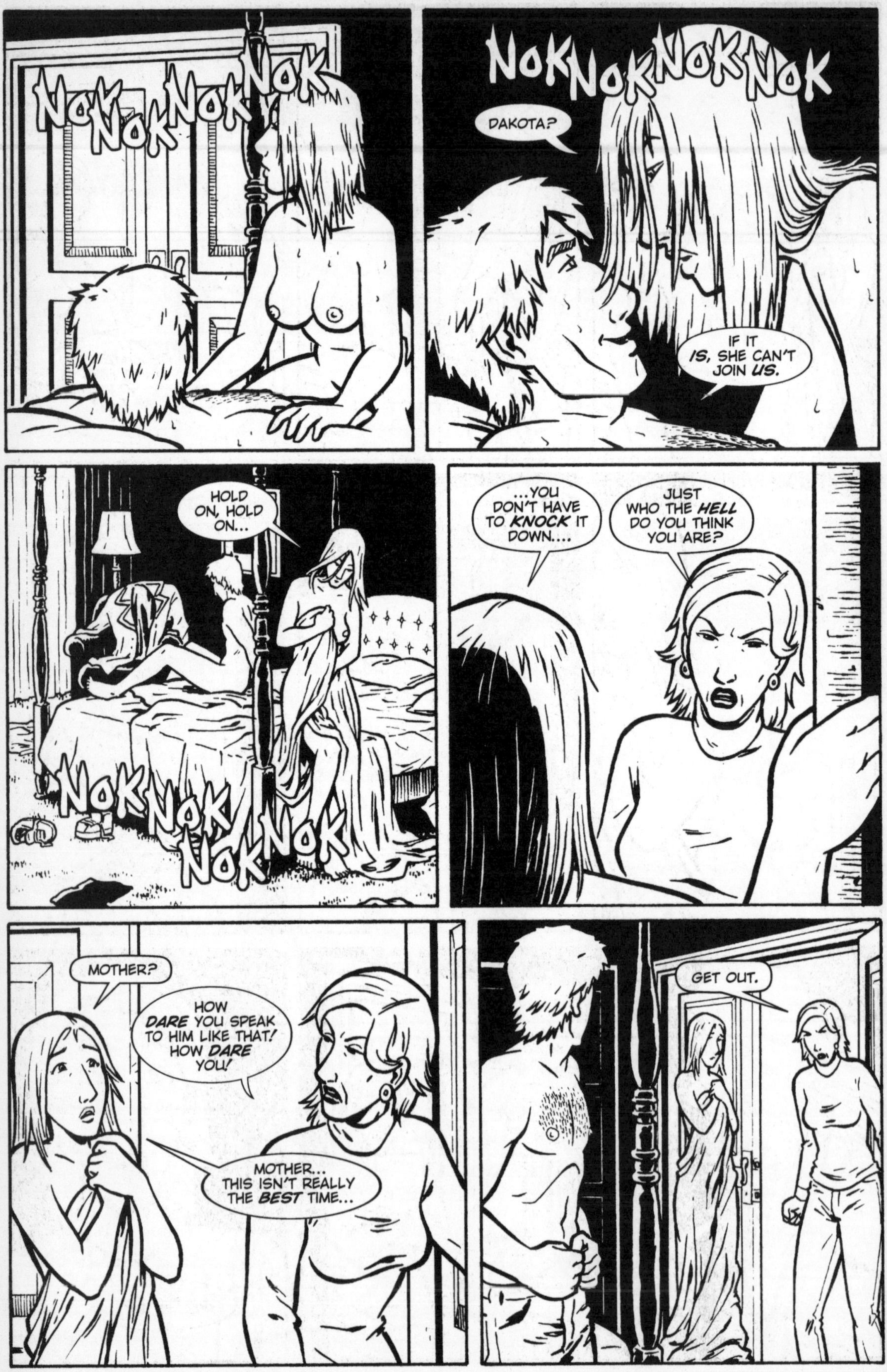
NOKNOKNOKNOK
NOKNOKNOKNOK
DAKOTA?
IF IT IS, SHE CAN'T JOIN US.
HOLD ON, HOLD ON...
NOKNOKNOKNOK
...YOU DON'T HAVE TO KNOCK IT DOWN....
JUST WHO THE HELL DO YOU THINK YOU ARE?
MOTHER?
HOW DARE YOU SPEAK TO HIM LIKE THAT! HOW DARE YOU!
MOTHER... THIS ISN'T REALLY THE BEST TIME...
GET OUT.

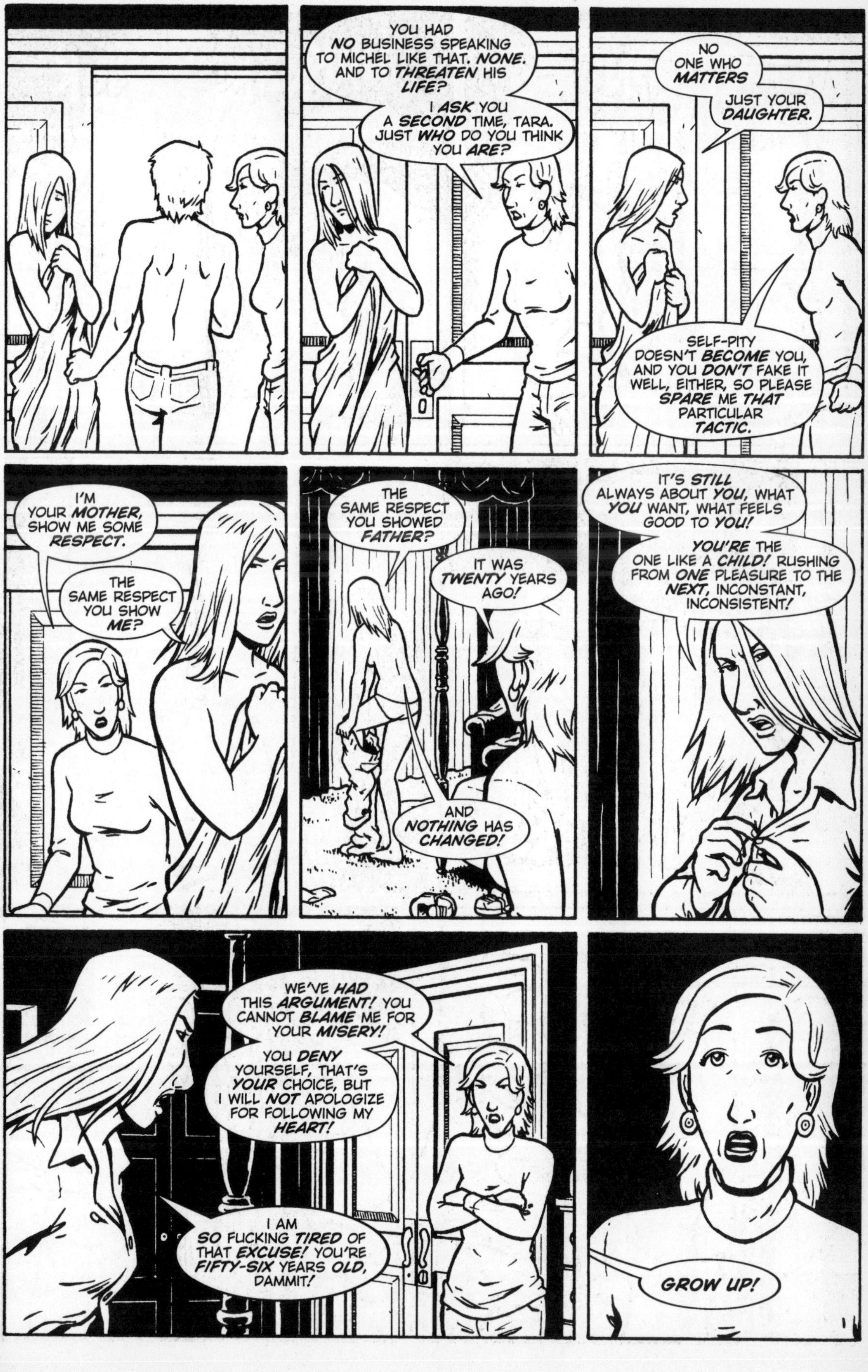
YOU HAD NO BUSINESS SPEAKING TO MICHEL LIKE THAT. NONE. AND TO THREATEN HIS LIFE?
I ASK YOU A SECOND TIME, TARA. JUST WHO DO YOU THINK YOU ARE?
NO ONE WHO MATTERS
JUST YOUR DAUGHTER.
SELF-PITY DOESN'T BECOME YOU, AND YOU DON'T FAKE IT WELL, EITHER, SO PLEASE SPARE ME THAT PARTICULAR TACTIC.
I'M YOUR MOTHER, SHOW ME SOME RESPECT.
THE SAME RESPECT YOU SHOW ME?
THE SAME RESPECT YOU SHOWED FATHER?
IT WAS TWENTY YEARS AGO!
AND NOTHING HAS CHANGED!
IT'S STILL ALWAYS ABOUT YOU, WHAT YOU WANT, WHAT FEELS GOOD TO YOU!
YOU'RE THE ONE LIKE A CHILD! RUSHING FROM ONE PLEASURE TO THE NEXT, INCONSTANT, INCONSISTENT!
WE'VE HAD THIS ARGUMENT! YOU CANNOT BLAME ME FOR YOUR MISERY!
YOU DENY YOURSELF, THAT'S YOUR CHOICE, BUT I WILL NOT APOLOGIZE FOR FOLLOWING MY HEART!
I AM SO FUCKING TIRED OF THAT EXCUSE! YOU'RE FIFTY-SIX YEARS OLD, DAMMIT!
GROW UP!

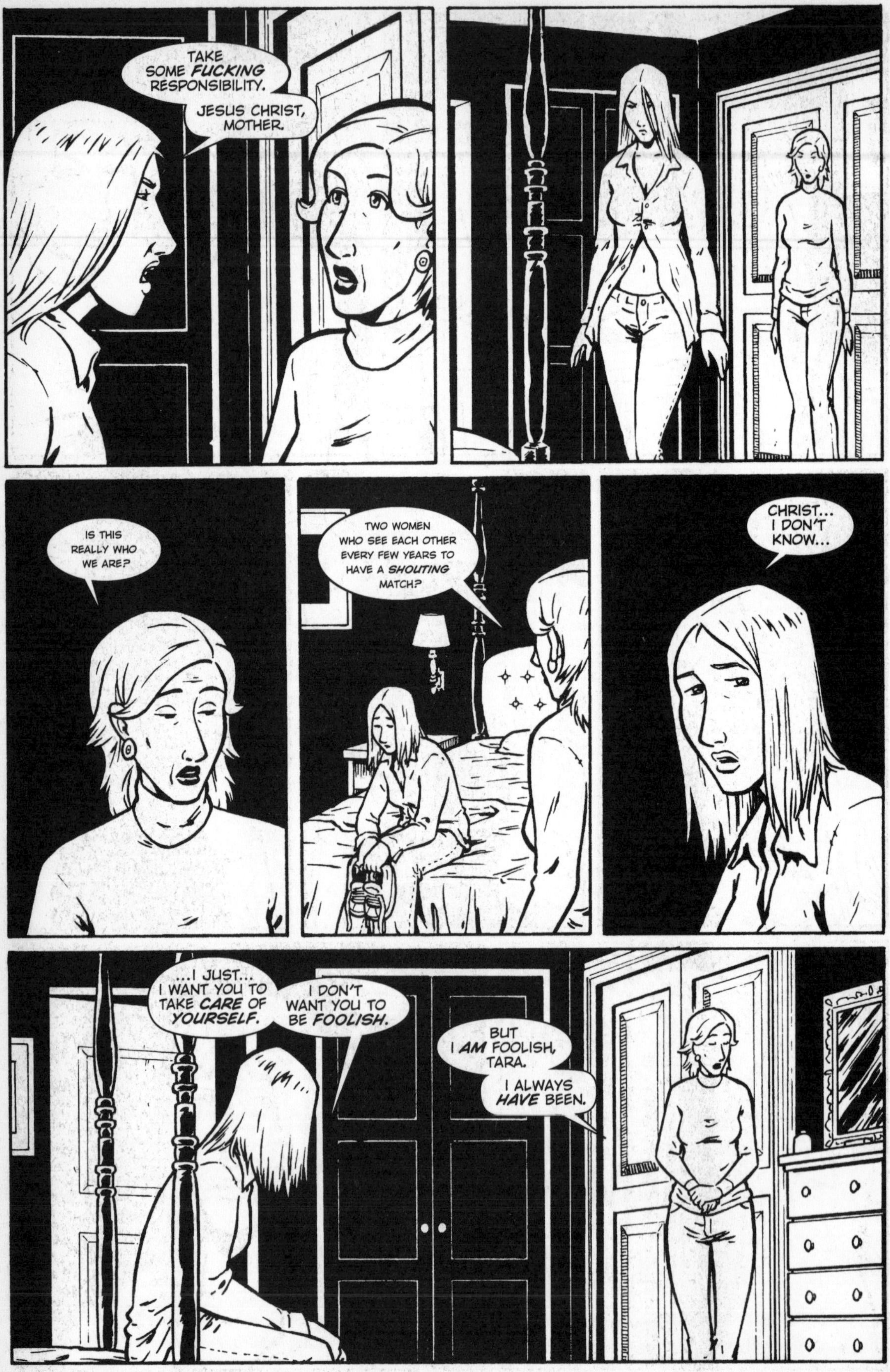
TAKE SOME FUCKING RESPONSIBILITY.
JESUS CHRIST, MOTHER.
IS THIS REALLY WHO WE ARE?
TWO WOMEN WHO SEE EACH OTHER EVERY FEW YEARS TO HAVE A SHOUTING MATCH?
CHRIST... I DON'T KNOW...
...I JUST... I WANT YOU TO TAKE CARE OF YOURSELF.
I DON'T WANT YOU TO BE FOOLISH.
BUT I AM FOOLISH, TARA.
I ALWAYS HAVE BEEN.

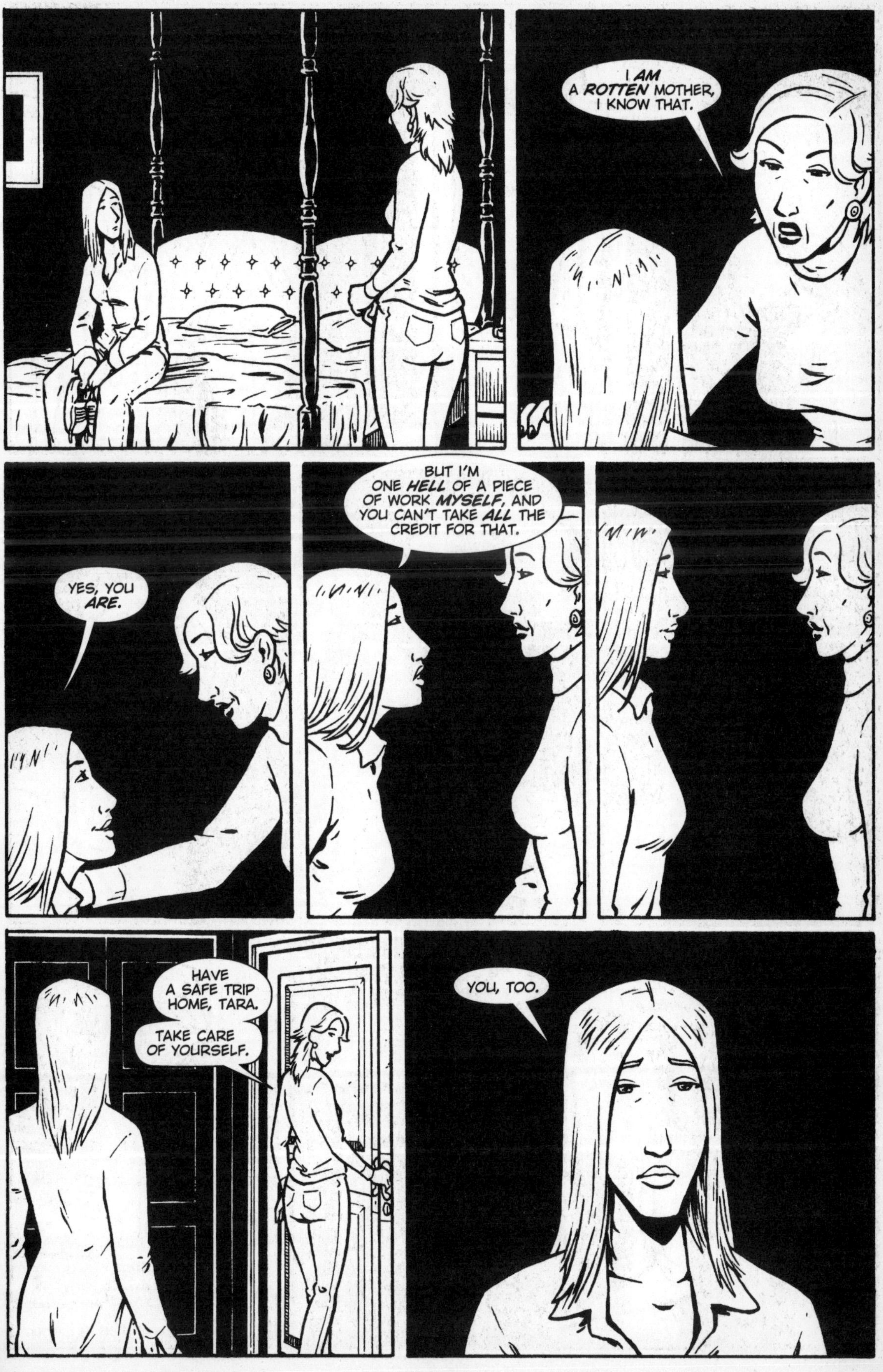
I AM A ROTTEN MOTHER, I KNOW THAT.
YES, YOU ARE.
BUT I'M ONE HELL OF A PIECE OF WORK MYSELF, AND YOU CAN'T TAKE ALL THE CREDIT FOR THAT.
HAVE A SAFE TRIP HOME, TARA.
TAKE CARE OF YOURSELF.
YOU, TOO.

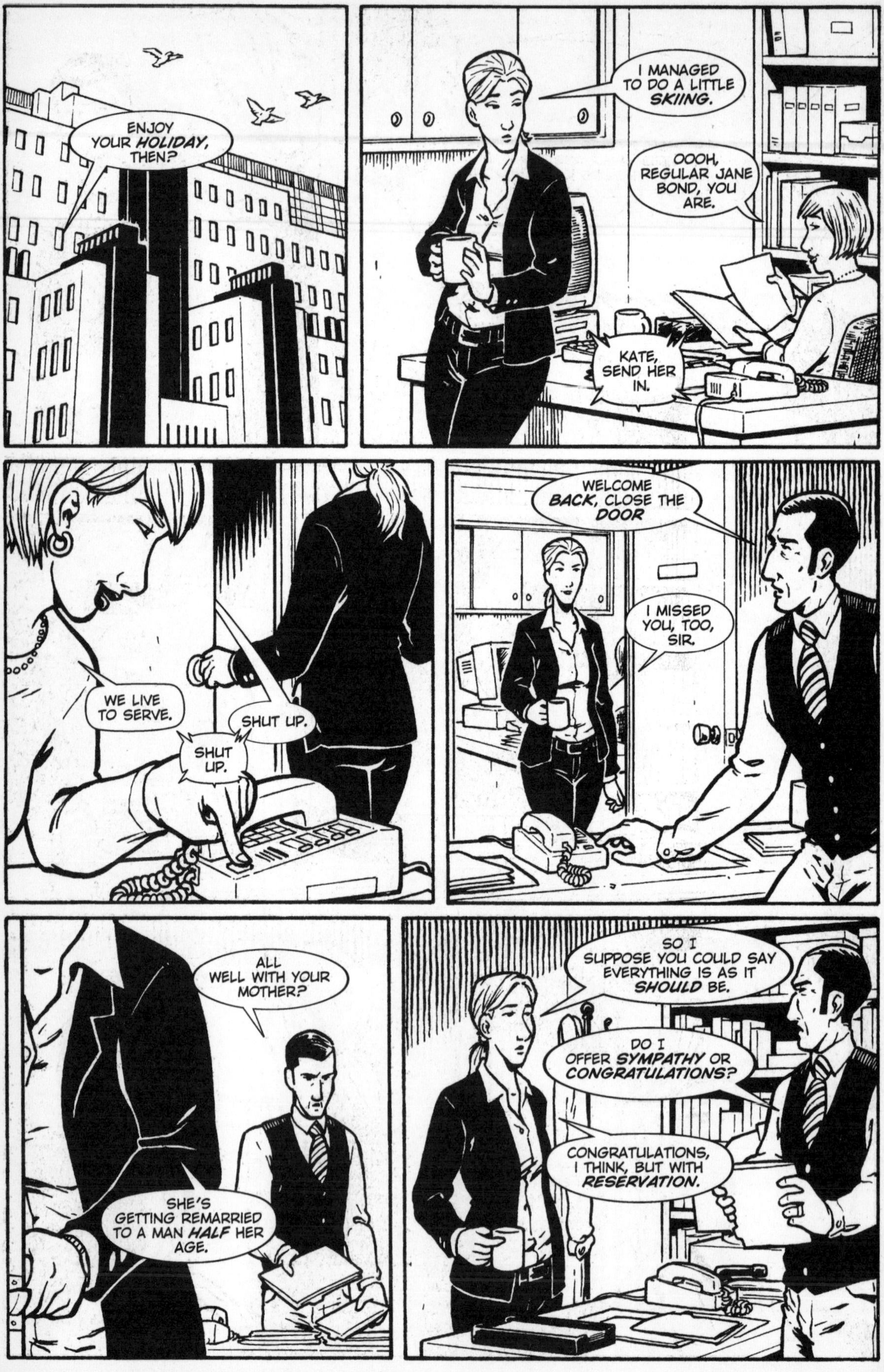
ENJOY YOUR HOLIDAY, THEN?
I MANAGED TO DO A LITTLE SKIING.
OOOH, REGULAR JANE BOND, YOU ARE.
KATE, SEND HER IN.
WE LIVE TO SERVE.
SHUT UP.
SHUT UP.
WELCOME BACK, CLOSE THE DOOR
I MISSED YOU, TOO, SIR.
ALL WELL WITH YOUR MOTHER?
SHE'S GETTING REMARRIED TO A MAN HALF HER AGE.
SO I SUPPOSE YOU COULD SAY EVERYTHING IS AS IT SHOULD BE.
DO I OFFER SYMPATHY OR CONGRATULATIONS?
CONGRATULATIONS, I THINK, BUT WITH RESERVATION.

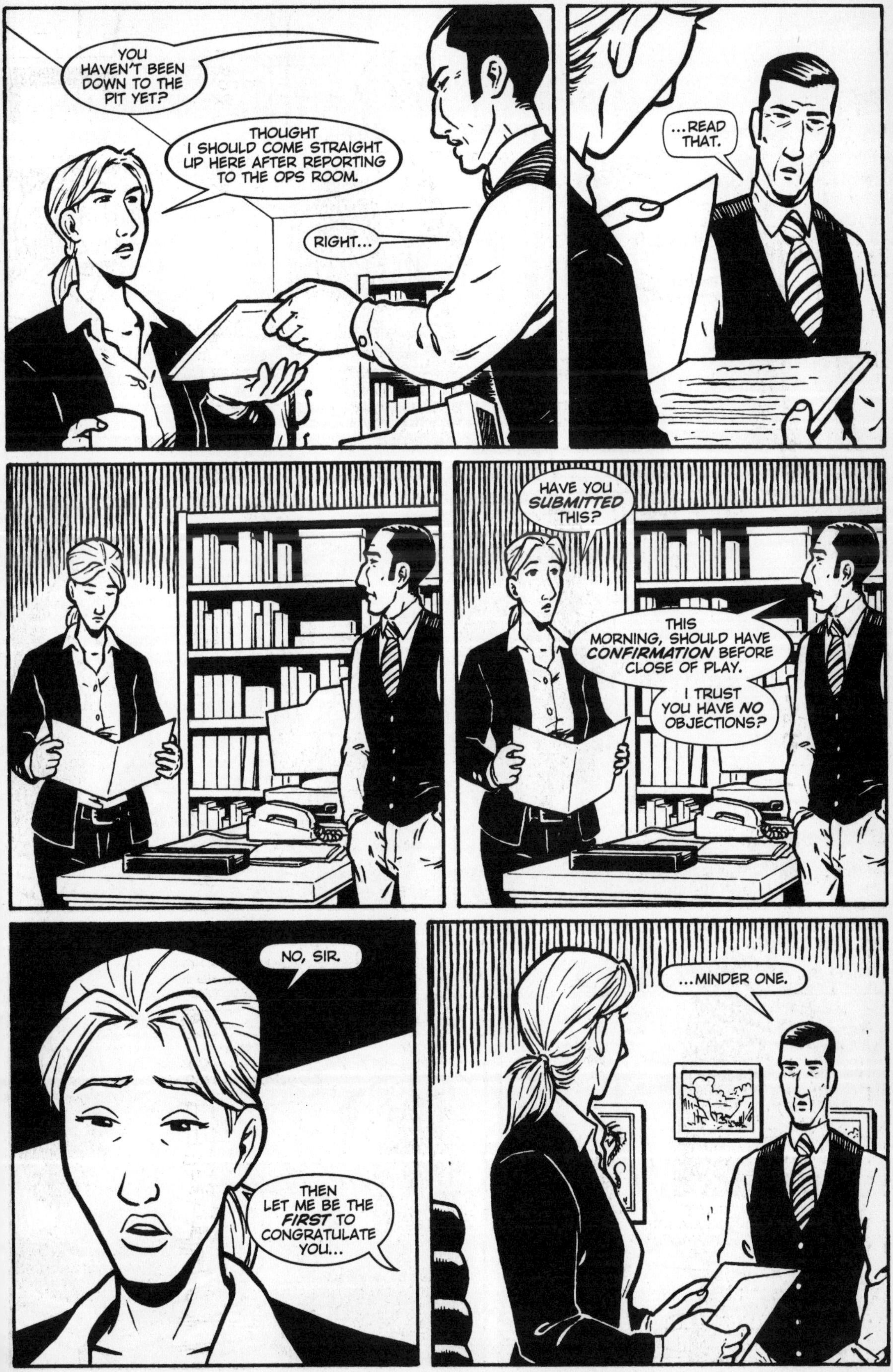
YOU HAVEN'T BEEN DOWN TO THE PIT YET?
THOUGHT I SHOULD COME STRAIGHT UP HERE AFTER REPORTING TO THE OPS ROOM.
RIGHT...
...READ THAT.
HAVE YOU SUBMITTED THIS?
THIS MORNING, SHOULD HAVE CONFIRMATION BEFORE CLOSE OF PLAY.
I TRUST YOU HAVE NO OBJECTIONS?
NO, SIR.
THEN LET ME BE THE FIRST TO CONGRATULATE YOU...
...MINDER ONE.

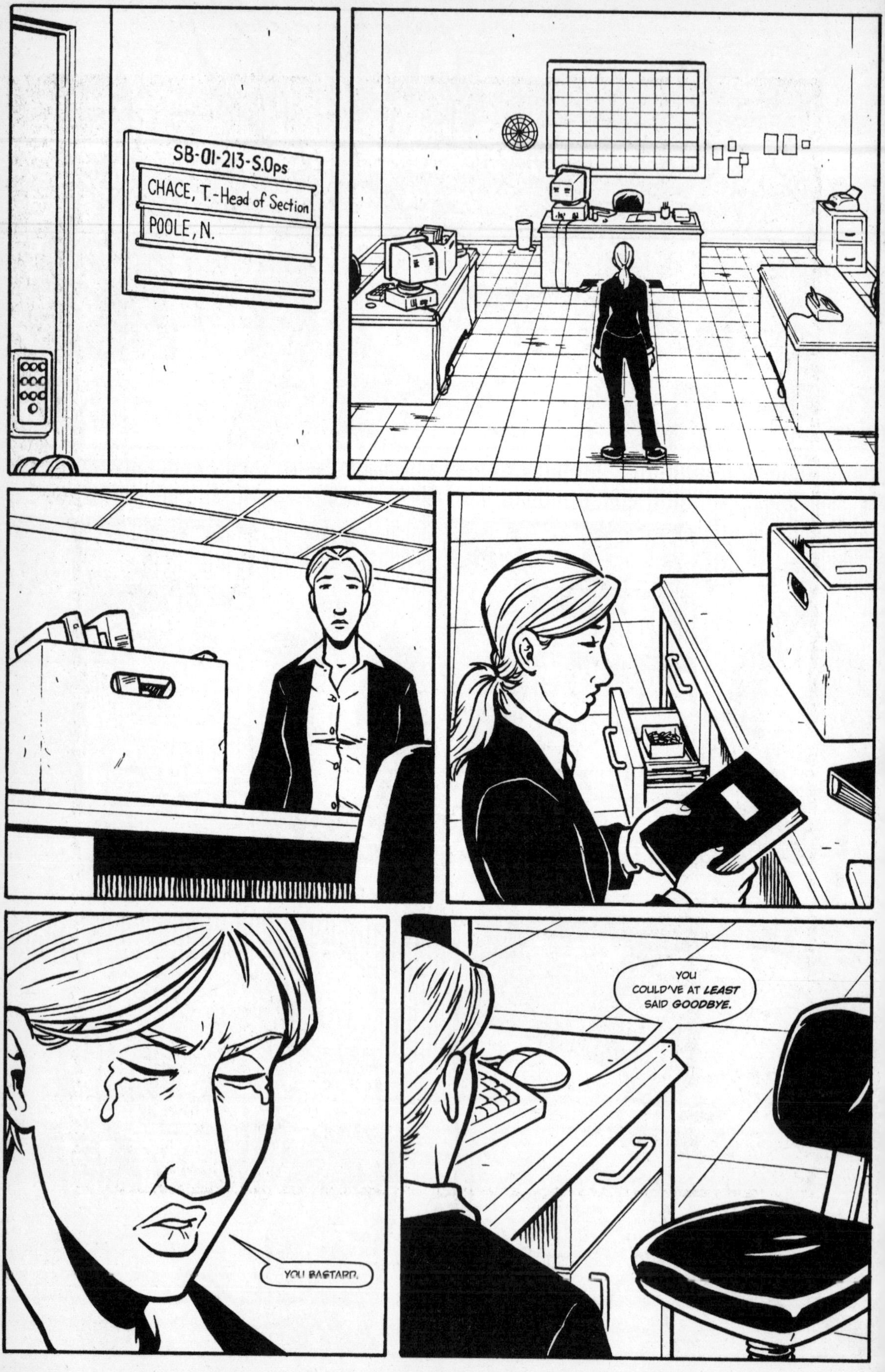

SB-01-213-S.Ops
CHACE, T.-Head of Section
POOLE, N.
YOU BASTARD.
YOU COULD'VE AT *LEAST* SAID *GOODBYE.*

# CHAPTER 1

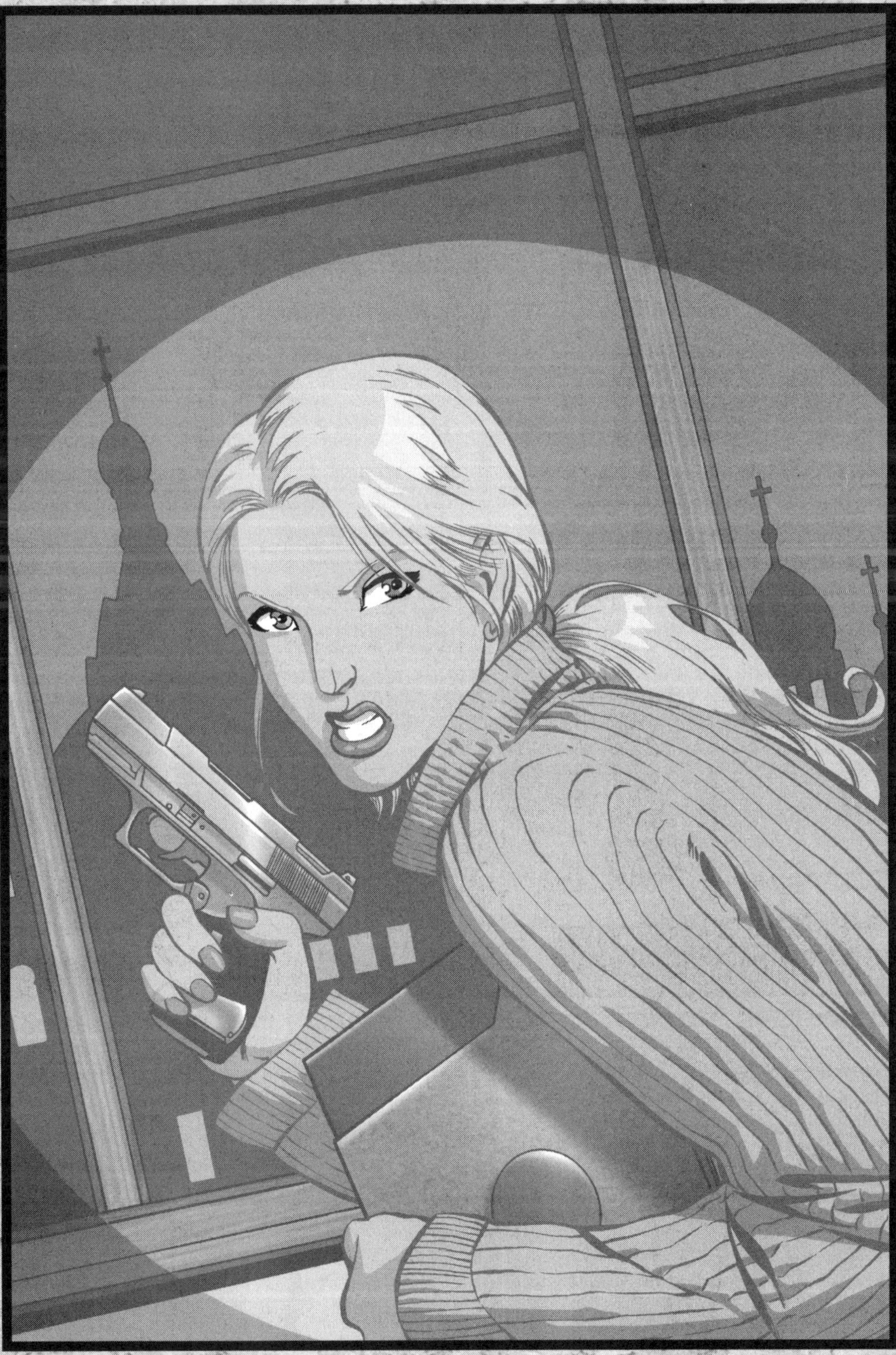

# ROSTER

### TARA CHACE

Head of Special Section, designate Minder 1.

### PAUL CROCKER

Director of Operations, encompassing all field work in all theaters of operations.

In addition to commanding individual stations, has direct command of the Special Section—sometimes referred to as Minders—used for special operations.

### NICK POOLE

Former S.A.S. officer and recently christened Minder 2.

### FRANCES BARCLAY

Chief of Service, also known as 'C.' Distinguished service as CIA-Liaison, Chairman of the Joint Intelligence Committee, and as Head of Station Prague (85-88), Saigon (89-91), and Paris (91-94).

### CHRIS LANKFORD

The fourth man to hold the title of Minder 3 in less than 18 months. Untested, Lankford's yet to spend significant time in the field.

### DONALD WELDON

Deputy Chief of Service, has oversight of all aspects of Intelligence gathering and operations. Immediate superior to Crocker.

# OPS ROOM STAFF:

### KATE

Personal Assistant to Paul Crocker, termed P.A. to D.Ops. Possibly the hardest and most important job in the Service.

### RON

Duty Operations Officer, responsible for monitoring the status and importance of all incoming intelligence, both from foreign stations and other sources.

### ALEXIS

Mission Control Officer (also called Main Communications Officer)—responsible for maintaining communications between the Operations Room and the agents in the field.

# OTHERS:

### TOM WALLACE

Former Head of Special Section and mentor of Tara Chace. Recently opted out of the Section in favor of a new career with a higher life expectancy.

### EDWARD KITTERING

Special Operations Officer, designated Minder Three. Has been with the Special Section for less than a year.

DECEASED

### BRIAN BUTLER

A former sergeant in one of the British Army's oldest and most respected regiments. An unique individual who actually requested assignment with special section.

DECEASED

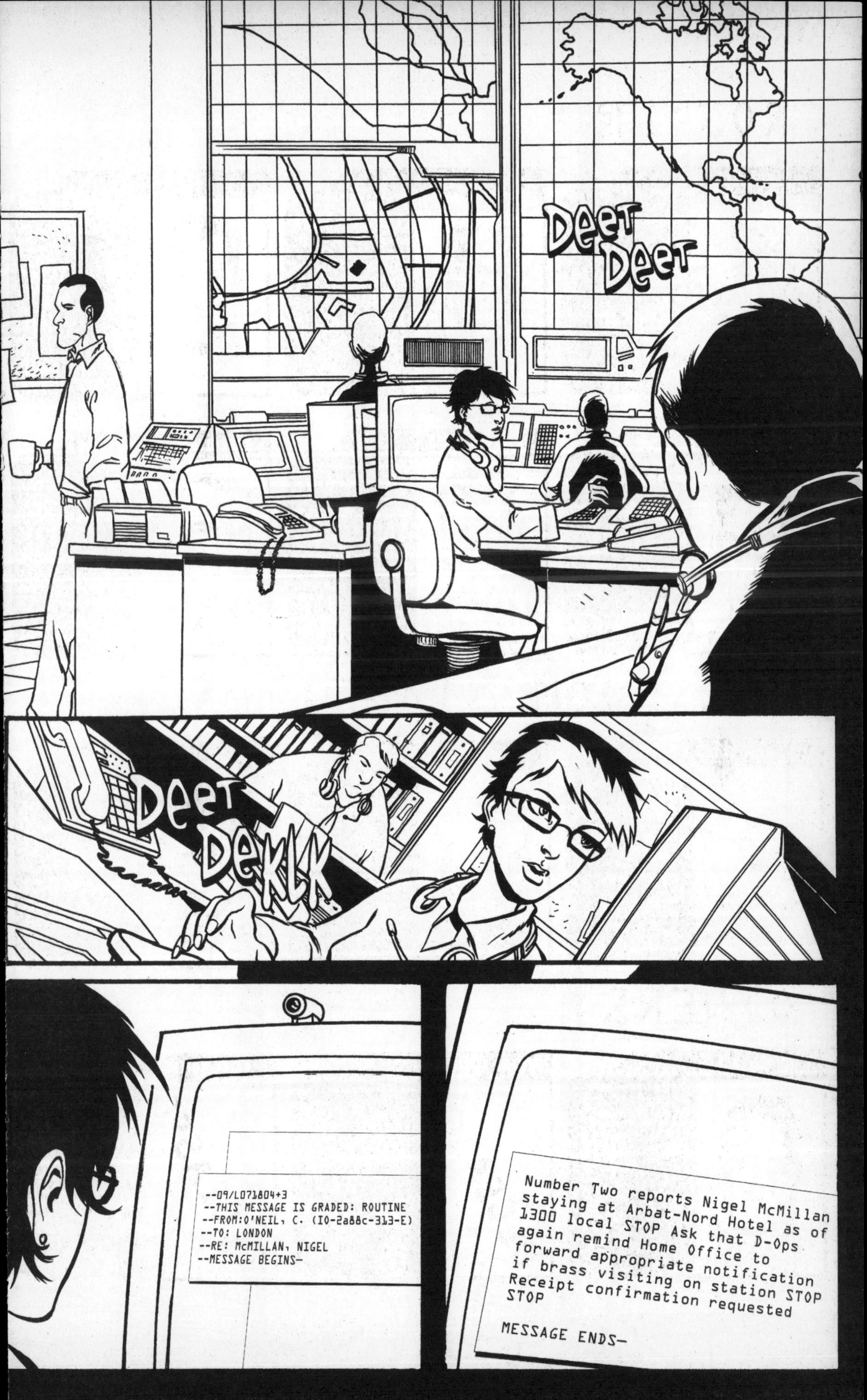
DEET DEET
DEET DEKLK
--09/L071804+3
--THIS MESSAGE IS GRADED: ROUTINE
--FROM:O'NEIL, C. (IO-2a88c-313-E)
--TO: LONDON
--RE: McMILLAN, NIGEL
--MESSAGE BEGINS-
Number Two reports Nigel McMillan staying at Arbat-Nord Hotel as of 1300 local STOP Ask that D-Ops again remind Home Office to forward appropriate notification if brass visiting on station STOP Receipt confirmation requested STOP
MESSAGE ENDS-

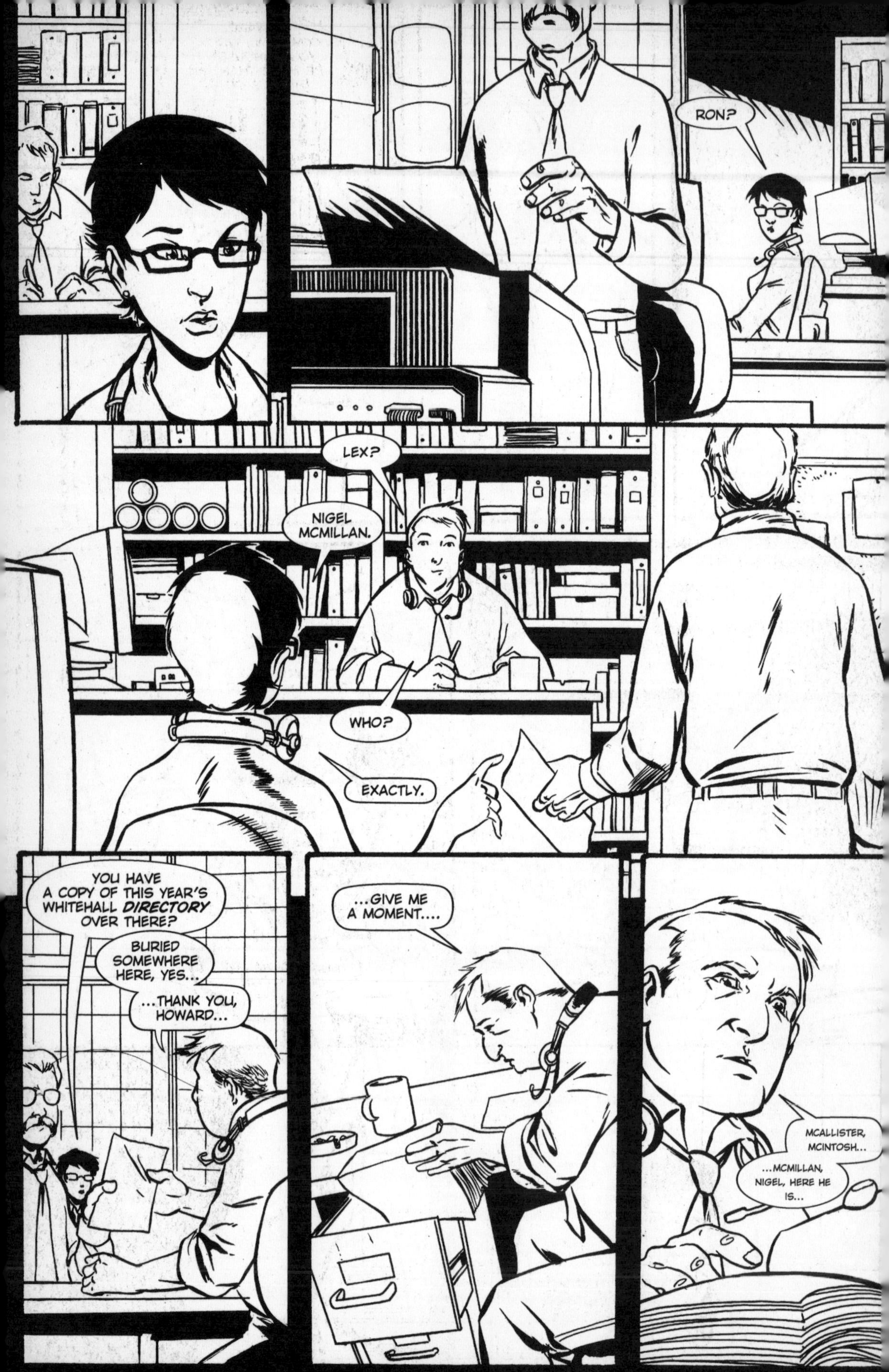
RON?
LEX?
NIGEL MCMILLAN.
WHO?
EXACTLY.
YOU HAVE A COPY OF THIS YEAR'S WHITEHALL *DIRECTORY* OVER THERE?
BURIED SOMEWHERE HERE, YES...
...THANK YOU, HOWARD...
...GIVE ME A MOMENT....
MCALLISTER, MCINTOSH...
...MCMILLAN, NIGEL, HERE HE IS...

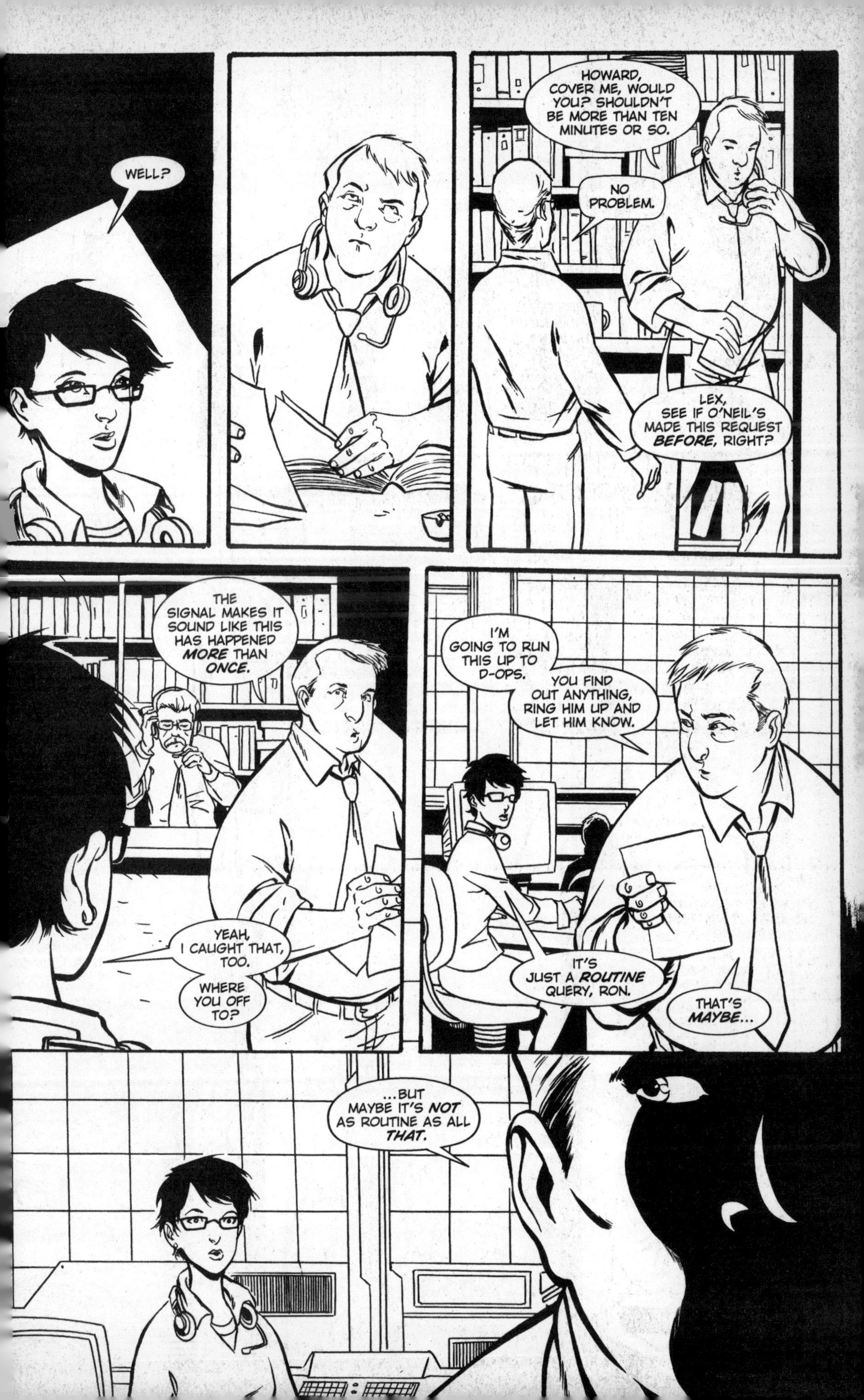
WELL?
HOWARD, COVER ME, WOULD YOU? SHOULDN'T BE MORE THAN TEN MINUTES OR SO.
NO PROBLEM.
LEX, SEE IF O'NEIL'S MADE THIS REQUEST BEFORE, RIGHT?
THE SIGNAL MAKES IT SOUND LIKE THIS HAS HAPPENED MORE THAN ONCE.
YEAH, I CAUGHT THAT, TOO.
WHERE YOU OFF TO?
I'M GOING TO RUN THIS UP TO D-OPS.
YOU FIND OUT ANYTHING, RING HIM UP AND LET HIM KNOW.
IT'S JUST A ROUTINE QUERY, RON.
THAT'S MAYBE...
...BUT MAYBE IT'S NOT AS ROUTINE AS ALL THAT.

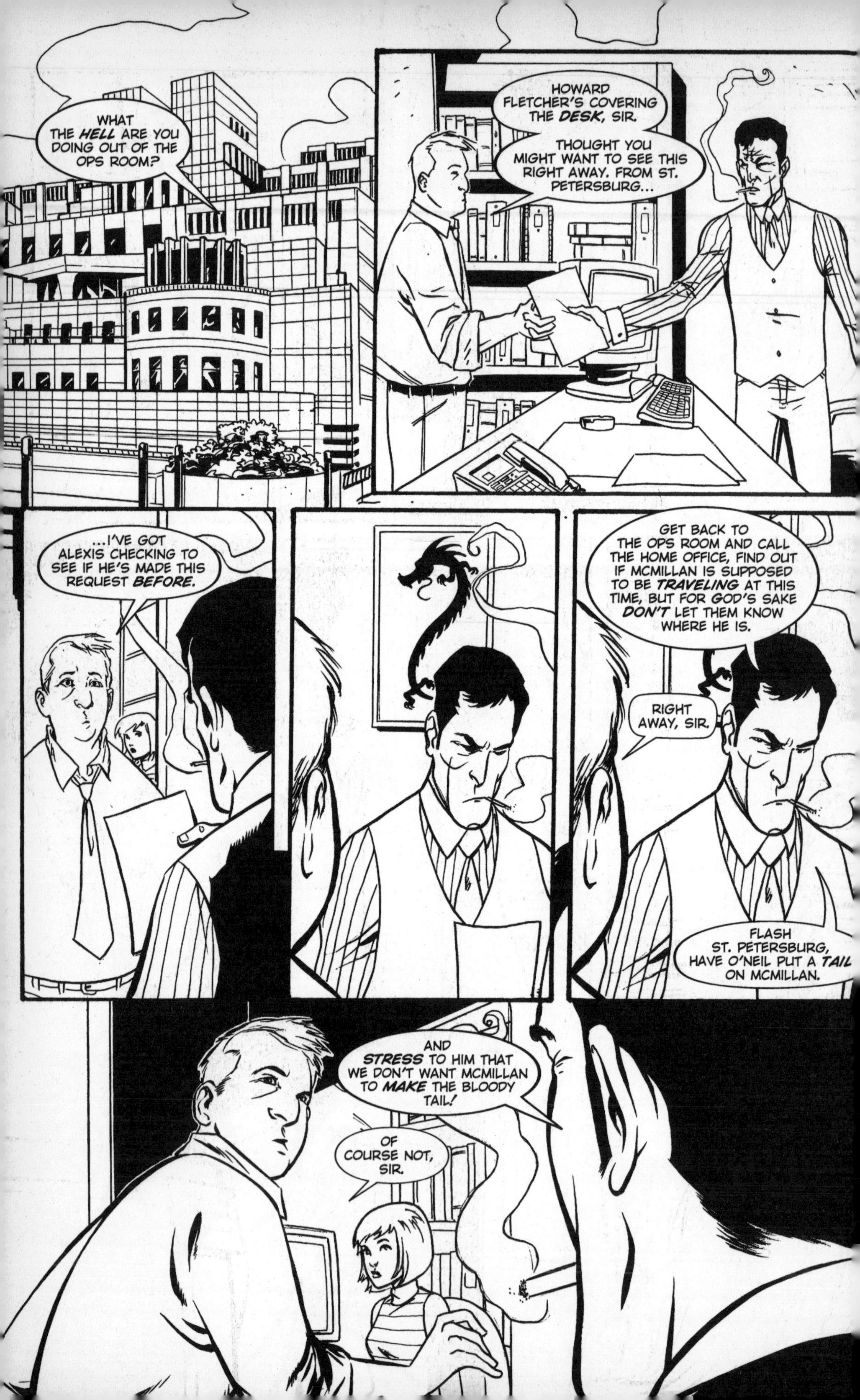
WHAT THE HELL ARE YOU DOING OUT OF THE OPS ROOM?
HOWARD FLETCHER'S COVERING THE DESK, SIR.
THOUGHT YOU MIGHT WANT TO SEE THIS RIGHT AWAY. FROM ST. PETERSBURG...
...I'VE GOT ALEXIS CHECKING TO SEE IF HE'S MADE THIS REQUEST BEFORE.
GET BACK TO THE OPS ROOM AND CALL THE HOME OFFICE, FIND OUT IF MCMILLAN IS SUPPOSED TO BE TRAVELING AT THIS TIME, BUT FOR GOD'S SAKE DON'T LET THEM KNOW WHERE HE IS.
RIGHT AWAY, SIR.
FLASH ST. PETERSBURG, HAVE O'NEIL PUT A TAIL ON MCMILLAN.
AND STRESS TO HIM THAT WE DON'T WANT MCMILLAN TO MAKE THE BLOODY TAIL!
OF COURSE NOT, SIR.

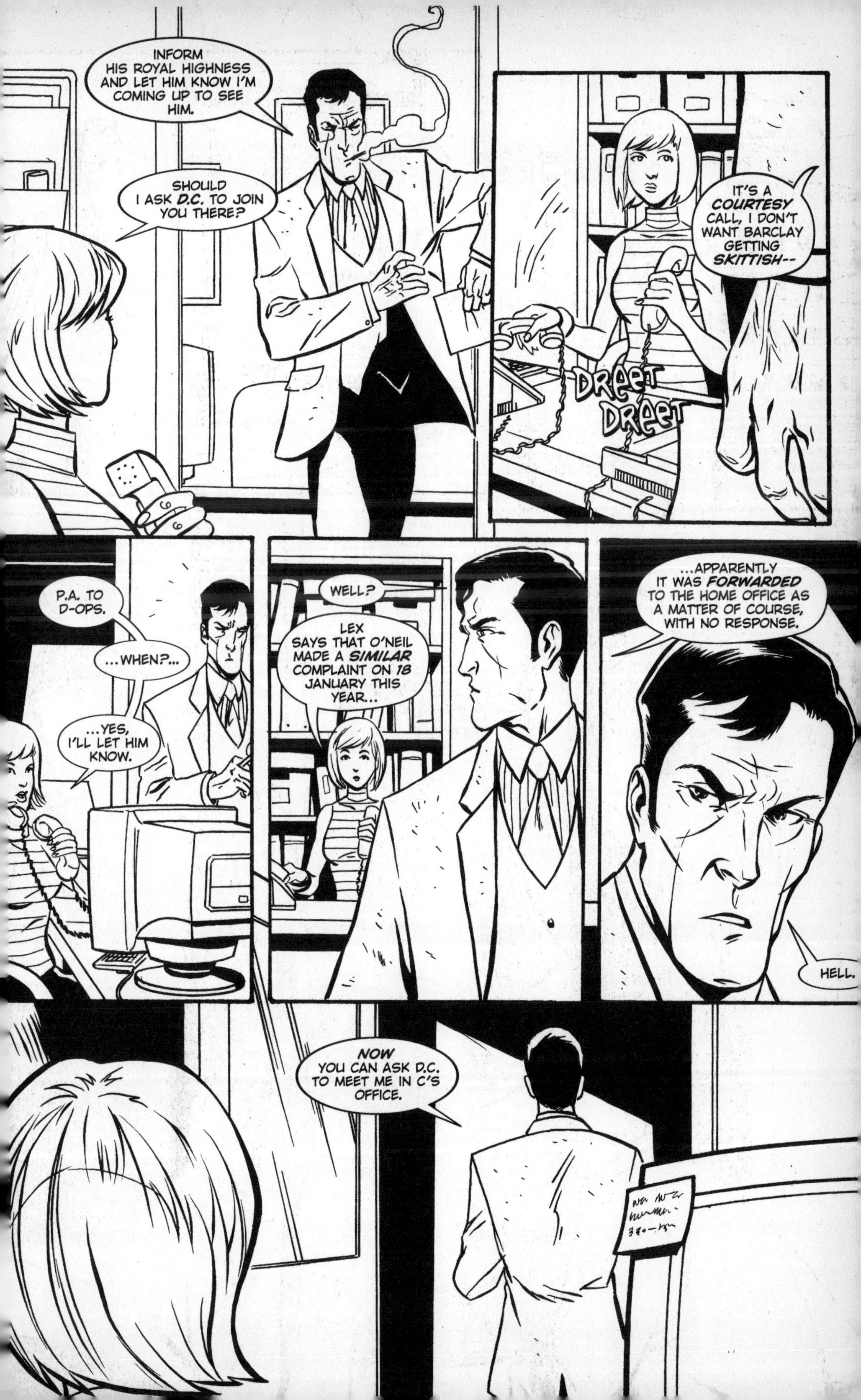
INFORM HIS ROYAL HIGHNESS AND LET HIM KNOW I'M COMING UP TO SEE HIM.
SHOULD I ASK D.C. TO JOIN YOU THERE?
IT'S A COURTESY CALL, I DON'T WANT BARCLAY GETTING SKITTISH--
DREET DREET
P.A. TO D-OPS.
...WHEN?...
...YES, I'LL LET HIM KNOW.
WELL?
LEX SAYS THAT O'NEIL MADE A SIMILAR COMPLAINT ON 18 JANUARY THIS YEAR...
...APPARENTLY IT WAS FORWARDED TO THE HOME OFFICE AS A MATTER OF COURSE, WITH NO RESPONSE.
HELL.
NOW YOU CAN ASK D.C. TO MEET ME IN C'S OFFICE.

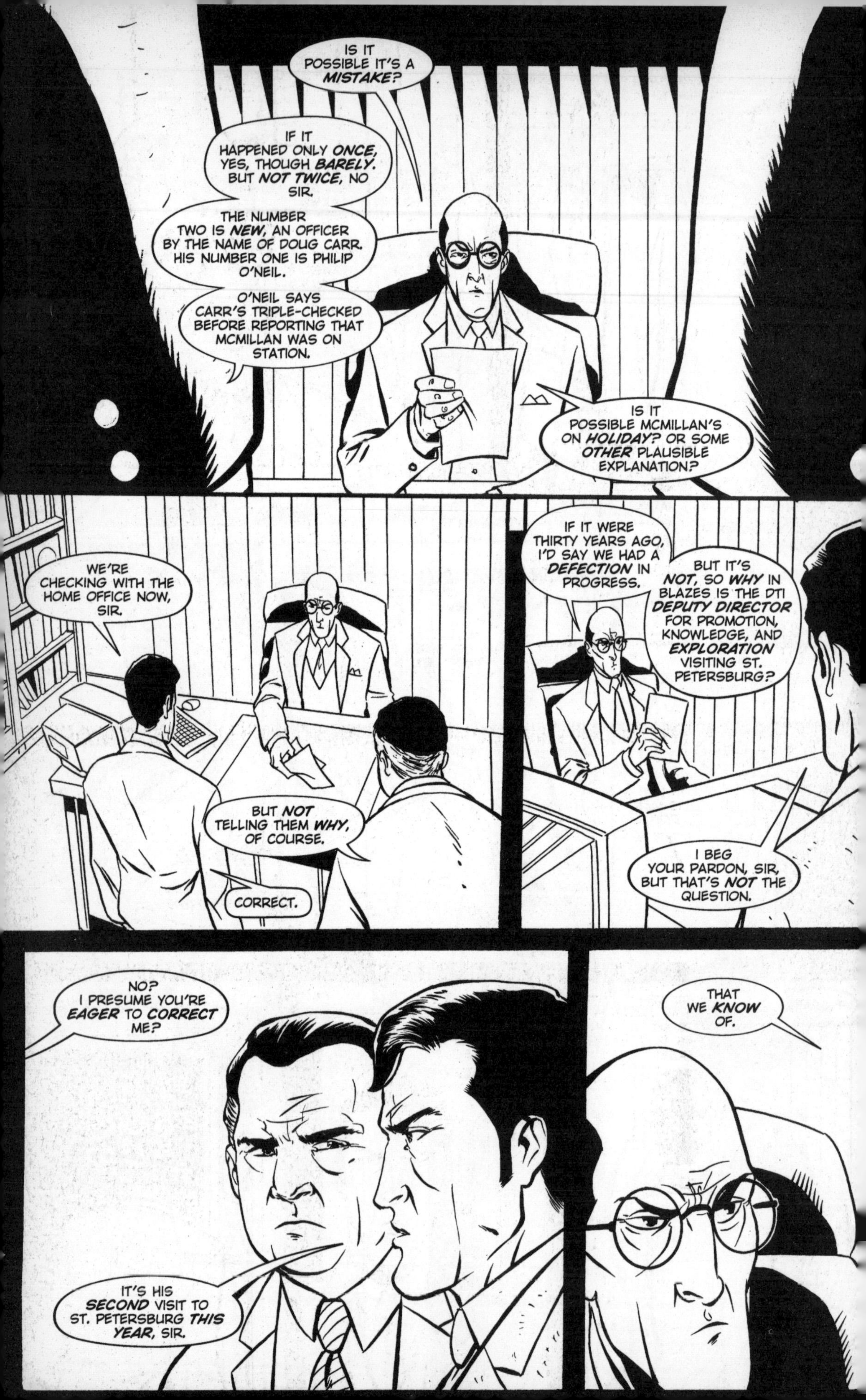
IS IT POSSIBLE IT'S A MISTAKE?
IF IT HAPPENED ONLY ONCE, YES, THOUGH BARELY. BUT NOT TWICE, NO SIR.
THE NUMBER TWO IS NEW, AN OFFICER BY THE NAME OF DOUG CARR. HIS NUMBER ONE IS PHILIP O'NEIL.
O'NEIL SAYS CARR'S TRIPLE-CHECKED BEFORE REPORTING THAT MCMILLAN WAS ON STATION.
IS IT POSSIBLE MCMILLAN'S ON HOLIDAY? OR SOME OTHER PLAUSIBLE EXPLANATION?
WE'RE CHECKING WITH THE HOME OFFICE NOW, SIR.
BUT NOT TELLING THEM WHY, OF COURSE.
CORRECT.
IF IT WERE THIRTY YEARS AGO, I'D SAY WE HAD A DEFECTION IN PROGRESS.
BUT IT'S NOT, SO WHY IN BLAZES IS THE DTI DEPUTY DIRECTOR FOR PROMOTION, KNOWLEDGE, AND EXPLORATION VISITING ST. PETERSBURG?
I BEG YOUR PARDON, SIR, BUT THAT'S NOT THE QUESTION.
NO? I PRESUME YOU'RE EAGER TO CORRECT ME?
IT'S HIS SECOND VISIT TO ST. PETERSBURG THIS YEAR, SIR.
THAT WE KNOW OF.

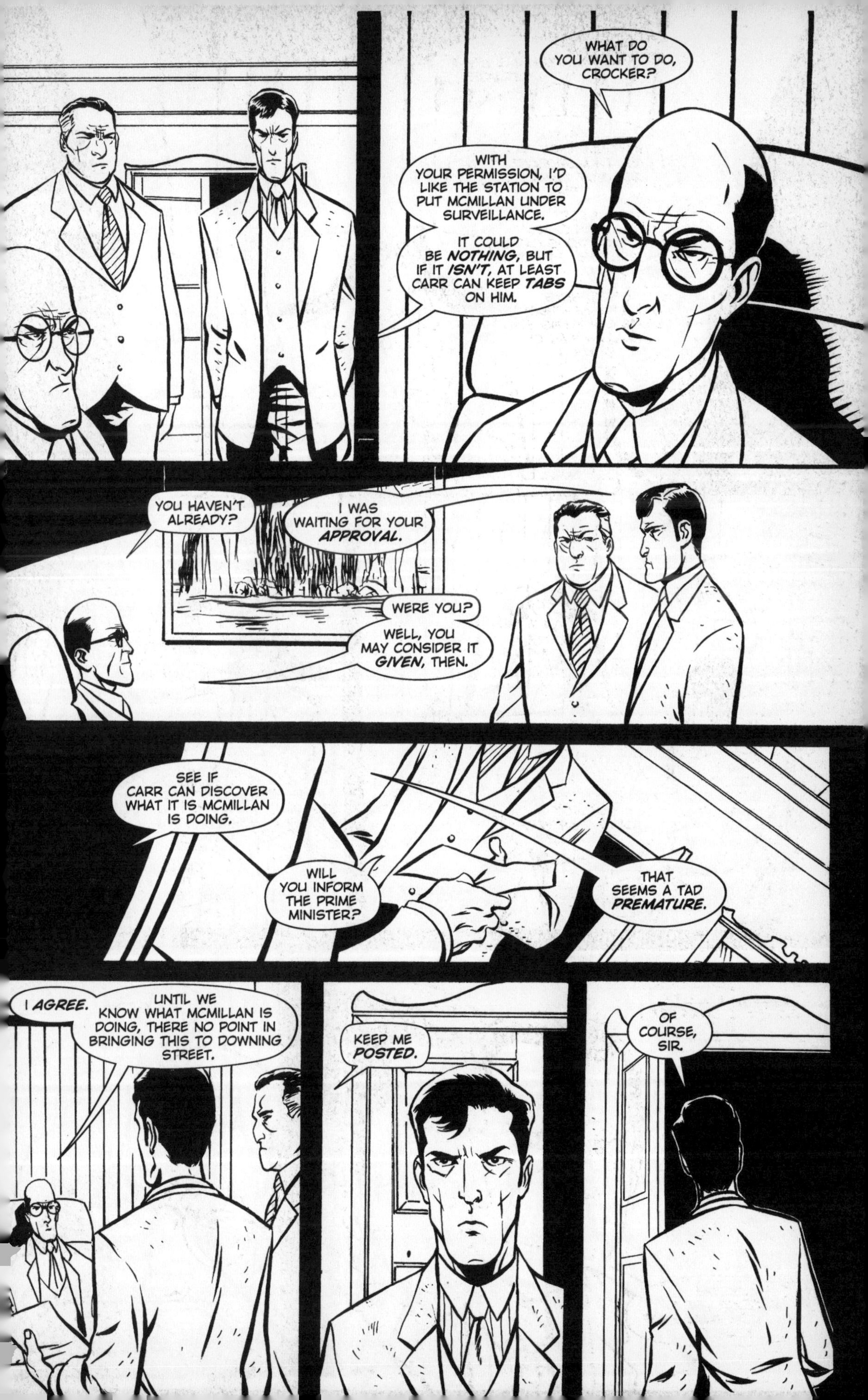
WHAT DO YOU WANT TO DO, CROCKER?
WITH YOUR PERMISSION, I'D LIKE THE STATION TO PUT MCMILLAN UNDER SURVEILLANCE.
IT COULD BE NOTHING, BUT IF IT ISN'T, AT LEAST CARR CAN KEEP TABS ON HIM.
YOU HAVEN'T ALREADY?
I WAS WAITING FOR YOUR APPROVAL.
WERE YOU?
WELL, YOU MAY CONSIDER IT GIVEN, THEN.
SEE IF CARR CAN DISCOVER WHAT IT IS MCMILLAN IS DOING.
WILL YOU INFORM THE PRIME MINISTER?
THAT SEEMS A TAD PREMATURE.
I AGREE.
UNTIL WE KNOW WHAT MCMILLAN IS DOING, THERE NO POINT IN BRINGING THIS TO DOWNING STREET.
KEEP ME POSTED.
OF COURSE, SIR.

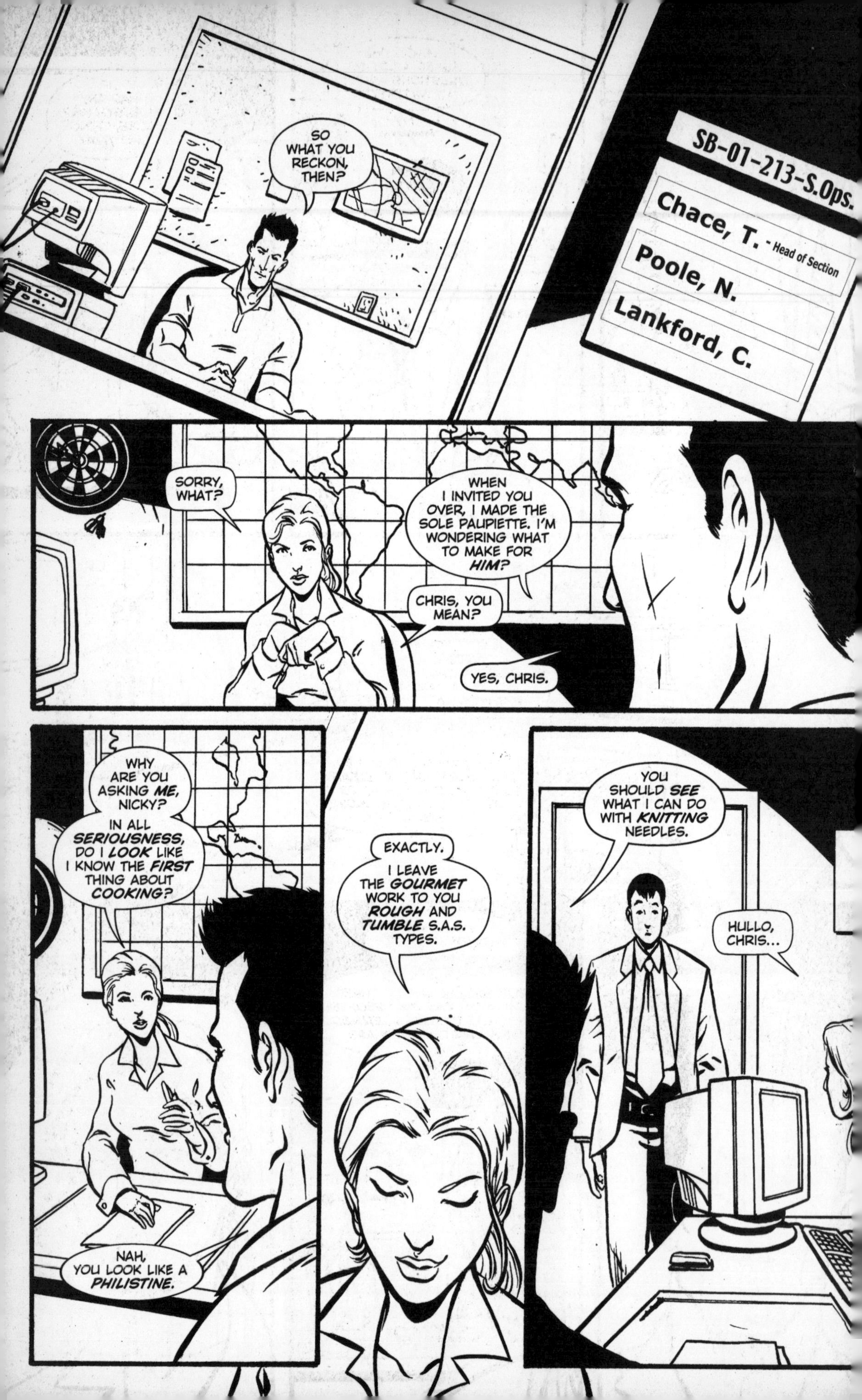
SO WHAT YOU RECKON, THEN?
SB-01-213-S.Ops.
Chace, T. - Head of Section
Poole, N.
Lankford, C.
SORRY, WHAT?
WHEN I INVITED YOU OVER, I MADE THE SOLE PAUPIETTE. I'M WONDERING WHAT TO MAKE FOR HIM?
CHRIS, YOU MEAN?
YES, CHRIS.
WHY ARE YOU ASKING ME, NICKY?
IN ALL SERIOUSNESS, DO I LOOK LIKE I KNOW THE FIRST THING ABOUT COOKING?
NAH, YOU LOOK LIKE A PHILISTINE.
EXACTLY.
I LEAVE THE GOURMET WORK TO YOU ROUGH AND TUMBLE S.A.S. TYPES.
YOU SHOULD SEE WHAT I CAN DO WITH KNITTING NEEDLES.
HULLO, CHRIS...

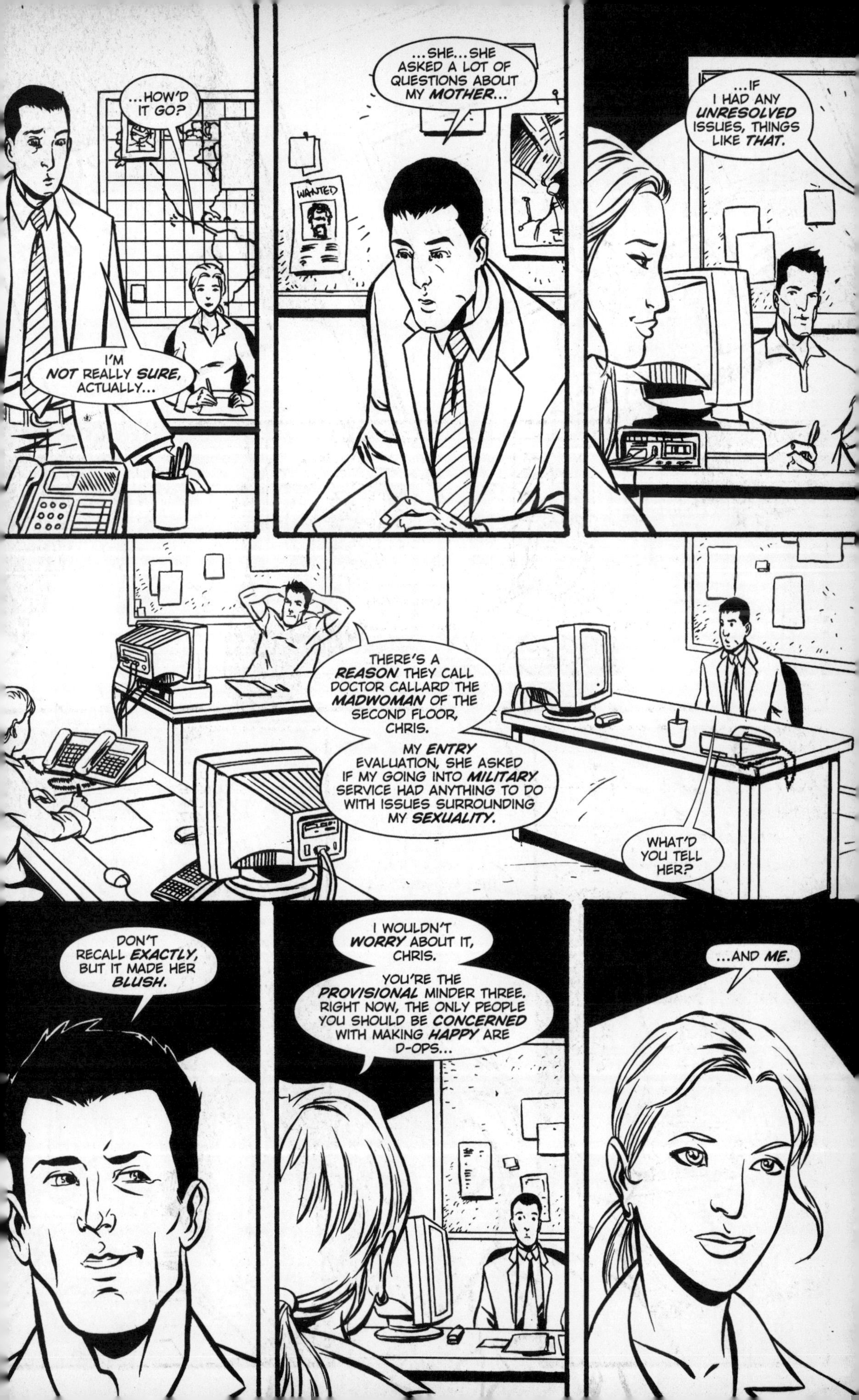
...HOW'D IT GO?
I'M NOT REALLY SURE, ACTUALLY...
...SHE...SHE ASKED A LOT OF QUESTIONS ABOUT MY MOTHER...
WANTED
...IF I HAD ANY UNRESOLVED ISSUES, THINGS LIKE THAT.
THERE'S A REASON THEY CALL DOCTOR CALLARD THE MADWOMAN OF THE SECOND FLOOR, CHRIS.
MY ENTRY EVALUATION, SHE ASKED IF MY GOING INTO MILITARY SERVICE HAD ANYTHING TO DO WITH ISSUES SURROUNDING MY SEXUALITY.
WHAT'D YOU TELL HER?
DON'T RECALL EXACTLY, BUT IT MADE HER BLUSH.
I WOULDN'T WORRY ABOUT IT, CHRIS.
YOU'RE THE PROVISIONAL MINDER THREE. RIGHT NOW, THE ONLY PEOPLE YOU SHOULD BE CONCERNED WITH MAKING HAPPY ARE D-OPS...
...AND ME.

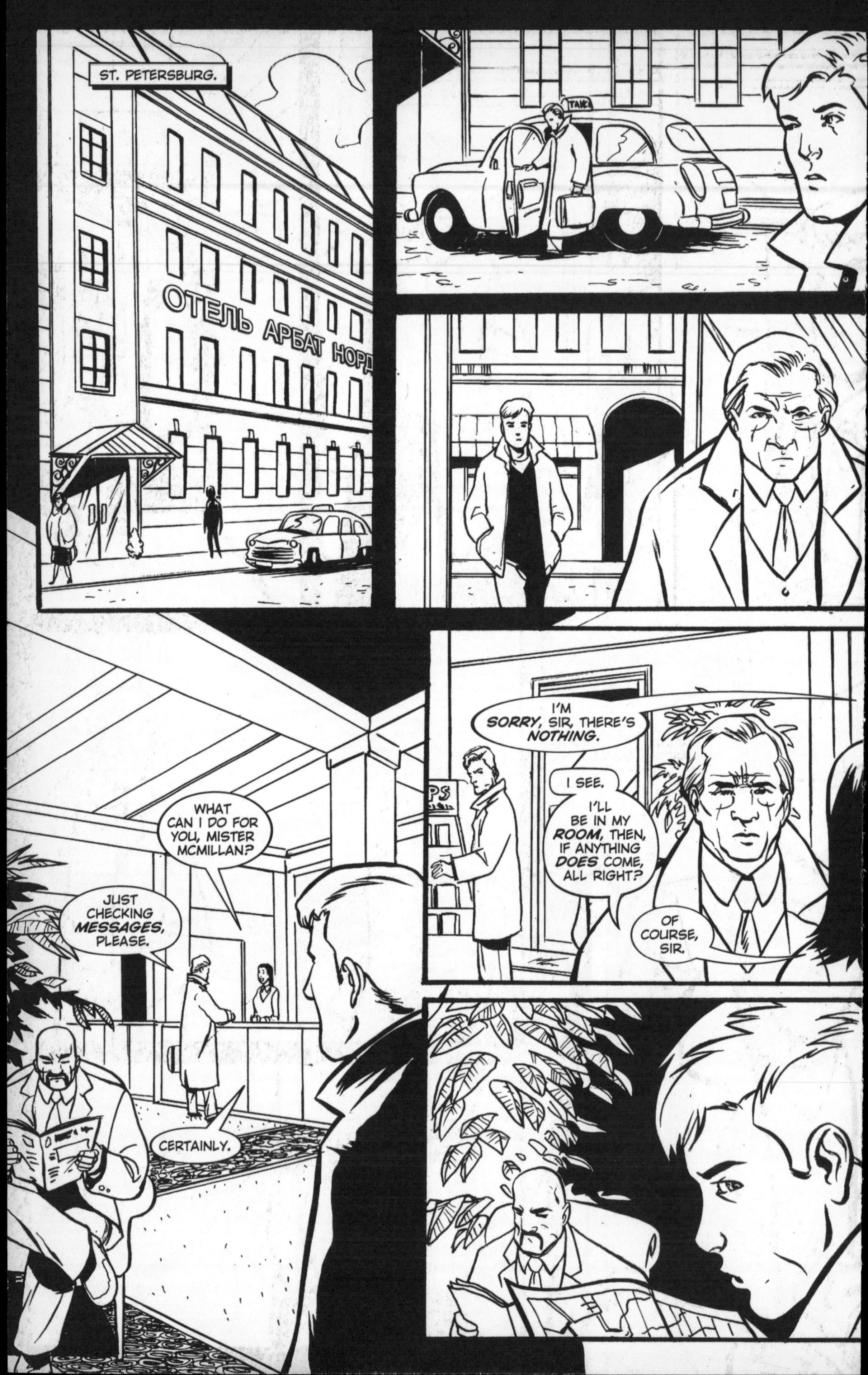
ST. PETERSBURG.
ОТЕЛЬ АРБАТ НОРД
WHAT CAN I DO FOR YOU, MISTER MCMILLAN?
JUST CHECKING MESSAGES, PLEASE.
CERTAINLY.
I'M SORRY, SIR, THERE'S NOTHING.
I SEE.
I'LL BE IN MY ROOM, THEN, IF ANYTHING DOES COME, ALL RIGHT?
OF COURSE, SIR.

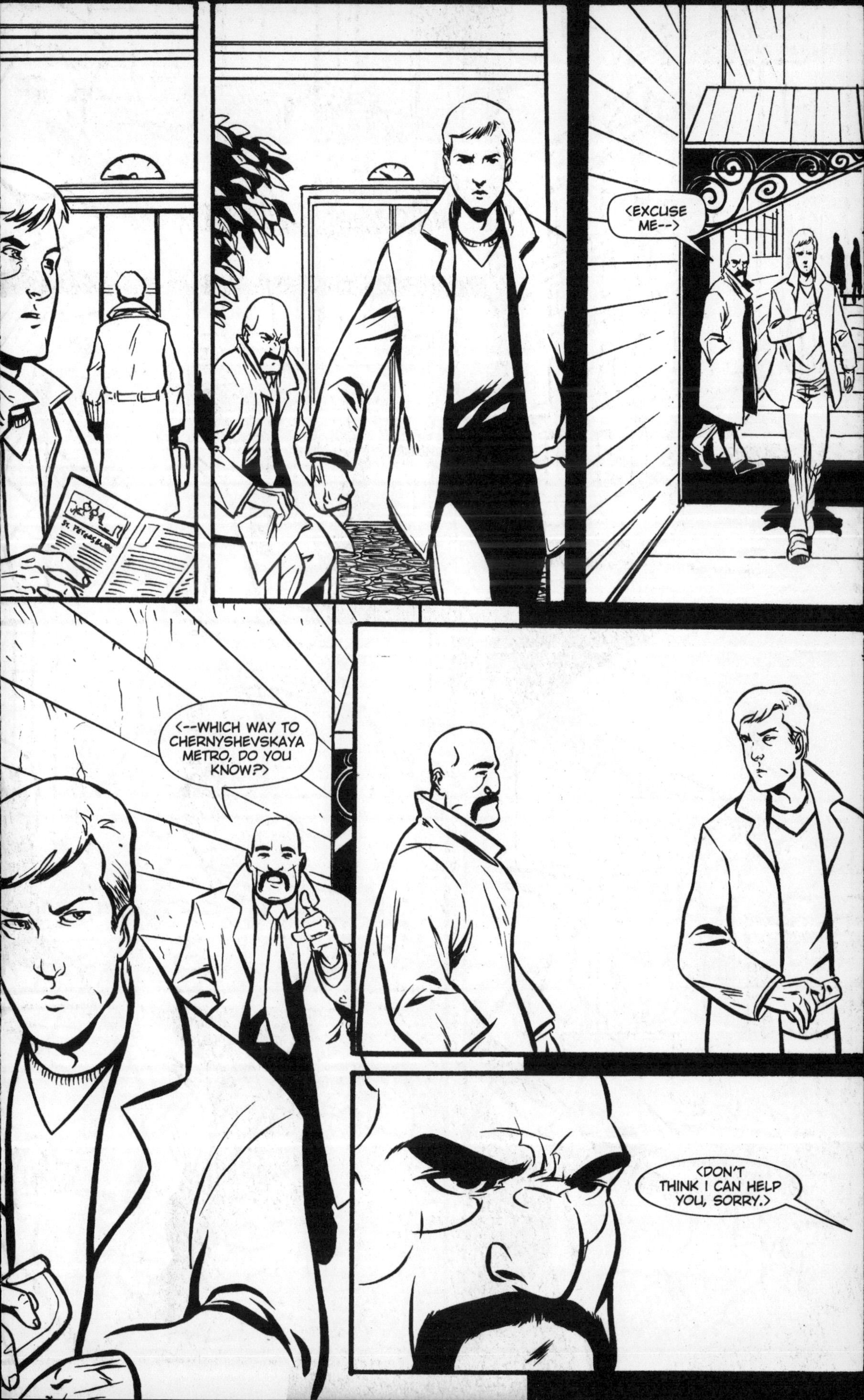
<EXCUSE ME-->
<--WHICH WAY TO CHERNYSHEVSKAYA METRO, DO YOU KNOW?>
<DON'T THINK I CAN HELP YOU, SORRY.>

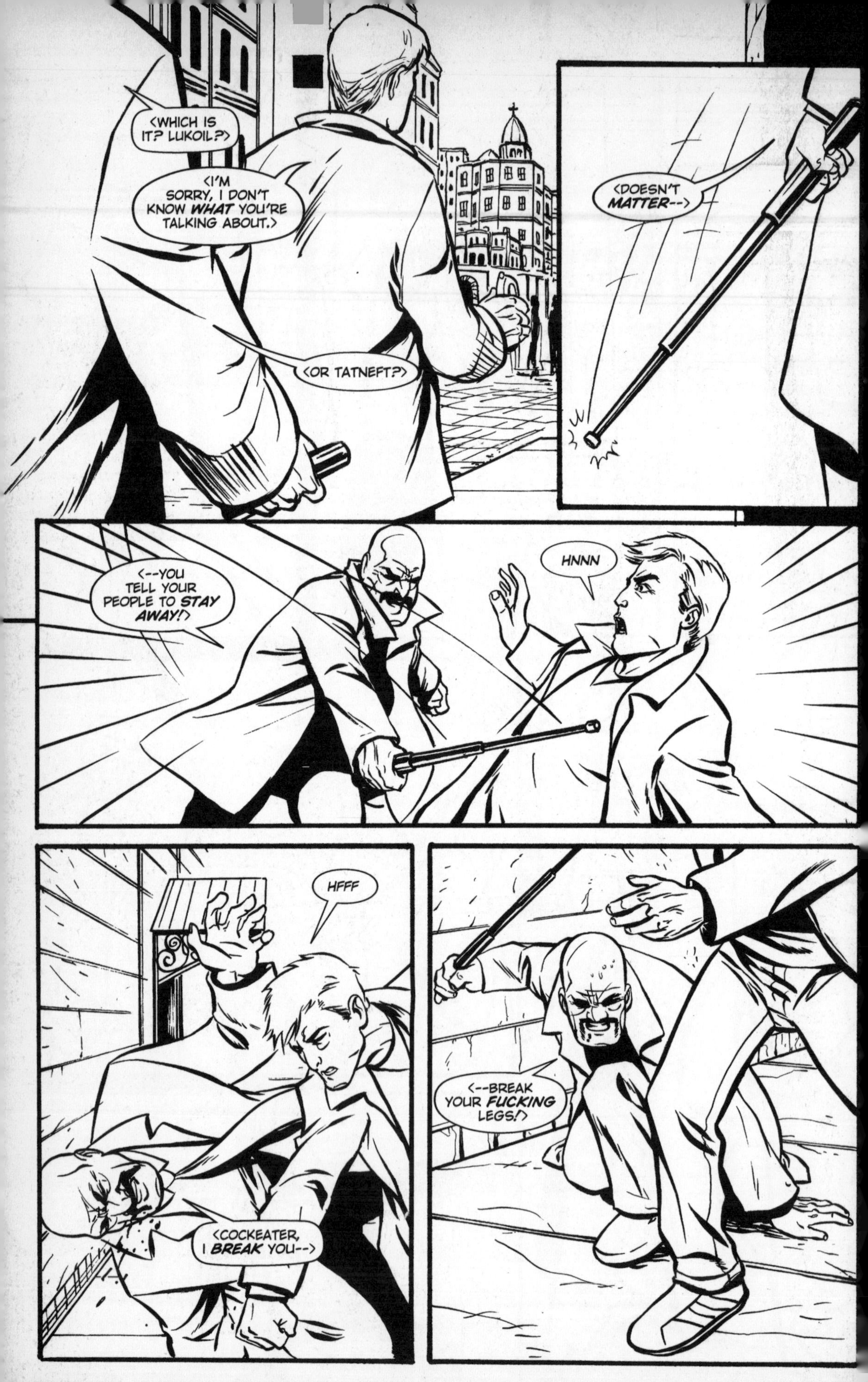
<WHICH IS IT? LUKOIL?>
<I'M SORRY, I DON'T KNOW **WHAT** YOU'RE TALKING ABOUT.>
<OR TATNEFT?>
<DOESN'T **MATTER**-->
<--YOU TELL YOUR PEOPLE TO **STAY AWAY!**>
HNNN
HFFF
<COCKEATER, I **BREAK** YOU-->
<--BREAK YOUR **FUCKING** LEGS!>

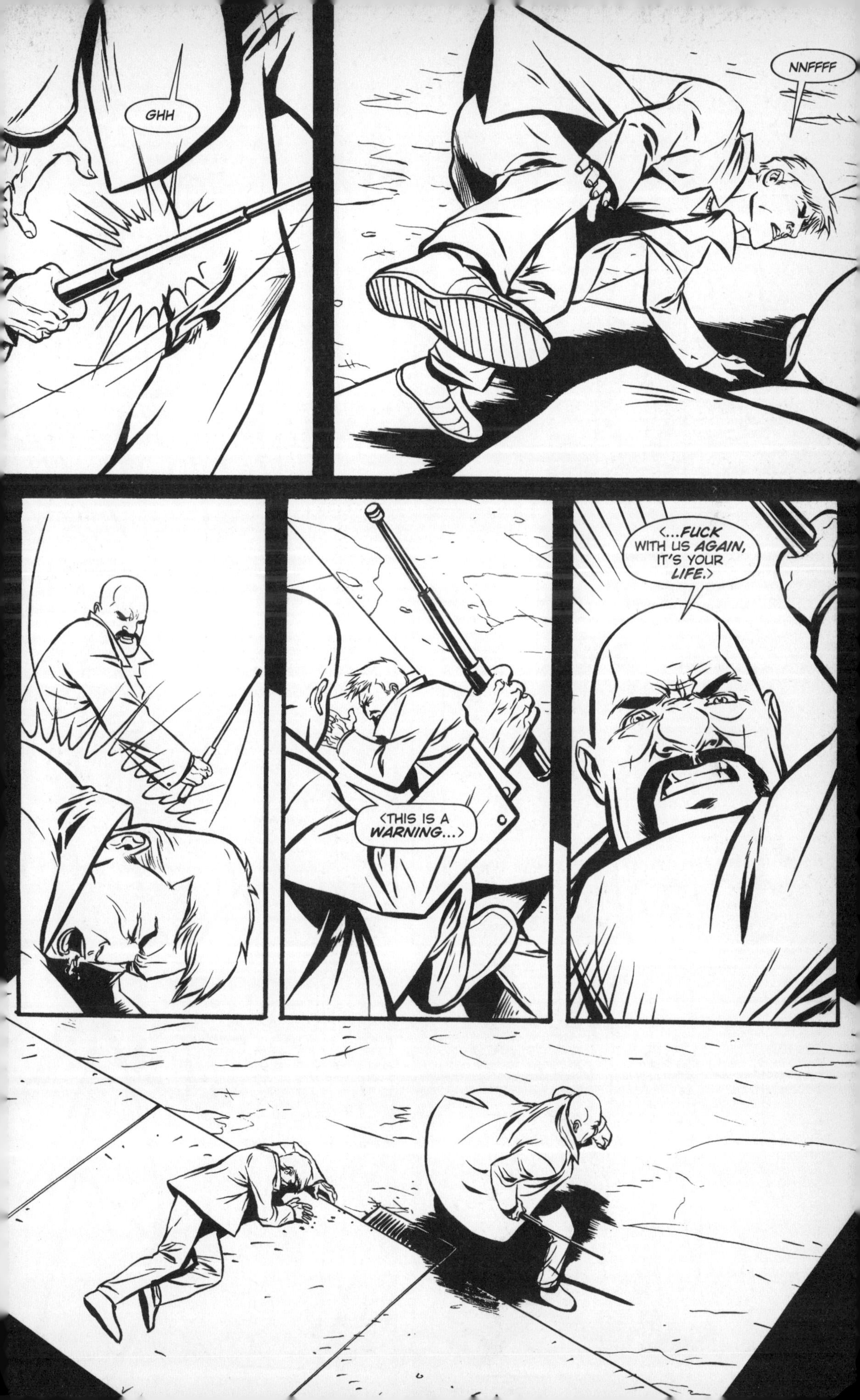
GHH
NNFFFF
<THIS IS A WARNING...>
<...FUCK WITH US AGAIN, IT'S YOUR LIFE.>

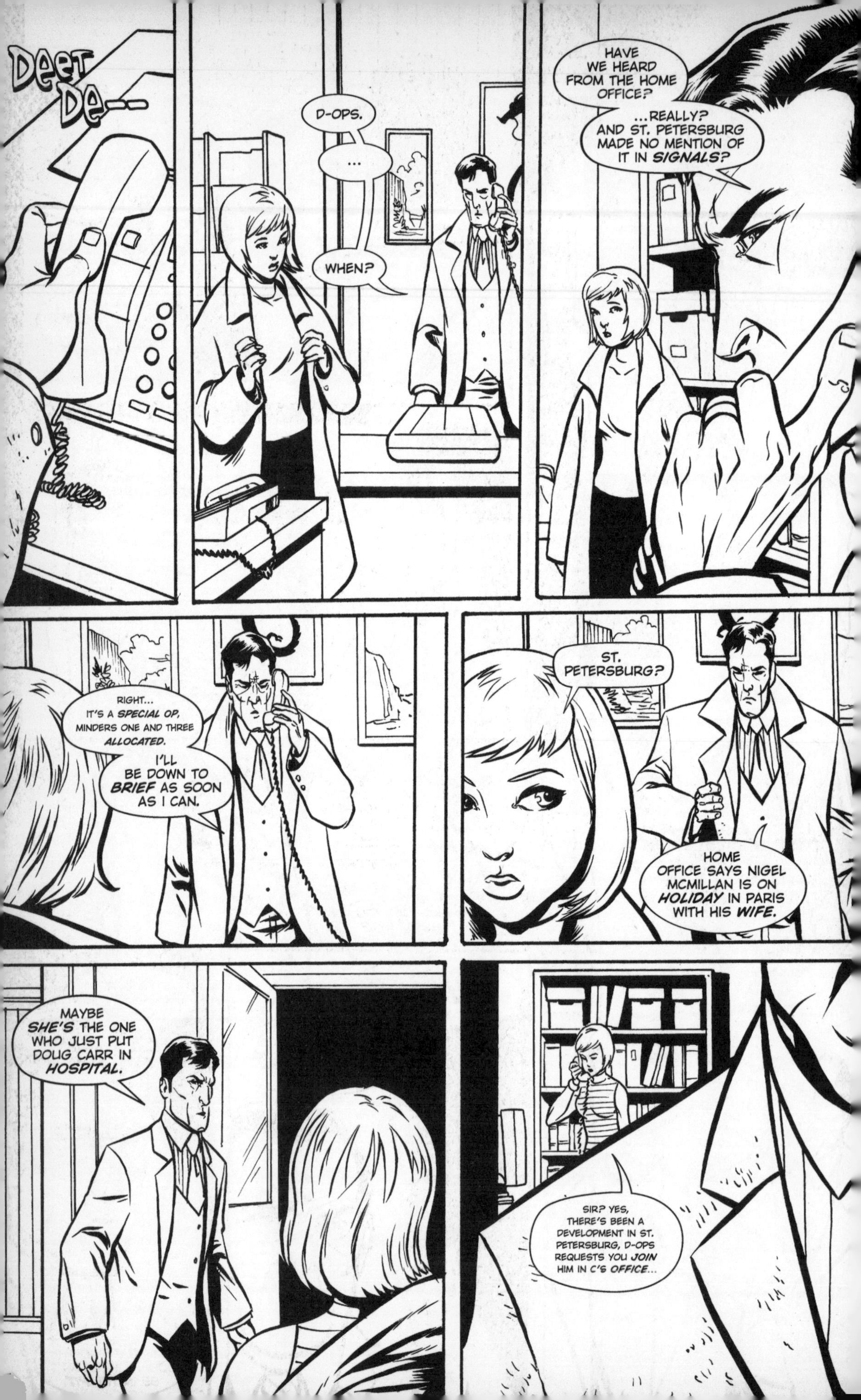
Deet De--
D-OPS.
...
WHEN?
HAVE WE HEARD FROM THE HOME OFFICE?
...REALLY? AND ST. PETERSBURG MADE NO MENTION OF IT IN SIGNALS?
RIGHT... IT'S A SPECIAL OP, MINDERS ONE AND THREE ALLOCATED.
I'LL BE DOWN TO BRIEF AS SOON AS I CAN.
ST. PETERSBURG?
HOME OFFICE SAYS NIGEL MCMILLAN IS ON HOLIDAY IN PARIS WITH HIS WIFE.
MAYBE SHE'S THE ONE WHO JUST PUT DOUG CARR IN HOSPITAL.
SIR? YES, THERE'S BEEN A DEVELOPMENT IN ST. PETERSBURG, D-OPS REQUESTS YOU JOIN HIM IN C'S OFFICE...

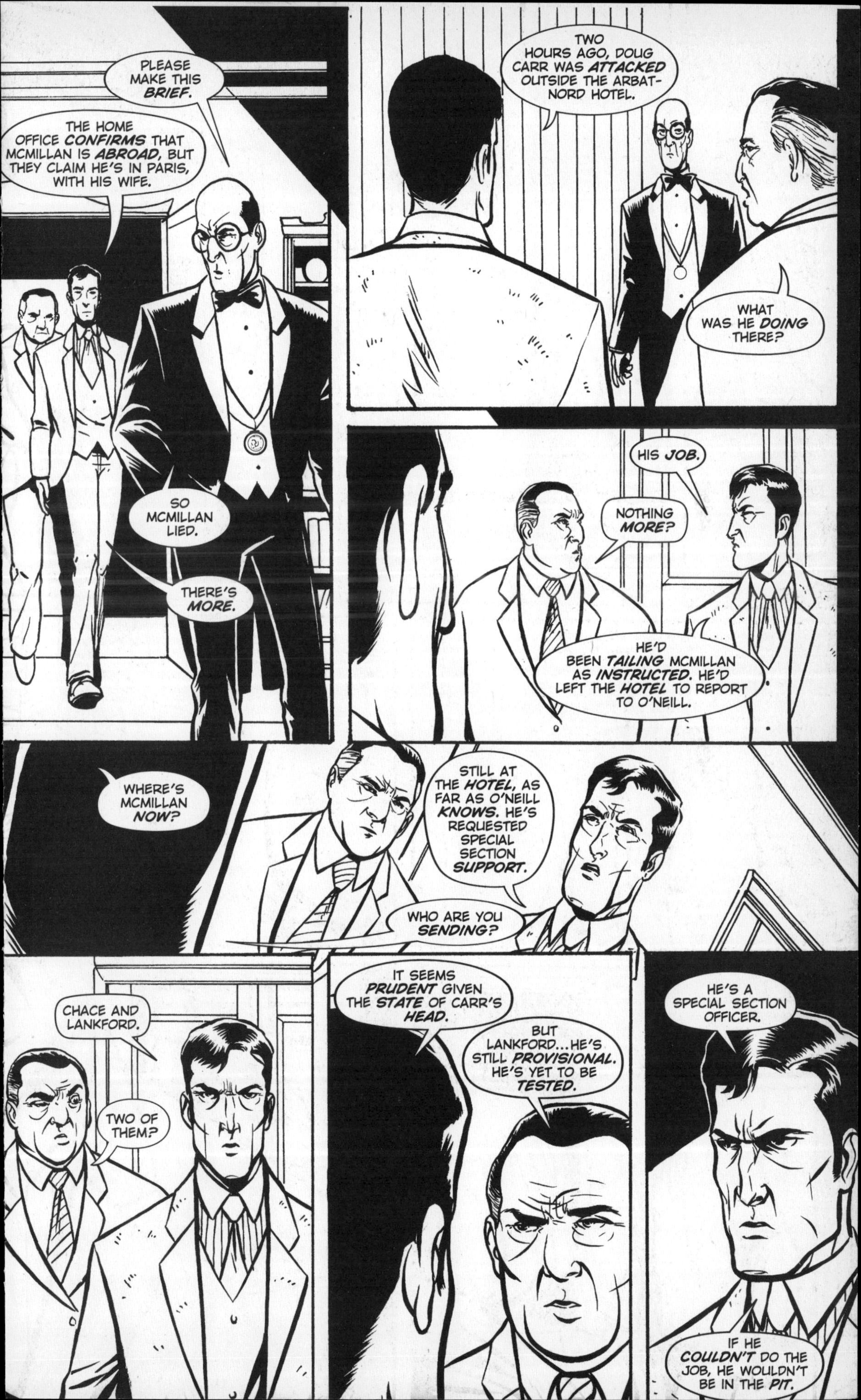
PLEASE MAKE THIS BRIEF.
THE HOME OFFICE CONFIRMS THAT MCMILLAN IS ABROAD, BUT THEY CLAIM HE'S IN PARIS, WITH HIS WIFE.
SO MCMILLAN LIED.
THERE'S MORE.
TWO HOURS AGO, DOUG CARR WAS ATTACKED OUTSIDE THE ARBAT-NORD HOTEL.
WHAT WAS HE DOING THERE?
HIS JOB.
NOTHING MORE?
HE'D BEEN TAILING MCMILLAN AS INSTRUCTED. HE'D LEFT THE HOTEL TO REPORT TO O'NEILL.
WHERE'S MCMILLAN NOW?
STILL AT THE HOTEL, AS FAR AS O'NEILL KNOWS. HE'S REQUESTED SPECIAL SECTION SUPPORT.
WHO ARE YOU SENDING?
CHACE AND LANKFORD.
TWO OF THEM?
IT SEEMS PRUDENT GIVEN THE STATE OF CARR'S HEAD.
BUT LANKFORD... HE'S STILL PROVISIONAL. HE'S YET TO BE TESTED.
HE'S A SPECIAL SECTION OFFICER.
IF HE COULDN'T DO THE JOB, HE WOULDN'T BE IN THE PIT.

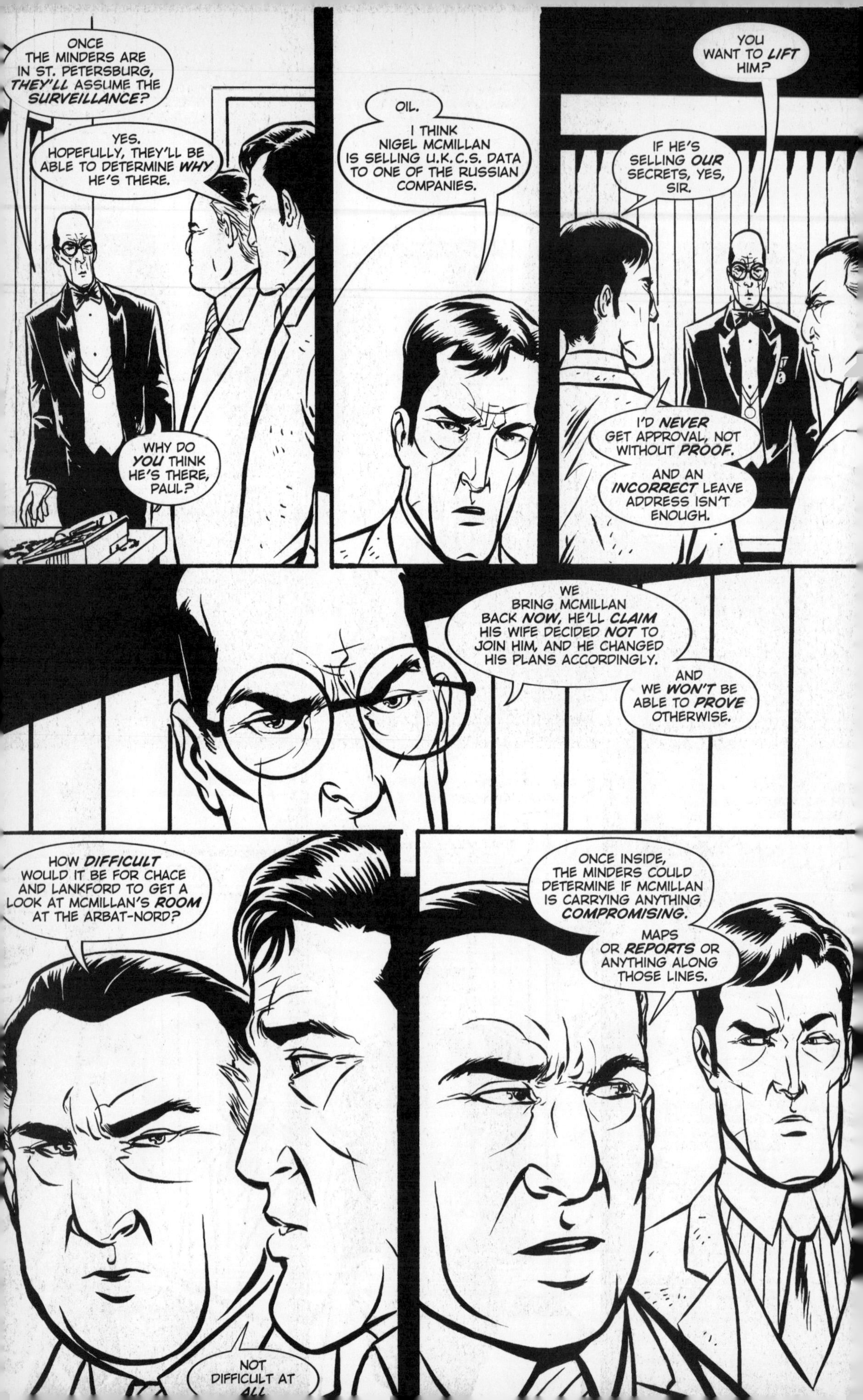
ONCE THE MINDERS ARE IN ST. PETERSBURG, THEY'LL ASSUME THE SURVEILLANCE?
YES. HOPEFULLY, THEY'LL BE ABLE TO DETERMINE WHY HE'S THERE.
WHY DO YOU THINK HE'S THERE, PAUL?
OIL.
I THINK NIGEL MCMILLAN IS SELLING U.K.C.S. DATA TO ONE OF THE RUSSIAN COMPANIES.
YOU WANT TO LIFT HIM?
IF HE'S SELLING OUR SECRETS, YES, SIR.
I'D NEVER GET APPROVAL, NOT WITHOUT PROOF.
AND AN INCORRECT LEAVE ADDRESS ISN'T ENOUGH.
WE BRING MCMILLAN BACK NOW, HE'LL CLAIM HIS WIFE DECIDED NOT TO JOIN HIM, AND HE CHANGED HIS PLANS ACCORDINGLY.
AND WE WON'T BE ABLE TO PROVE OTHERWISE.
HOW DIFFICULT WOULD IT BE FOR CHACE AND LANKFORD TO GET A LOOK AT MCMILLAN'S ROOM AT THE ARBAT-NORD?
NOT DIFFICULT AT ALL
ONCE INSIDE, THE MINDERS COULD DETERMINE IF MCMILLAN IS CARRYING ANYTHING COMPROMISING.
MAPS OR REPORTS OR ANYTHING ALONG THOSE LINES.

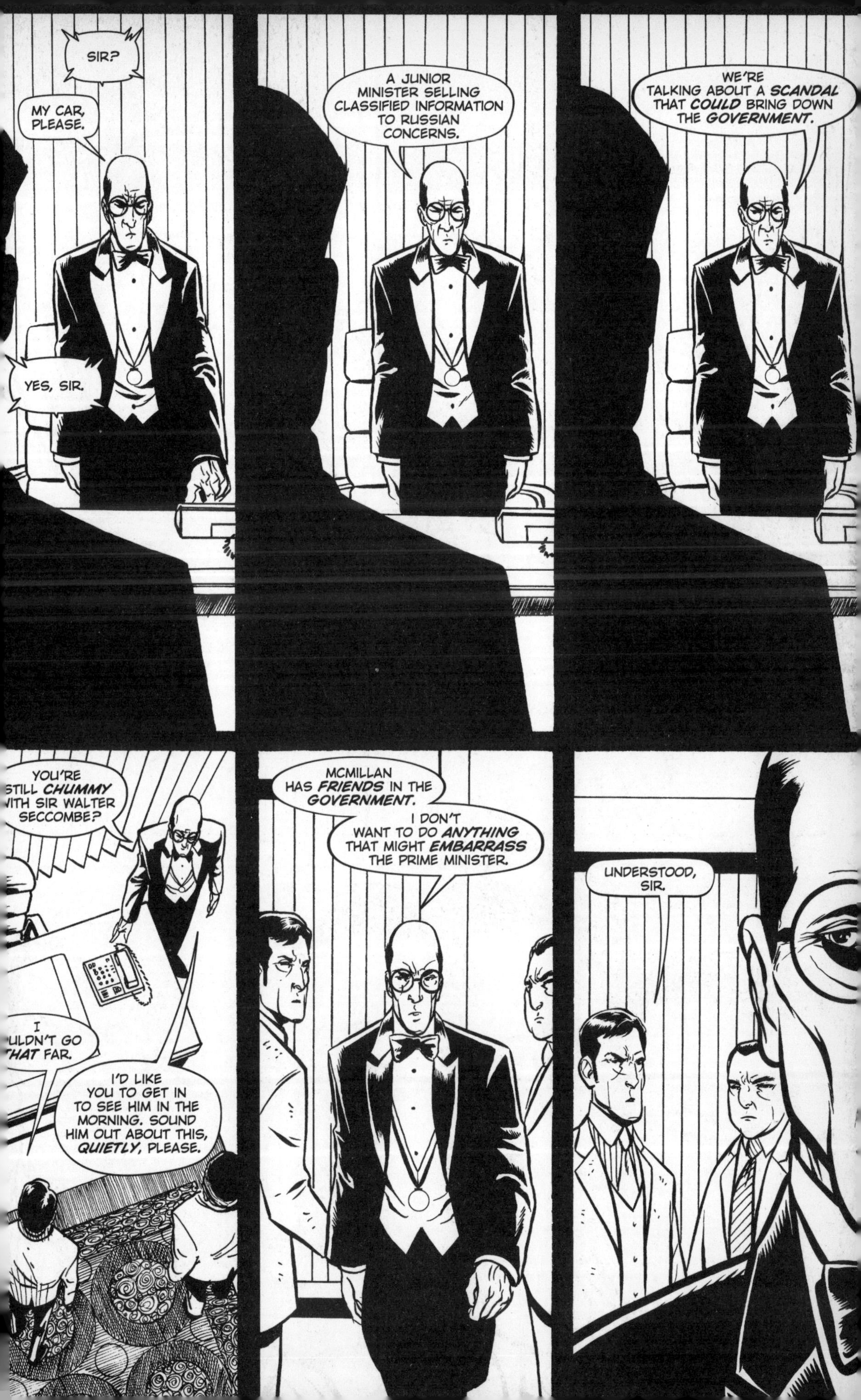
SIR?
MY CAR, PLEASE.
YES, SIR.
A JUNIOR MINISTER SELLING CLASSIFIED INFORMATION TO RUSSIAN CONCERNS.
WE'RE TALKING ABOUT A SCANDAL THAT COULD BRING DOWN THE GOVERNMENT.
YOU'RE STILL CHUMMY WITH SIR WALTER SECCOMBE?
I ULDN'T GO THAT FAR.
I'D LIKE YOU TO GET IN TO SEE HIM IN THE MORNING. SOUND HIM OUT ABOUT THIS, QUIETLY, PLEASE.
MCMILLAN HAS FRIENDS IN THE GOVERNMENT.
I DON'T WANT TO DO ANYTHING THAT MIGHT EMBARRASS THE PRIME MINISTER.
UNDERSTOOD, SIR.

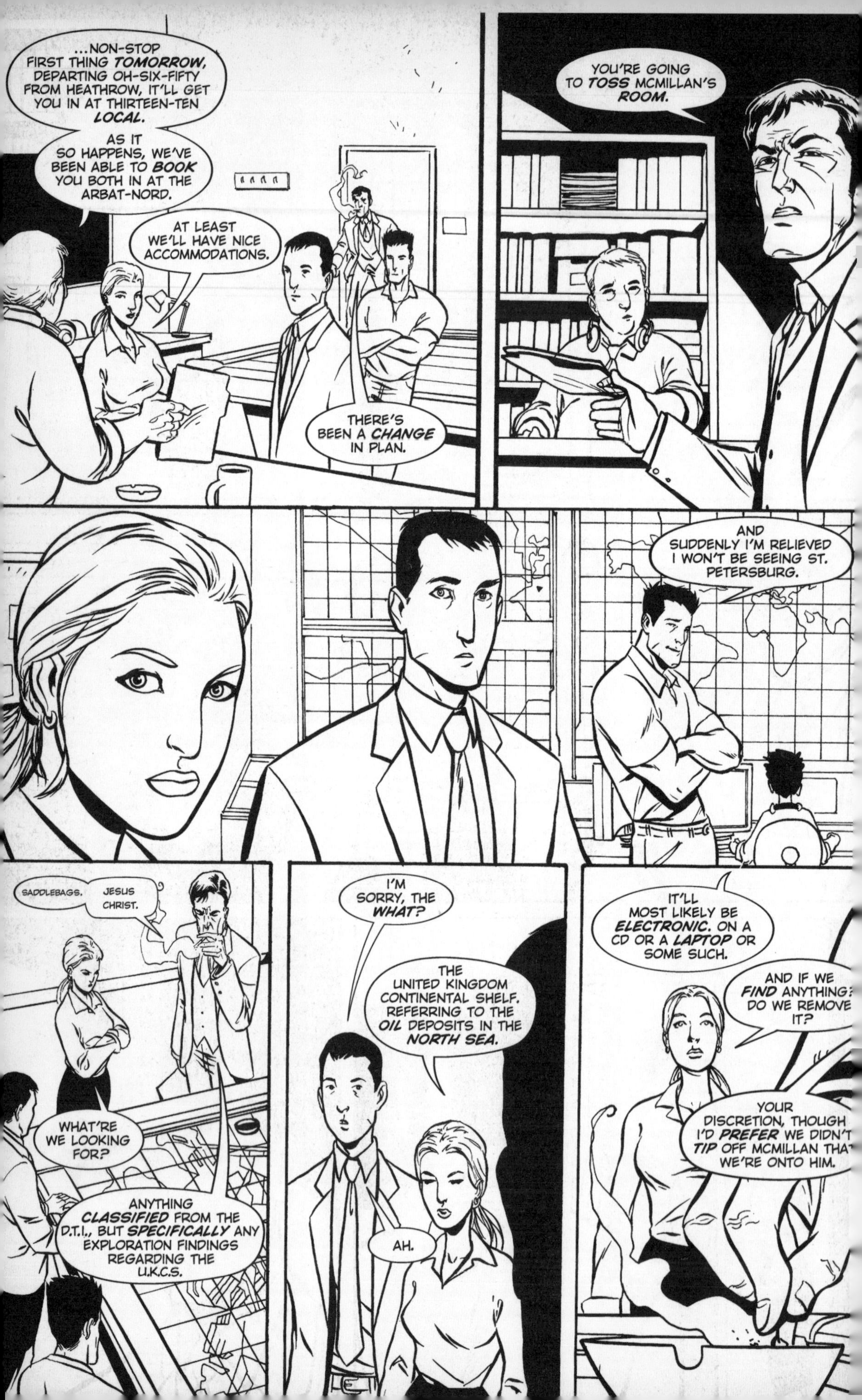
...NON-STOP FIRST THING TOMORROW, DEPARTING OH-SIX-FIFTY FROM HEATHROW, IT'LL GET YOU IN AT THIRTEEN-TEN LOCAL.
AS IT SO HAPPENS, WE'VE BEEN ABLE TO BOOK YOU BOTH IN AT THE ARBAT-NORD.
AT LEAST WE'LL HAVE NICE ACCOMMODATIONS.
THERE'S BEEN A CHANGE IN PLAN.
YOU'RE GOING TO TOSS MCMILLAN'S ROOM.
AND SUDDENLY I'M RELIEVED I WON'T BE SEEING ST. PETERSBURG.
SADDLEBAGS.
JESUS CHRIST.
WHAT'RE WE LOOKING FOR?
ANYTHING CLASSIFIED FROM THE D.T.I., BUT SPECIFICALLY ANY EXPLORATION FINDINGS REGARDING THE U.K.C.S.
I'M SORRY, THE WHAT?
THE UNITED KINGDOM CONTINENTAL SHELF. REFERRING TO THE OIL DEPOSITS IN THE NORTH SEA.
AH.
IT'LL MOST LIKELY BE ELECTRONIC. ON A CD OR A LAPTOP OR SOME SUCH.
AND IF WE FIND ANYTHING? DO WE REMOVE IT?
YOUR DISCRETION, THOUGH I'D PREFER WE DIDN'T TIP OFF MCMILLAN THAT WE'RE ONTO HIM.

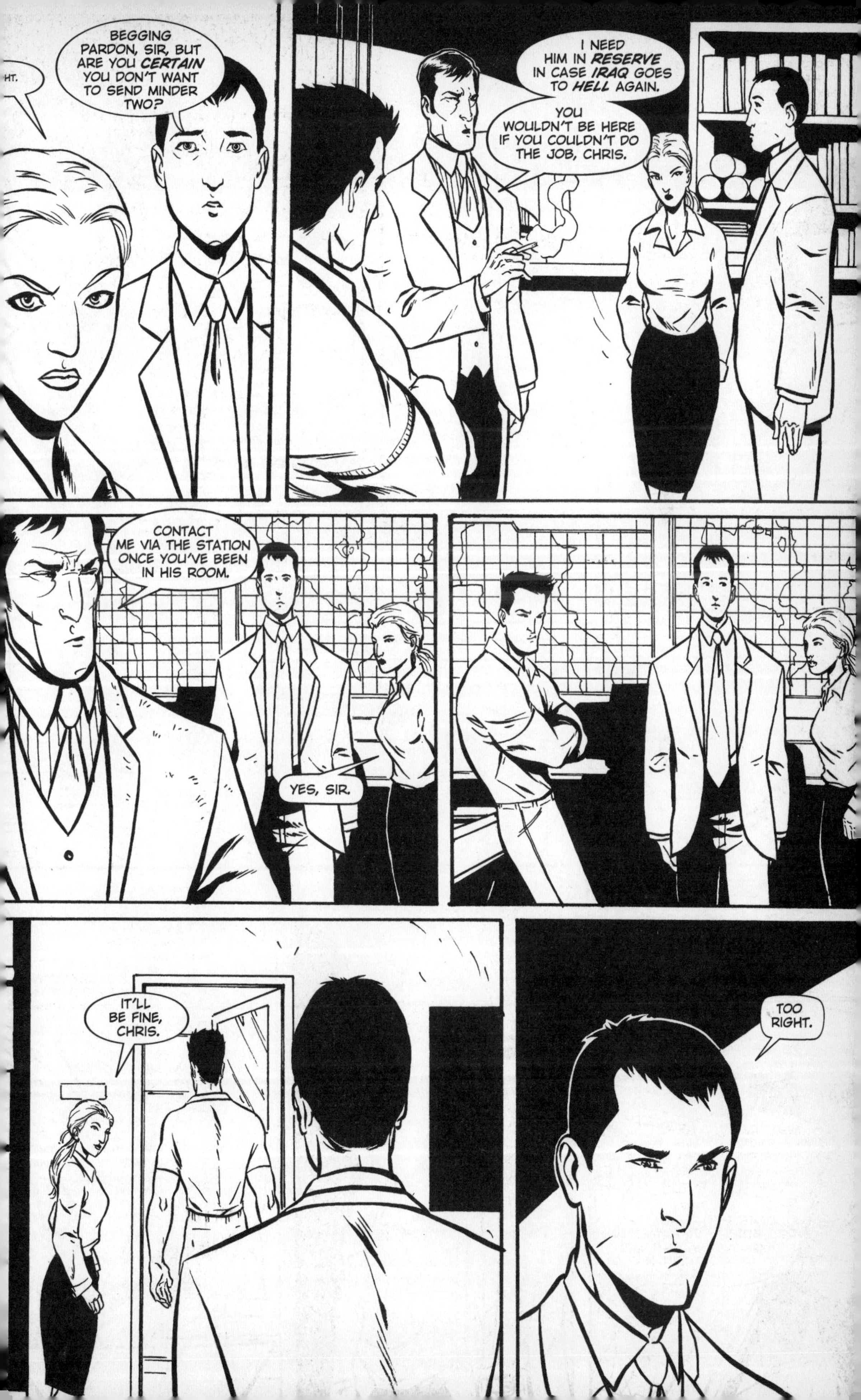
HT.
BEGGING PARDON, SIR, BUT ARE YOU CERTAIN YOU DON'T WANT TO SEND MINDER TWO?
I NEED HIM IN RESERVE IN CASE IRAQ GOES TO HELL AGAIN.
YOU WOULDN'T BE HERE IF YOU COULDN'T DO THE JOB, CHRIS.
CONTACT ME VIA THE STATION ONCE YOU'VE BEEN IN HIS ROOM.
YES, SIR.
IT'LL BE FINE, CHRIS.
TOO RIGHT.

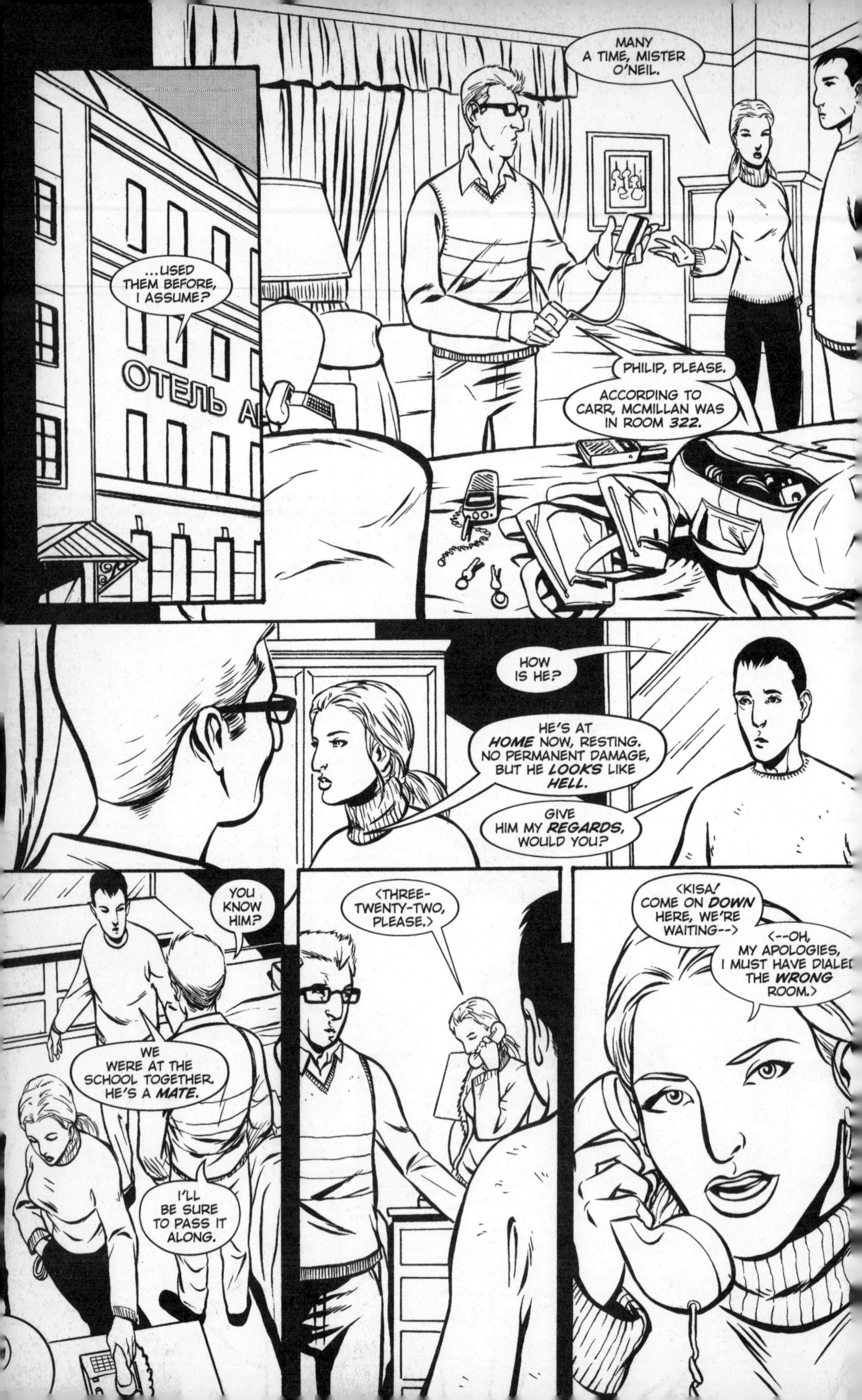
ОТЕЛЬ А
...USED THEM BEFORE, I ASSUME?
MANY A TIME, MISTER O'NEIL.
PHILIP, PLEASE.
ACCORDING TO CARR, MCMILLAN WAS IN ROOM 322.
HOW IS HE?
HE'S AT HOME NOW, RESTING. NO PERMANENT DAMAGE, BUT HE LOOKS LIKE HELL.
GIVE HIM MY REGARDS, WOULD YOU?
YOU KNOW HIM?
WE WERE AT THE SCHOOL TOGETHER. HE'S A MATE.
I'LL BE SURE TO PASS IT ALONG.
<THREE-TWENTY-TWO, PLEASE.>
<KISA! COME ON DOWN HERE, WE'RE WAITING-->
<--OH, MY APOLOGIES, I MUST HAVE DIALED THE WRONG ROOM.>

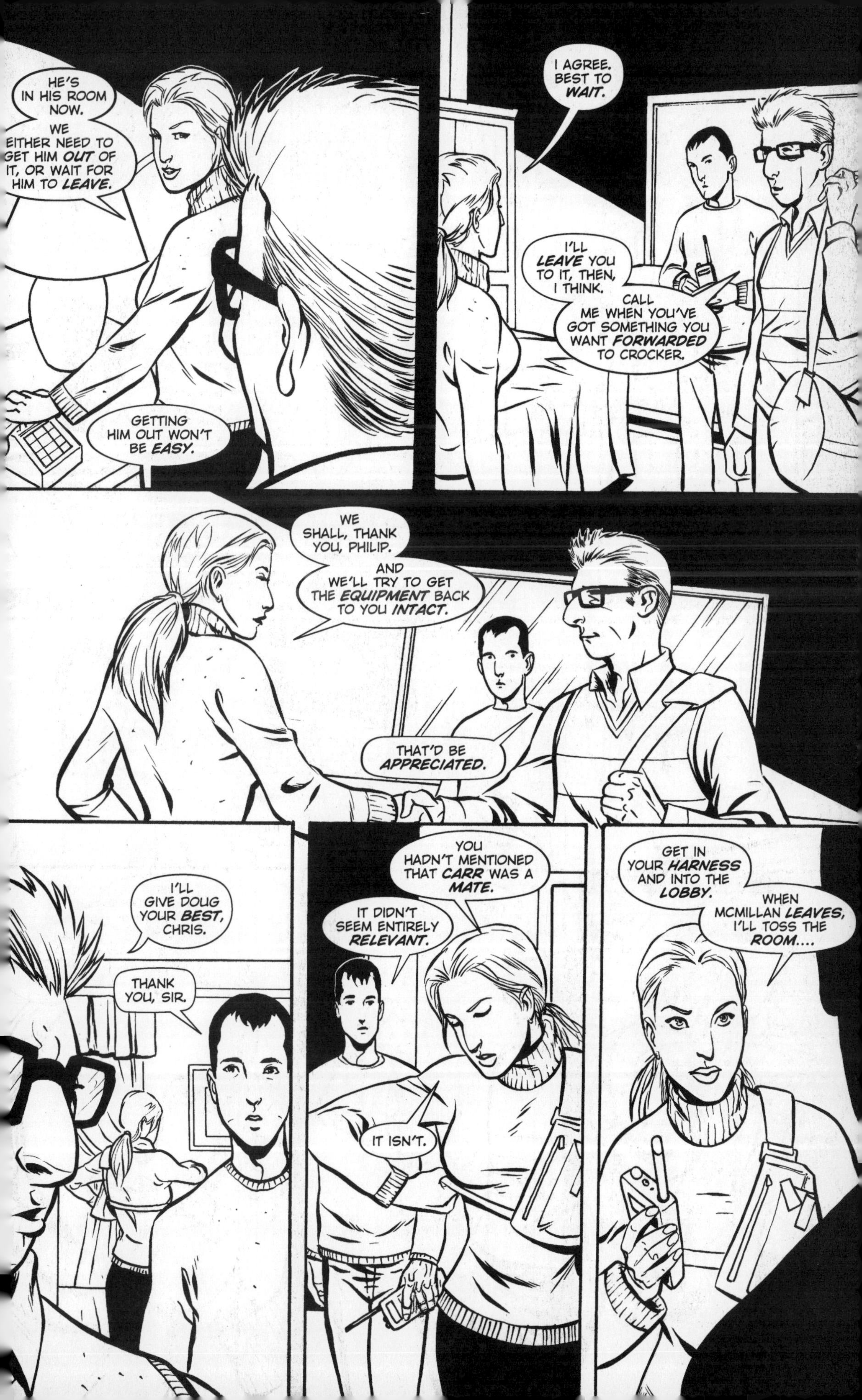
HE'S IN HIS ROOM NOW.
WE EITHER NEED TO GET HIM OUT OF IT, OR WAIT FOR HIM TO LEAVE.
GETTING HIM OUT WON'T BE EASY.
I AGREE. BEST TO WAIT.
I'LL LEAVE YOU TO IT, THEN, I THINK.
CALL ME WHEN YOU'VE GOT SOMETHING YOU WANT FORWARDED TO CROCKER.
WE SHALL, THANK YOU, PHILIP.
AND WE'LL TRY TO GET THE EQUIPMENT BACK TO YOU INTACT.
THAT'D BE APPRECIATED.
I'LL GIVE DOUG YOUR BEST, CHRIS.
THANK YOU, SIR.
YOU HADN'T MENTIONED THAT CARR WAS A MATE.
IT DIDN'T SEEM ENTIRELY RELEVANT.
IT ISN'T.
GET IN YOUR HARNESS AND INTO THE LOBBY.
WHEN MCMILLAN LEAVES, I'LL TOSS THE ROOM....

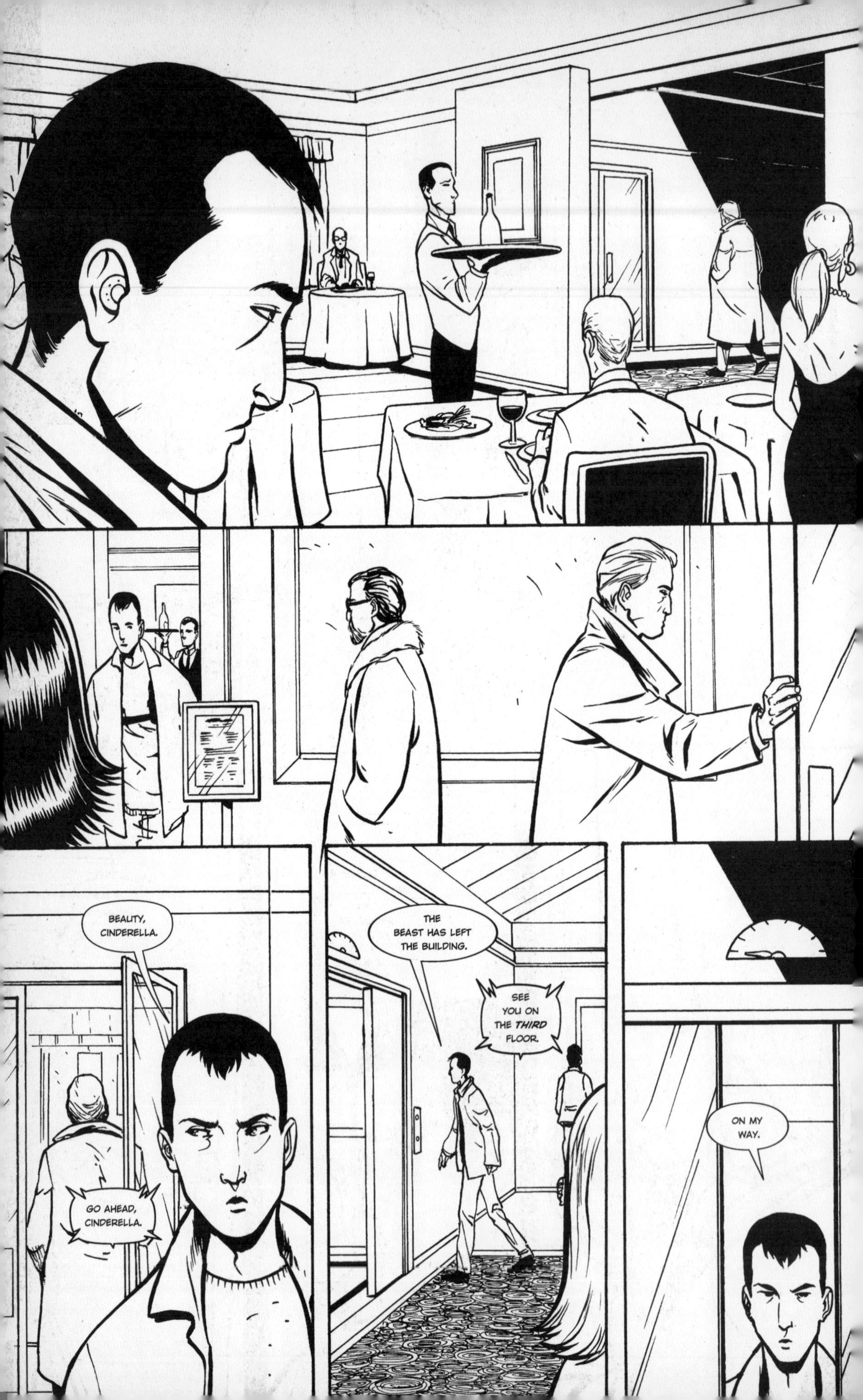
BEAUTY, CINDERELLA.
GO AHEAD, CINDERELLA.
THE BEAST HAS LEFT THE BUILDING.
SEE YOU ON THE *THIRD* FLOOR.
ON MY WAY.

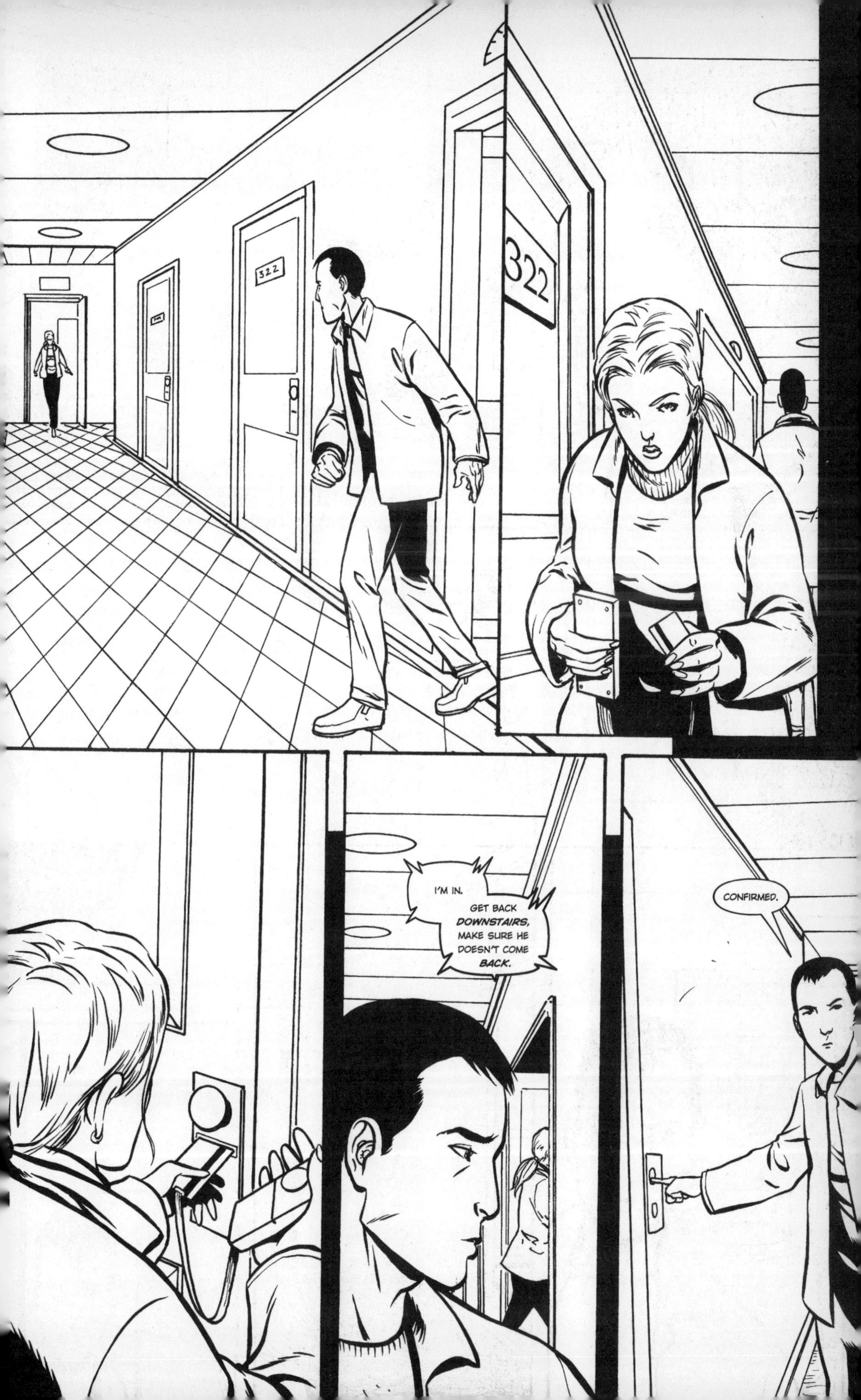

I'M IN.
GET BACK DOWNSTAIRS, MAKE SURE HE DOESN'T COME BACK.
CONFIRMED.

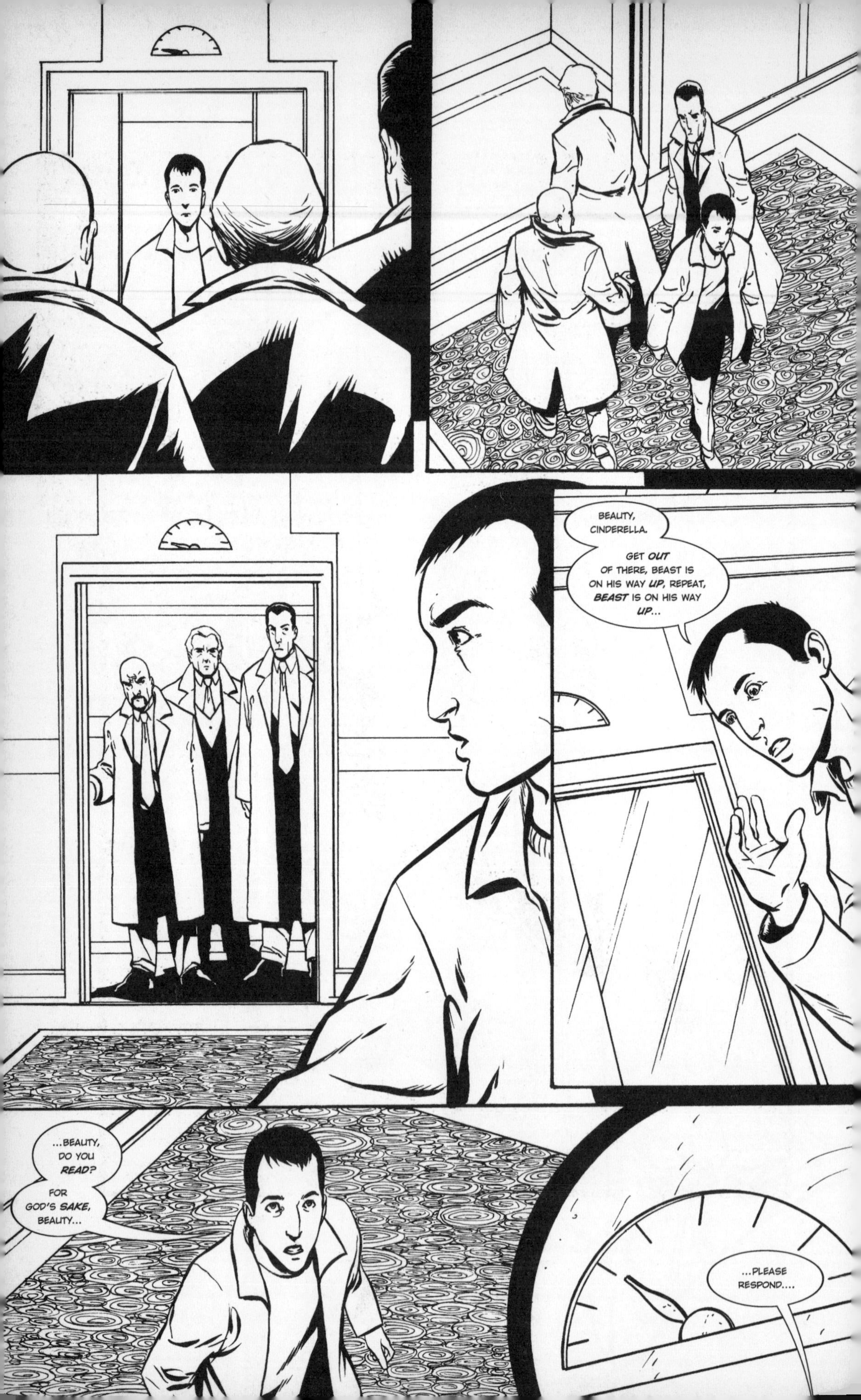
BEAUTY, CINDERELLA.
GET OUT OF THERE, BEAST IS ON HIS WAY UP, REPEAT, BEAST IS ON HIS WAY UP...
...BEAUTY, DO YOU READ?
FOR GOD'S SAKE, BEAUTY...
...PLEASE RESPOND....

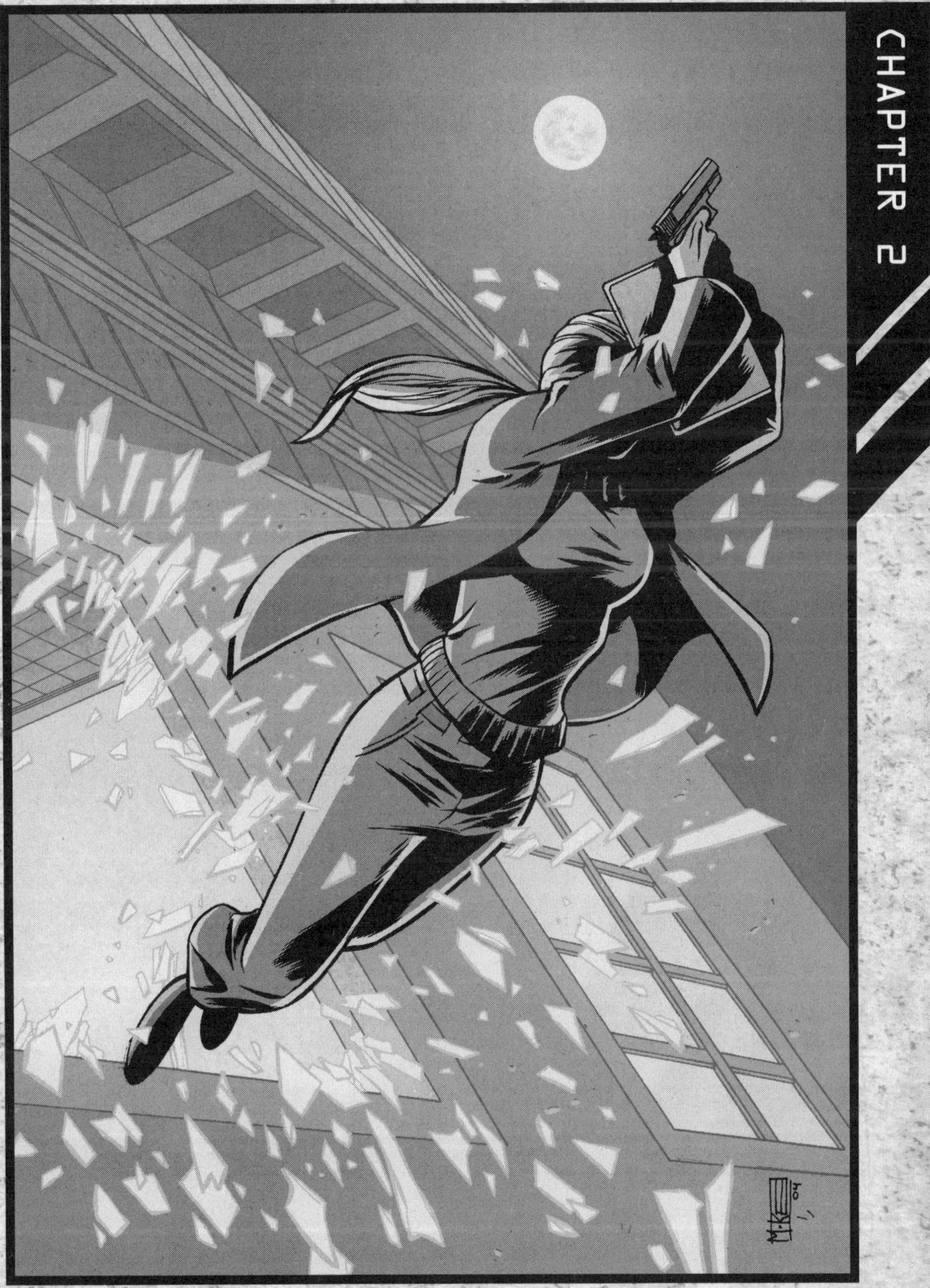
CHAPTER 2

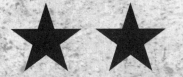

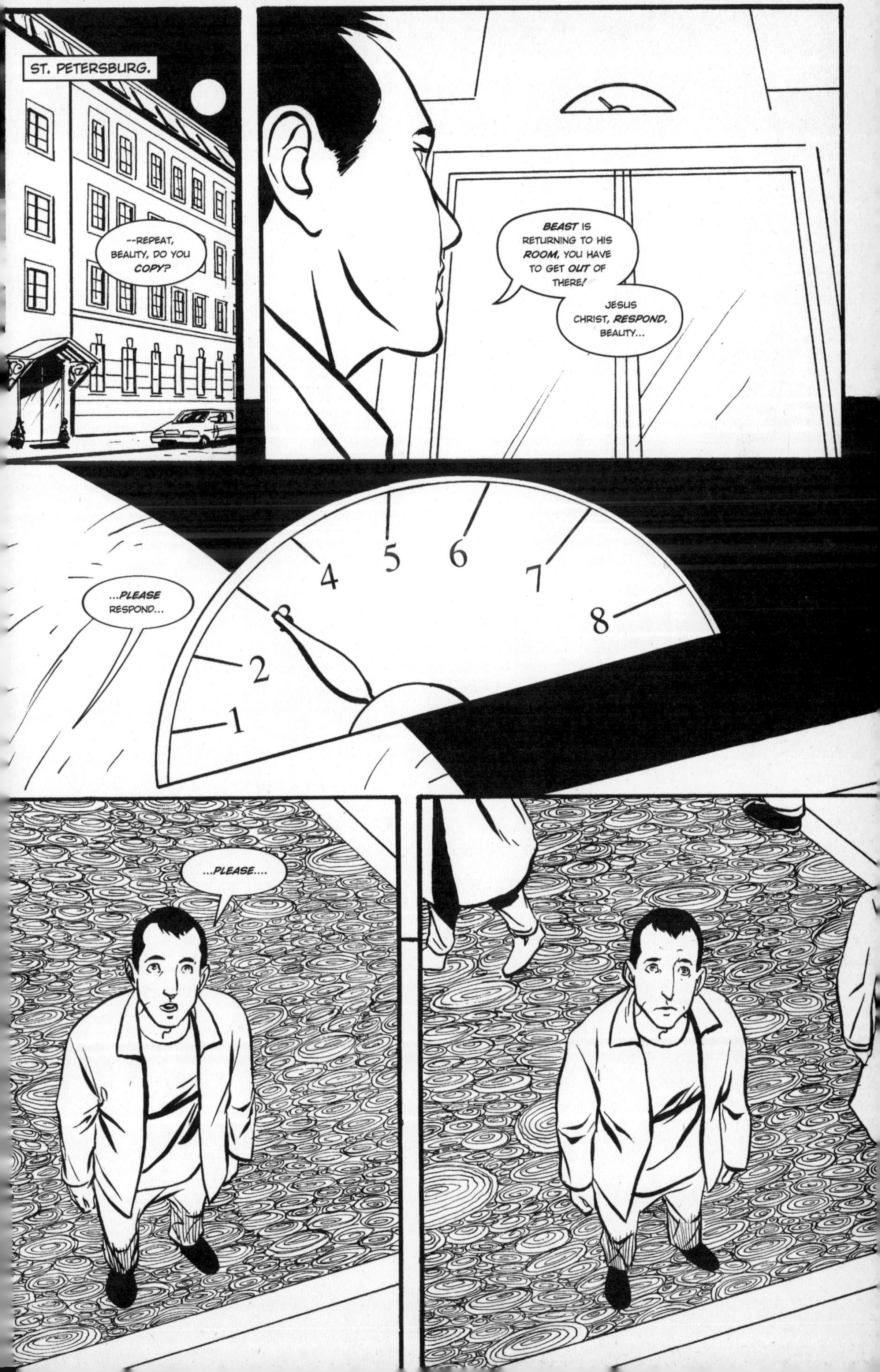
ST. PETERSBURG.
--REPEAT, BEAUTY, DO YOU COPY?
BEAST IS RETURNING TO HIS ROOM, YOU HAVE TO GET OUT OF THERE!
JESUS CHRIST, RESPOND, BEAUTY...
...PLEASE RESPOND...
1
2
3
4
5
6
7
8
...PLEASE....

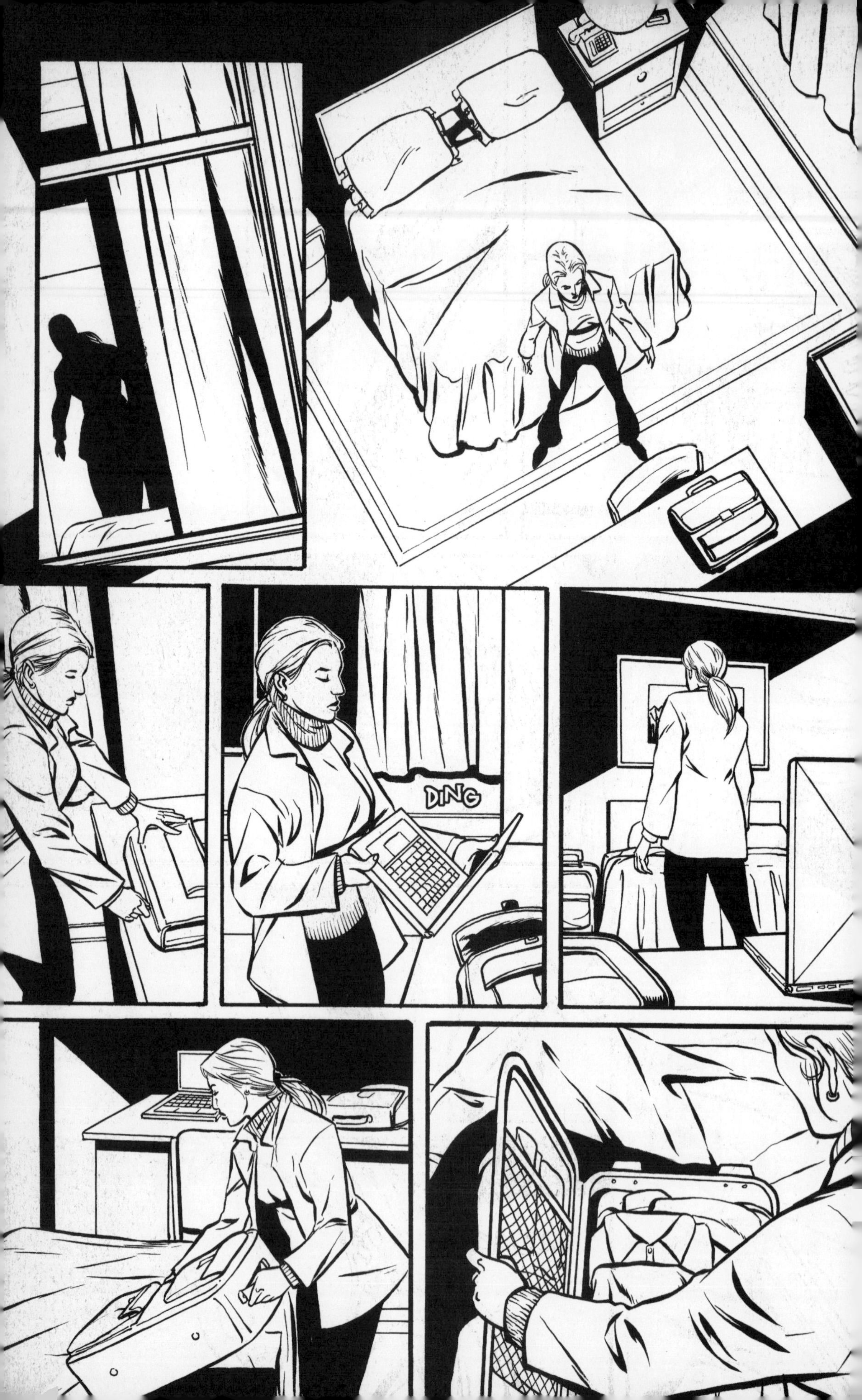
DING

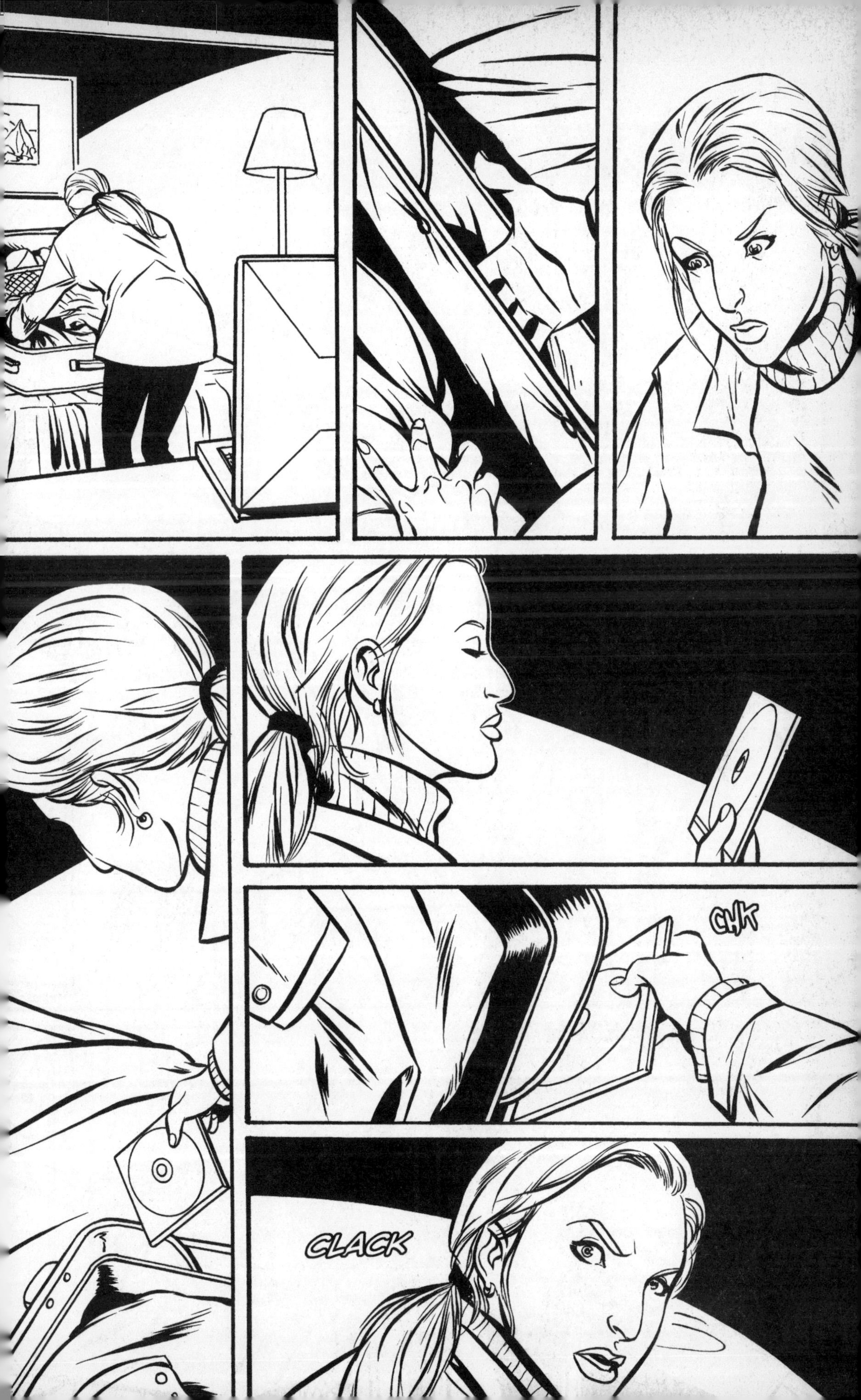
CHK
CLACK

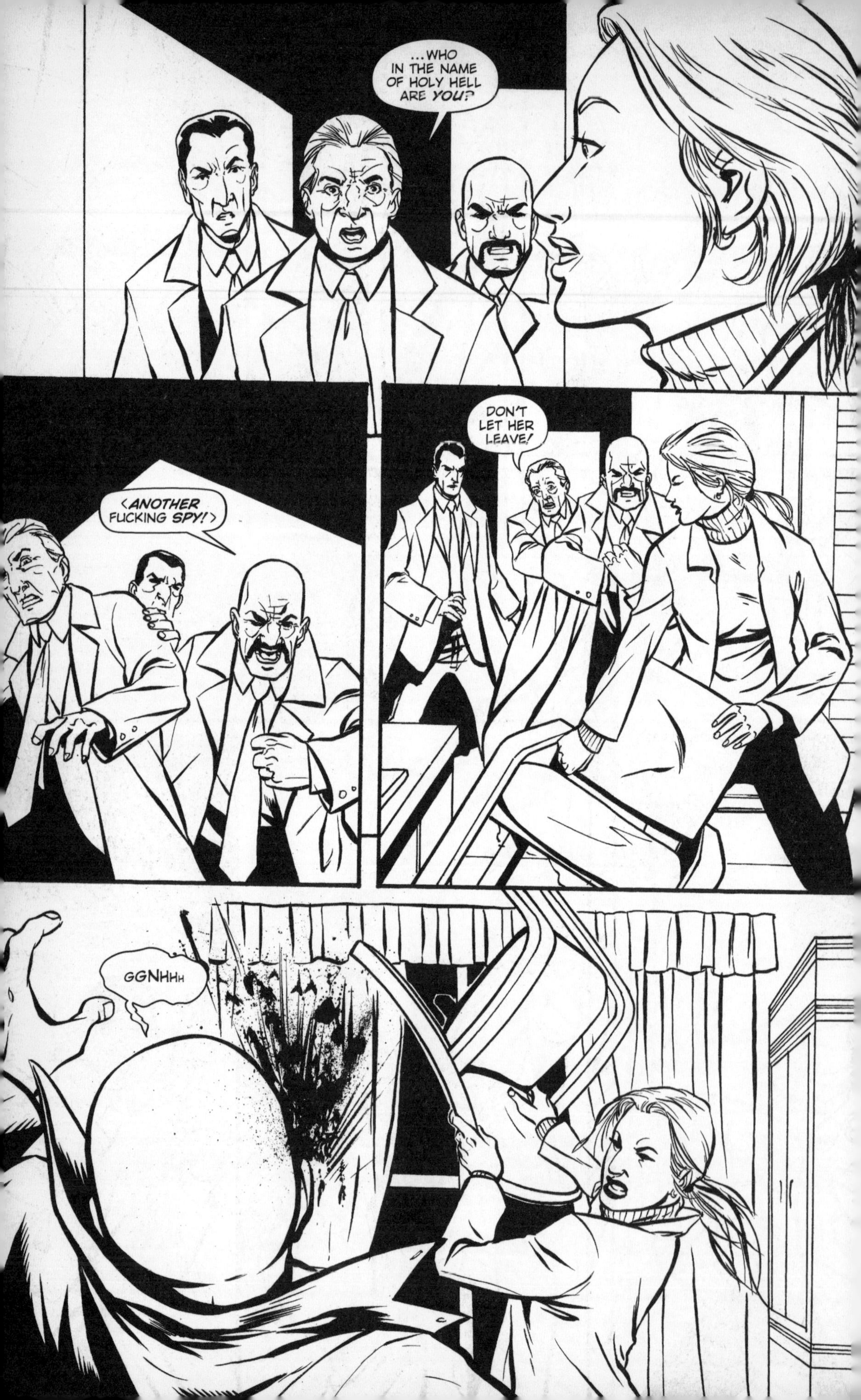
...WHO IN THE NAME OF HOLY HELL ARE YOU?
<ANOTHER FUCKING SPY!>
DON'T LET HER LEAVE!
GGNHHH

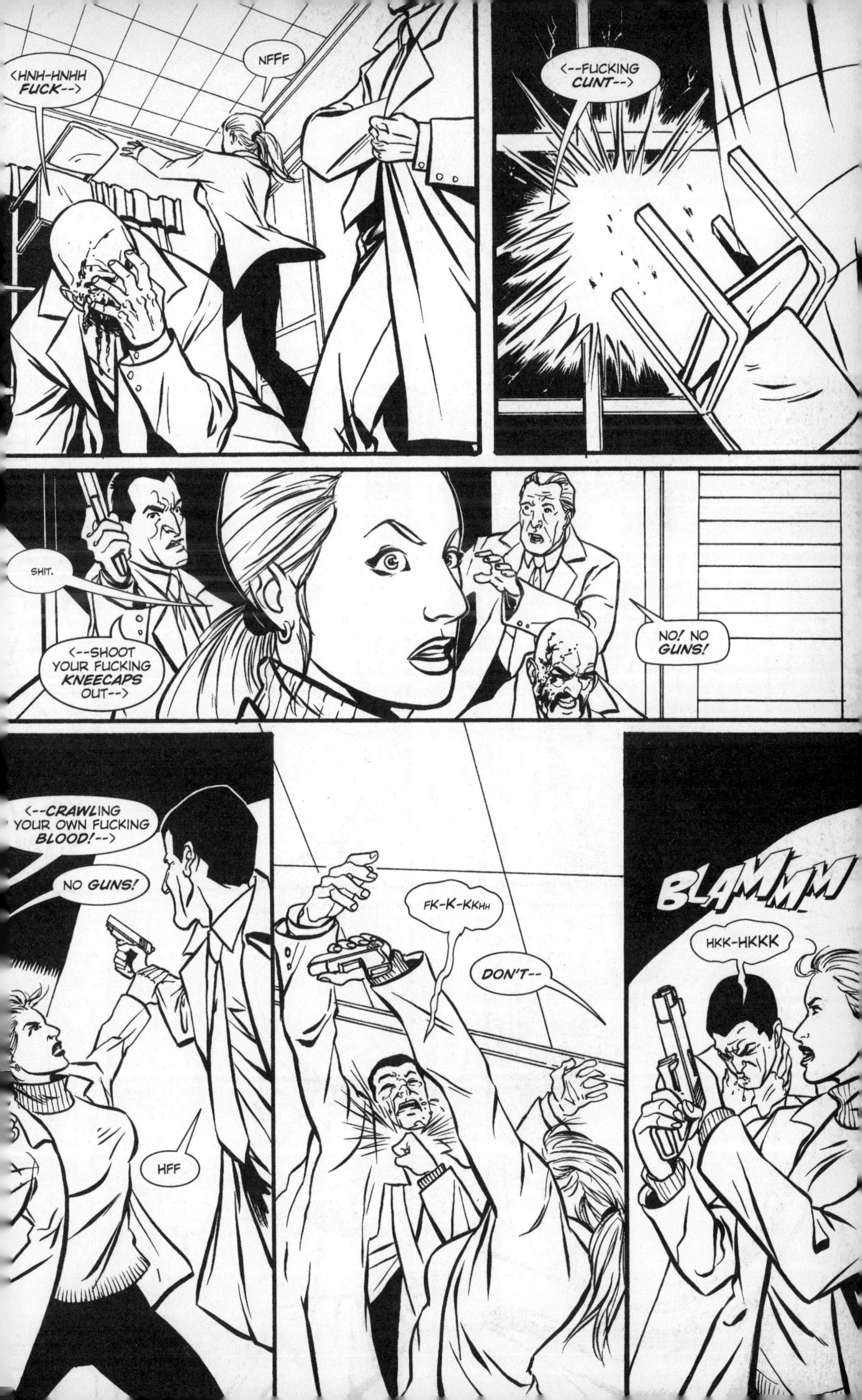
<HNH-HNHH FUCK-->
NFFF
<--FUCKING CUNT-->
SHIT.
<--SHOOT YOUR FUCKING KNEECAPS OUT-->
NO! NO GUNS!
<--CRAWLING YOUR OWN FUCKING BLOOD!-->
NO GUNS!
HFF
FK-K-KKHH
DON'T--
BLAMMM
HKK-HKKK

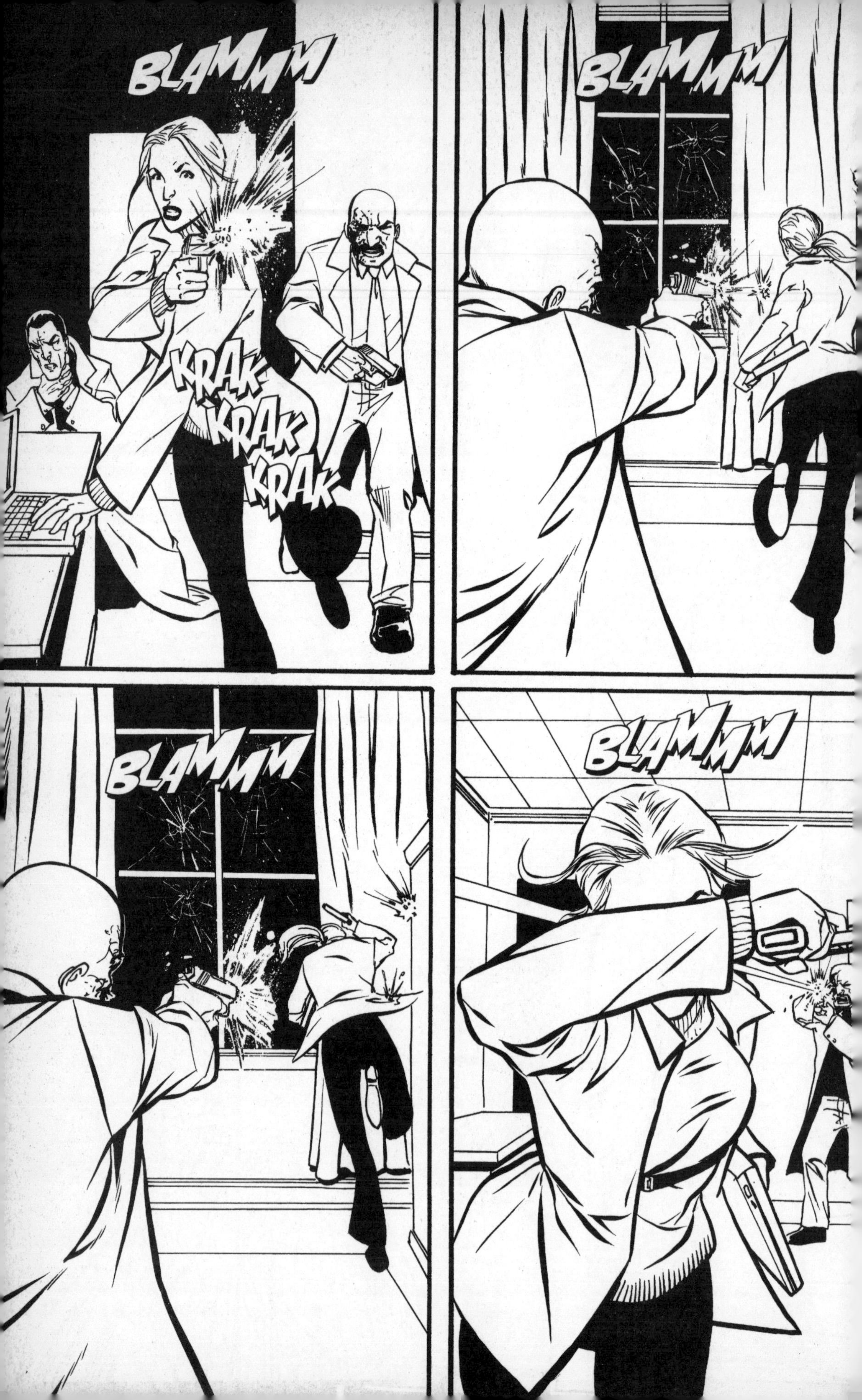
BLAMMM
KRAK
KRAK
KRAK
BLAMMM
BLAMMM
BLAMMM

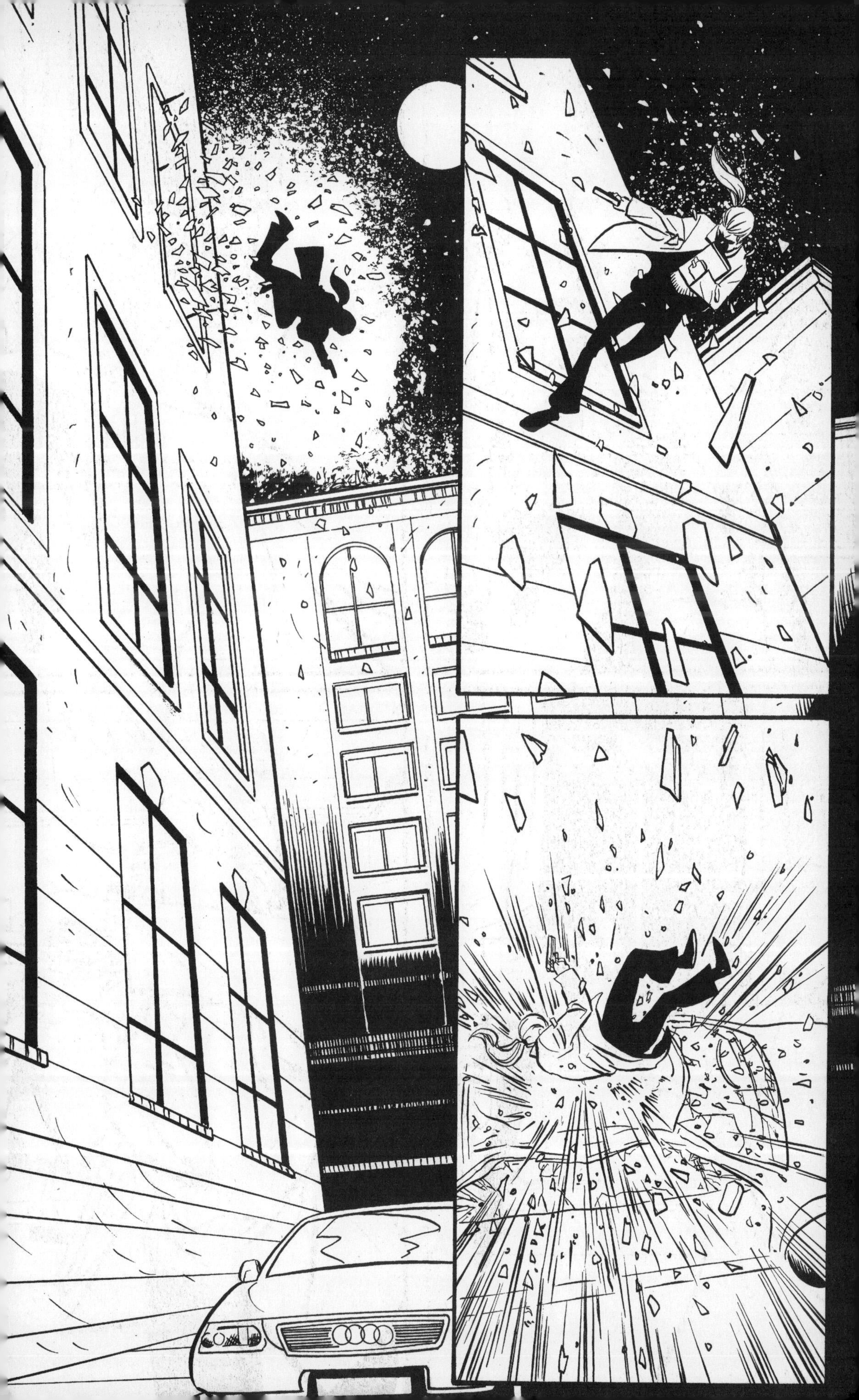

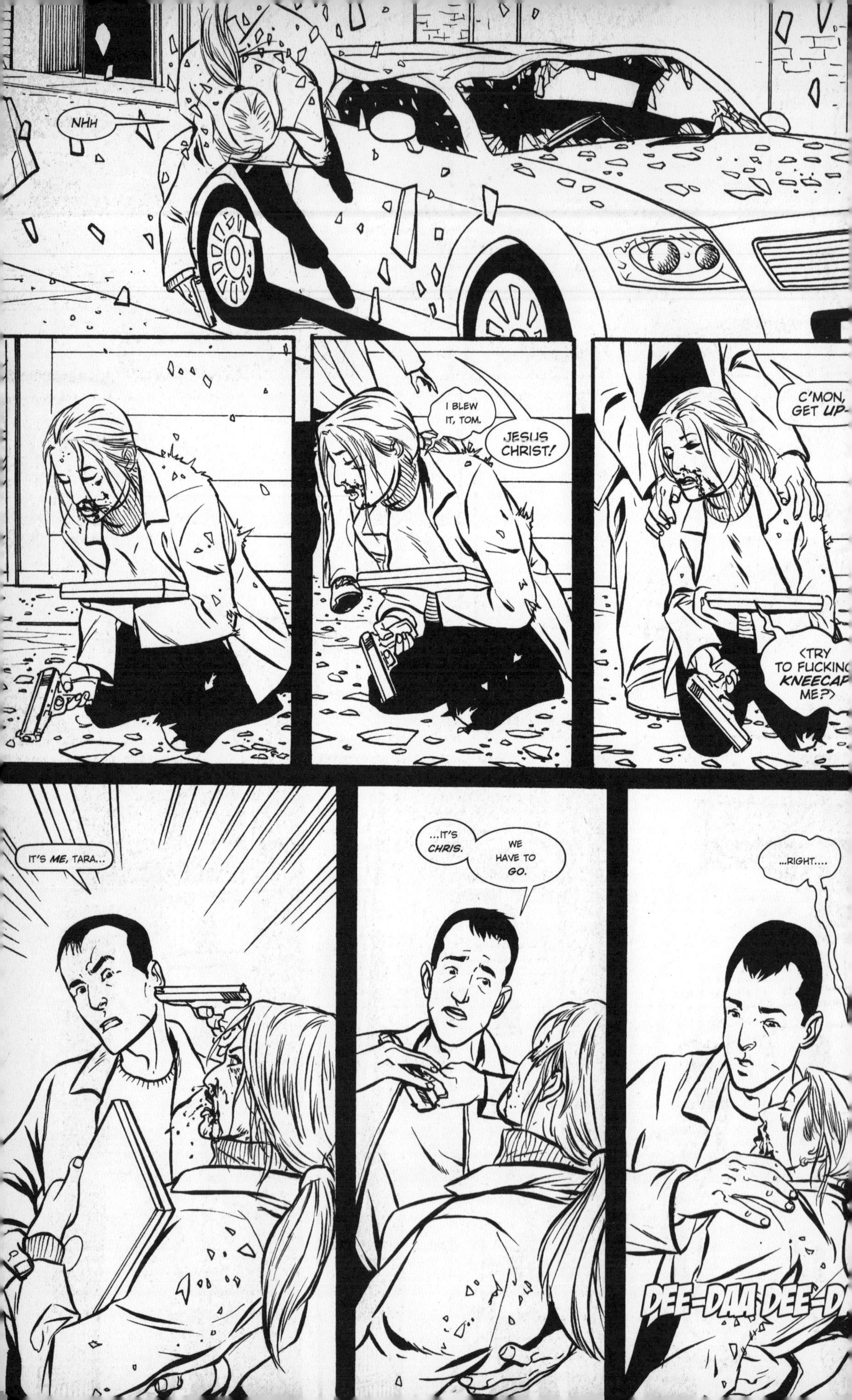
NHH
I BLEW IT, TOM.
JESUS CHRIST!
C'MON, GET UP-
<TRY TO FUCKING KNEECAP ME?>
IT'S ME, TARA...
...IT'S CHRIS.
WE HAVE TO GO.
...RIGHT....
DEE-DAA DEE-D

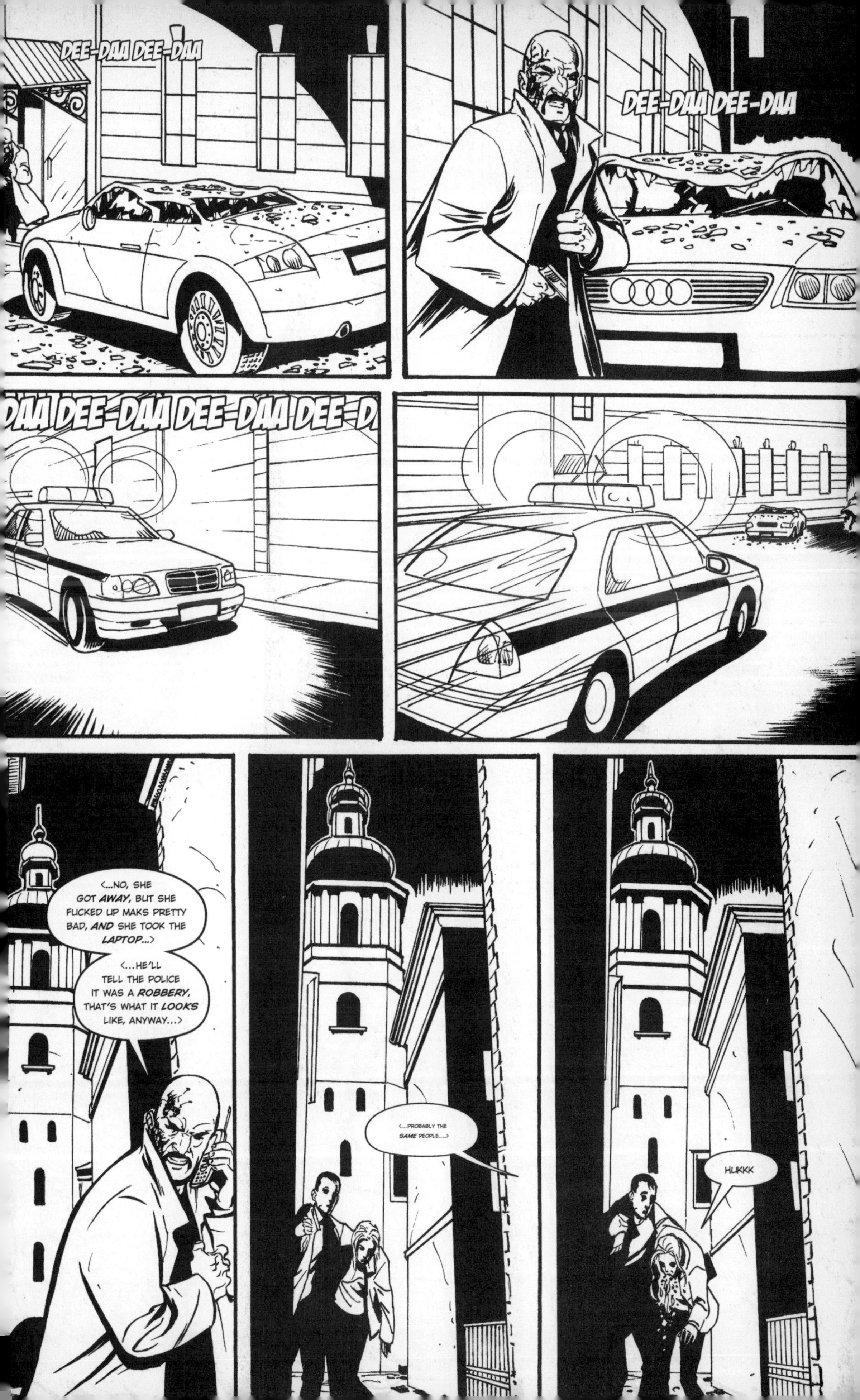
DEE-DAA DEE-DAA
DEE-DAA DEE-DAA
DAA DEE-DAA DEE-DAA DEE-D
<...NO, SHE GOT AWAY, BUT SHE FUCKED UP MAKS PRETTY BAD, AND SHE TOOK THE LAPTOP...>
<...HE'LL TELL THE POLICE IT WAS A ROBBERY, THAT'S WHAT IT LOOKS LIKE, ANYWAY...>
<...PROBABLY THE SAME PEOPLE....>
HUKKK

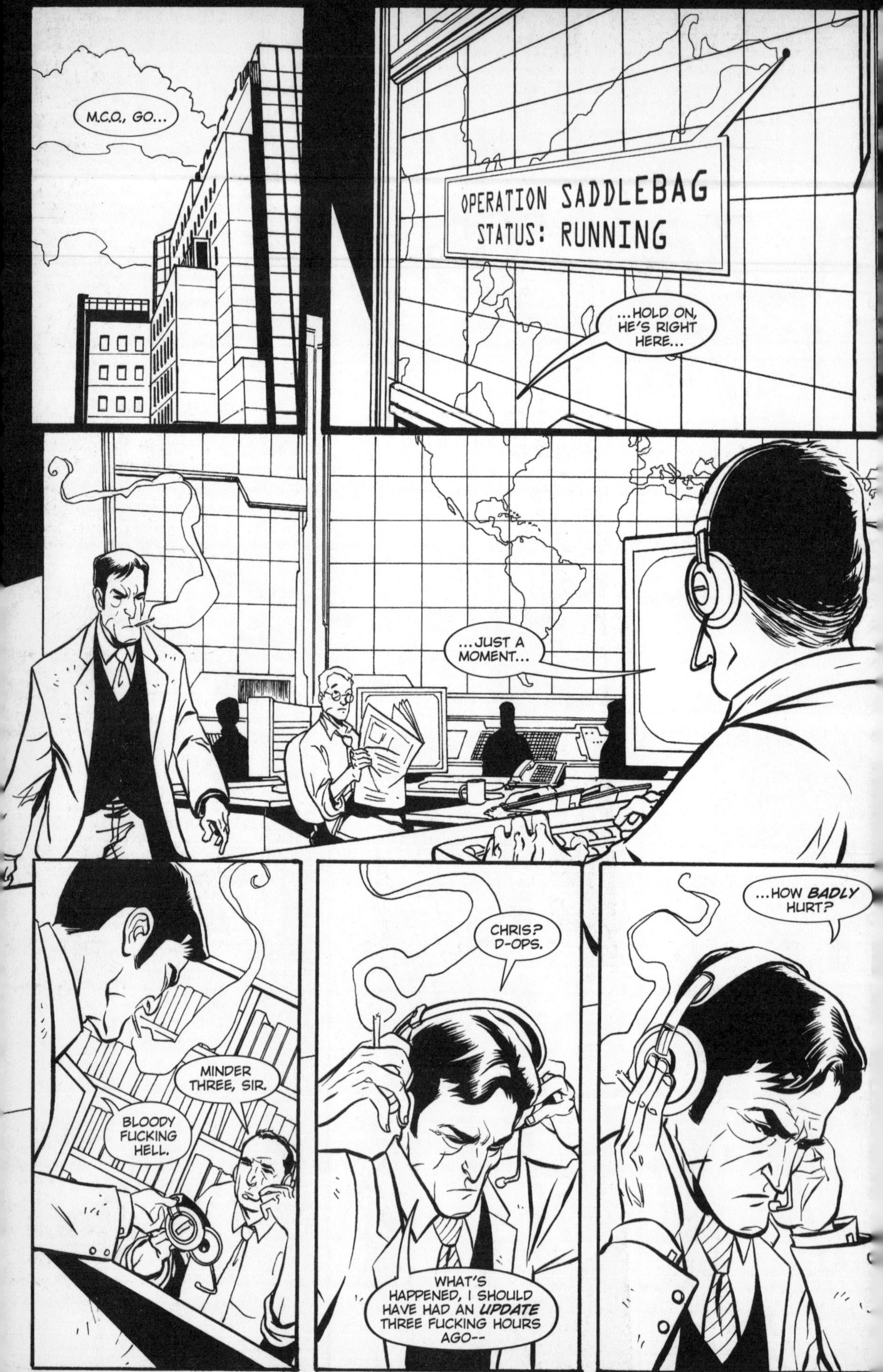
M.C.O., GO...
OPERATION SADDLEBAG
STATUS: RUNNING
...HOLD ON, HE'S RIGHT HERE...
...JUST A MOMENT...
MINDER THREE, SIR.
BLOODY FUCKING HELL.
CHRIS? D-OPS.
WHAT'S HAPPENED, I SHOULD HAVE HAD AN *UPDATE* THREE FUCKING HOURS AGO--
...HOW *BADLY* HURT?

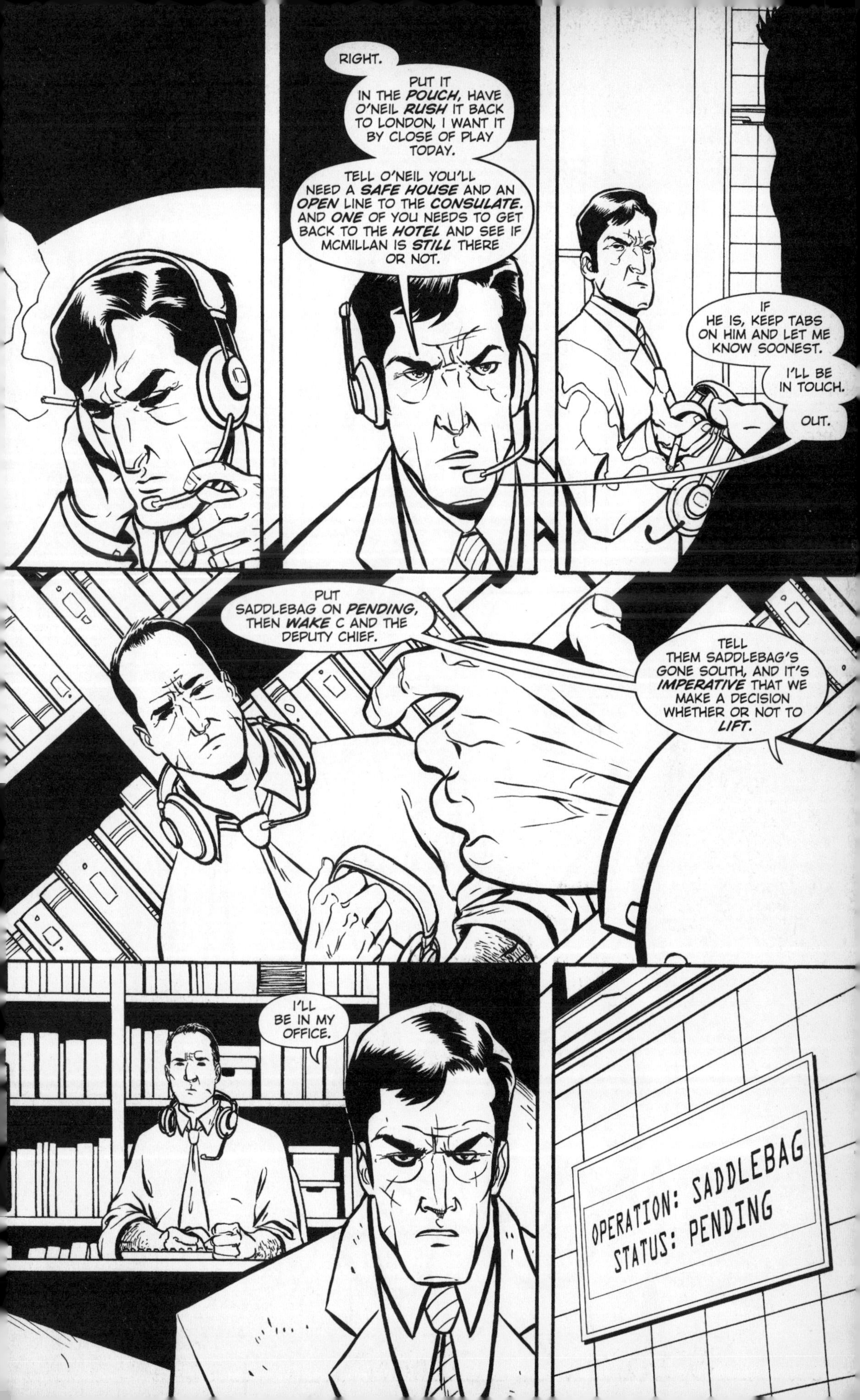
RIGHT.
PUT IT IN THE POUCH, HAVE O'NEIL RUSH IT BACK TO LONDON, I WANT IT BY CLOSE OF PLAY TODAY.
TELL O'NEIL YOU'LL NEED A SAFE HOUSE AND AN OPEN LINE TO THE CONSULATE. AND ONE OF YOU NEEDS TO GET BACK TO THE HOTEL AND SEE IF MCMILLAN IS STILL THERE OR NOT.
IF HE IS, KEEP TABS ON HIM AND LET ME KNOW SOONEST.
I'LL BE IN TOUCH.
OUT.
PUT SADDLEBAG ON PENDING, THEN WAKE C AND THE DEPUTY CHIEF.
TELL THEM SADDLEBAG'S GONE SOUTH, AND IT'S IMPERATIVE THAT WE MAKE A DECISION WHETHER OR NOT TO LIFT.
I'LL BE IN MY OFFICE.
OPERATION: SADDLEBAG
STATUS: PENDING

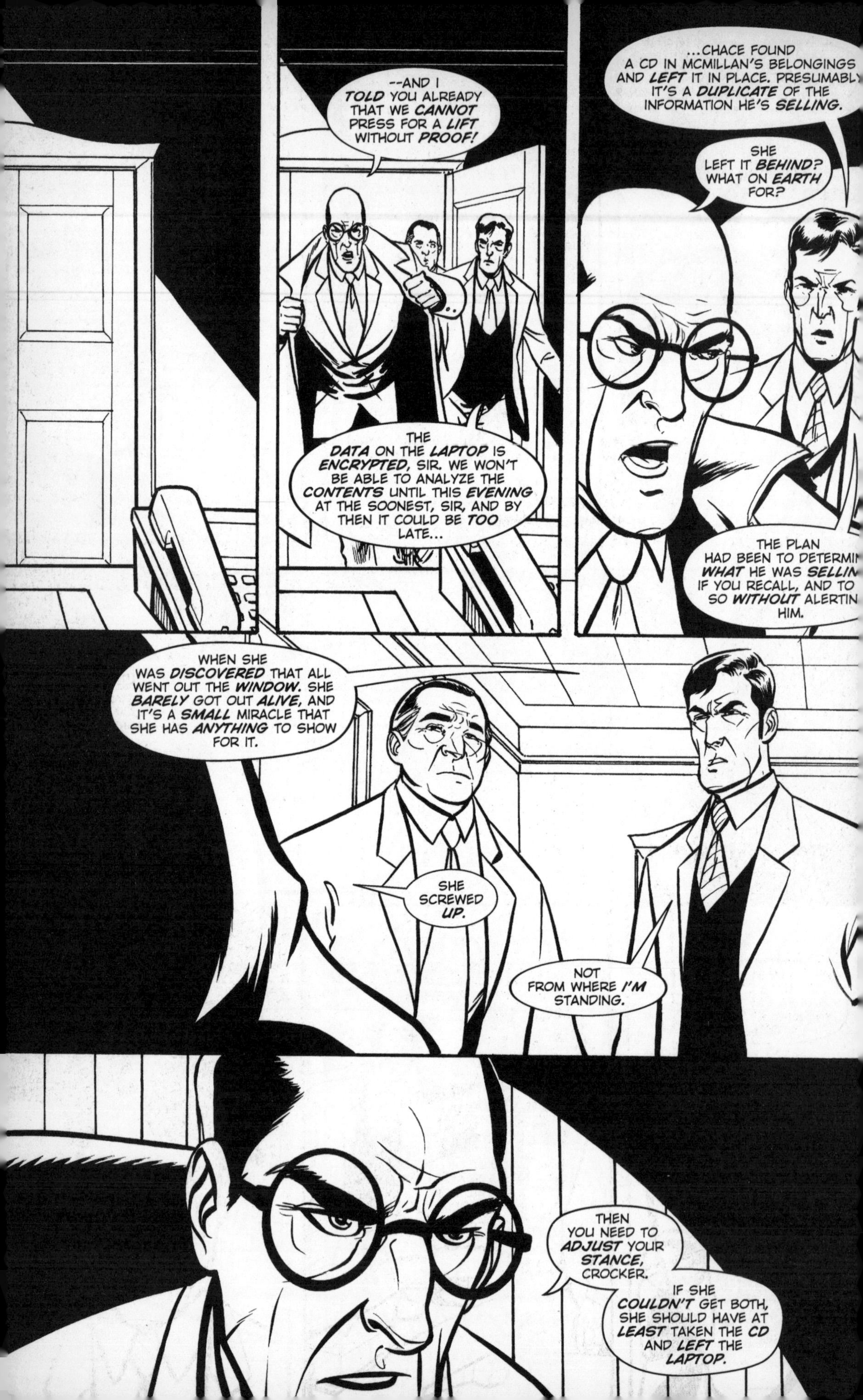
--AND I TOLD YOU ALREADY THAT WE CANNOT PRESS FOR A LIFT WITHOUT PROOF!
THE DATA ON THE LAPTOP IS ENCRYPTED, SIR. WE WON'T BE ABLE TO ANALYZE THE CONTENTS UNTIL THIS EVENING AT THE SOONEST, SIR, AND BY THEN IT COULD BE TOO LATE...
...CHACE FOUND A CD IN MCMILLAN'S BELONGINGS AND LEFT IT IN PLACE. PRESUMABLY IT'S A DUPLICATE OF THE INFORMATION HE'S SELLING.
SHE LEFT IT BEHIND? WHAT ON EARTH FOR?
THE PLAN HAD BEEN TO DETERMIN WHAT HE WAS SELLIN IF YOU RECALL, AND TO SO WITHOUT ALERTIN HIM.
WHEN SHE WAS DISCOVERED THAT ALL WENT OUT THE WINDOW. SHE BARELY GOT OUT ALIVE, AND IT'S A SMALL MIRACLE THAT SHE HAS ANYTHING TO SHOW FOR IT.
SHE SCREWED UP.
NOT FROM WHERE I'M STANDING.
THEN YOU NEED TO ADJUST YOUR STANCE, CROCKER.
IF SHE COULDN'T GET BOTH, SHE SHOULD HAVE AT LEAST TAKEN THE CD AND LEFT THE LAPTOP.

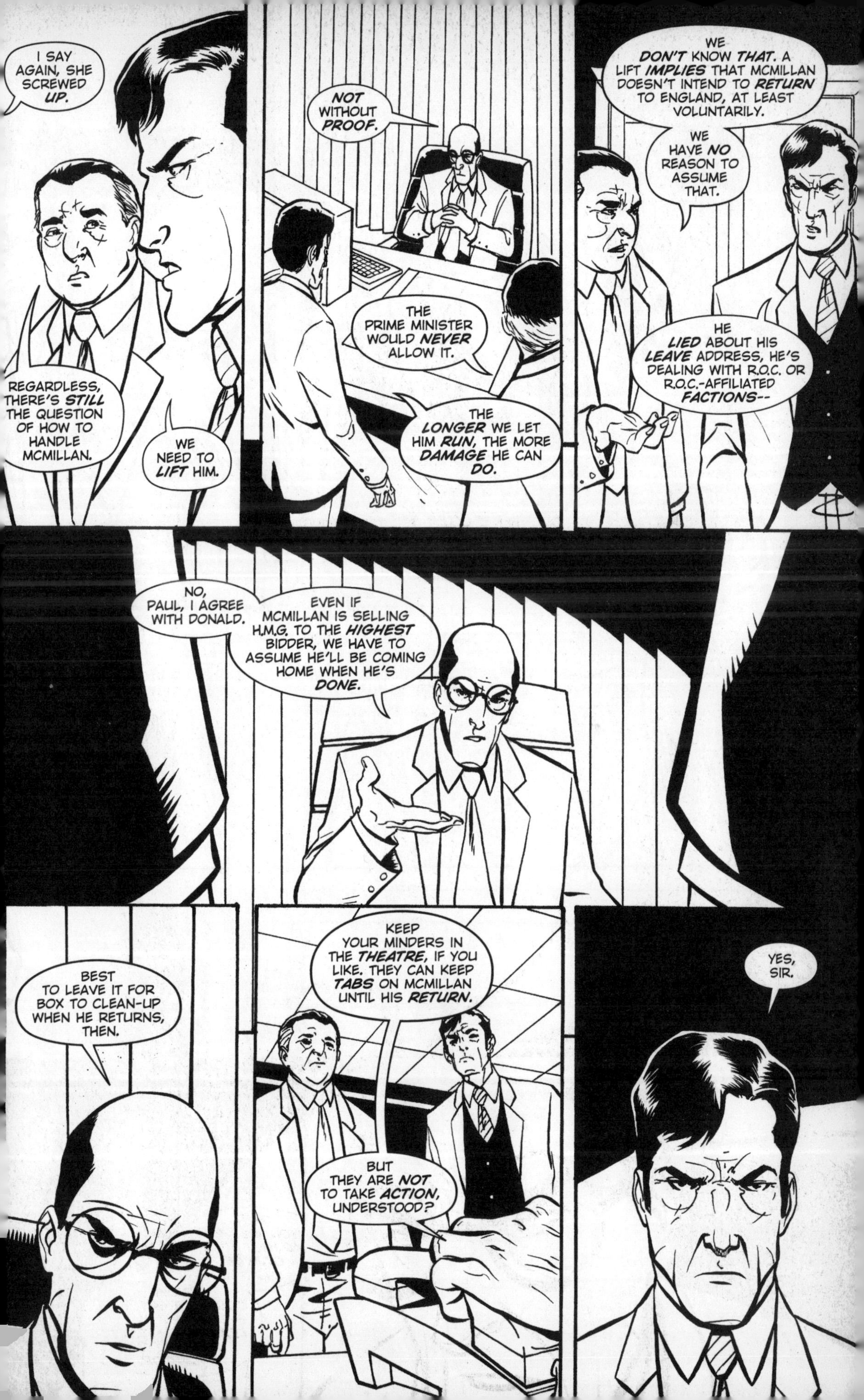
I SAY AGAIN, SHE SCREWED UP.
REGARDLESS, THERE'S STILL THE QUESTION OF HOW TO HANDLE MCMILLAN.
WE NEED TO LIFT HIM.
NOT WITHOUT PROOF.
THE PRIME MINISTER WOULD NEVER ALLOW IT.
THE LONGER WE LET HIM RUN, THE MORE DAMAGE HE CAN DO.
WE DON'T KNOW THAT. A LIFT IMPLIES THAT MCMILLAN DOESN'T INTEND TO RETURN TO ENGLAND, AT LEAST VOLUNTARILY.
WE HAVE NO REASON TO ASSUME THAT.
HE LIED ABOUT HIS LEAVE ADDRESS, HE'S DEALING WITH R.O.C. OR R.O.C.-AFFILIATED FACTIONS--
NO, PAUL, I AGREE WITH DONALD.
EVEN IF MCMILLAN IS SELLING H.M.G. TO THE HIGHEST BIDDER, WE HAVE TO ASSUME HE'LL BE COMING HOME WHEN HE'S DONE.
BEST TO LEAVE IT FOR BOX TO CLEAN-UP WHEN HE RETURNS, THEN.
KEEP YOUR MINDERS IN THE THEATRE, IF YOU LIKE. THEY CAN KEEP TABS ON MCMILLAN UNTIL HIS RETURN.
BUT THEY ARE NOT TO TAKE ACTION, UNDERSTOOD?
YES, SIR.

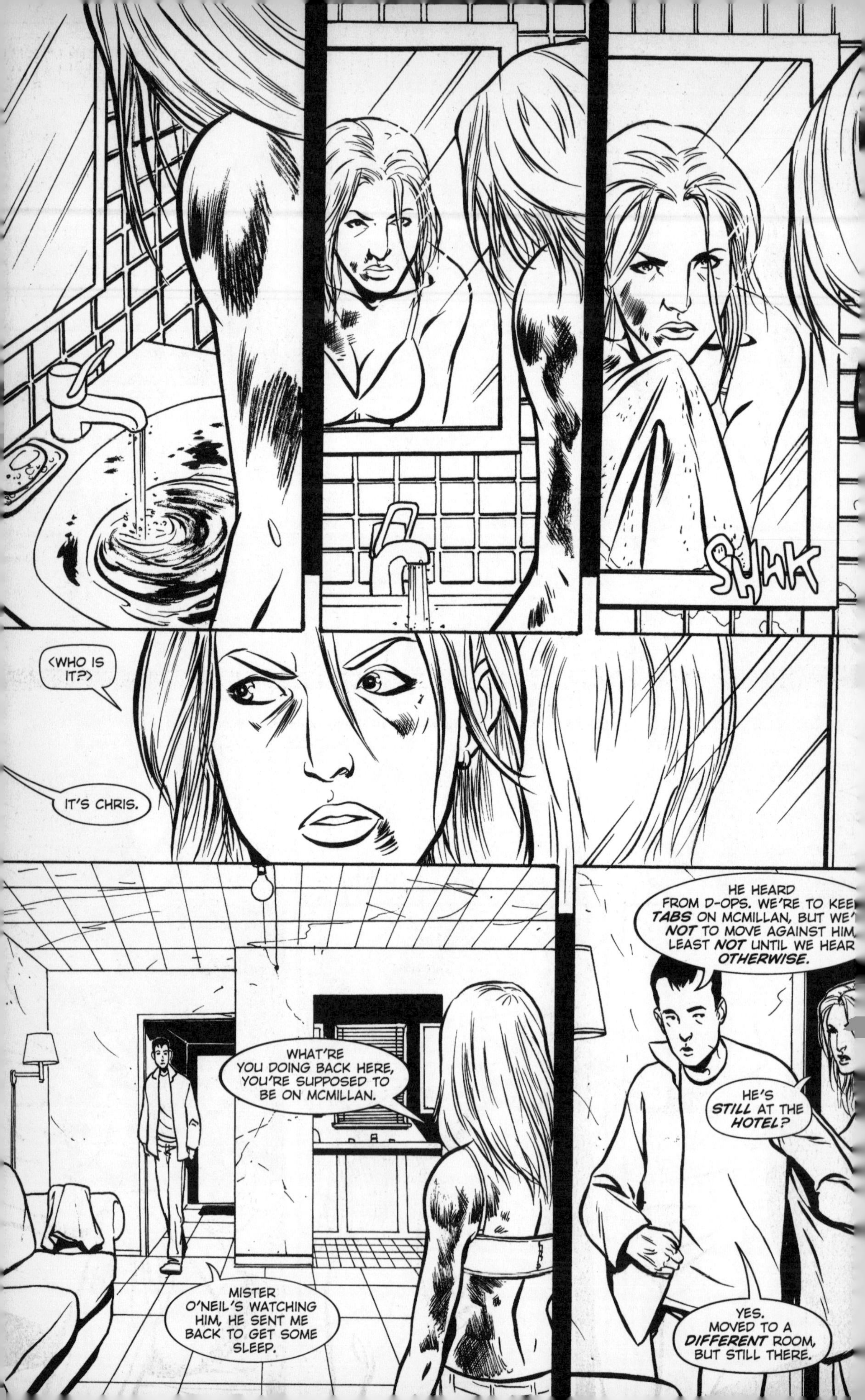
SHHK
<WHO IS IT?>
IT'S CHRIS.
WHAT'RE YOU DOING BACK HERE, YOU'RE SUPPOSED TO BE ON MCMILLAN.
MISTER O'NEIL'S WATCHING HIM, HE SENT ME BACK TO GET SOME SLEEP.
HE HEARD FROM D-OPS. WE'RE TO KEE TABS ON MCMILLAN, BUT WE' NOT TO MOVE AGAINST HIM, LEAST NOT UNTIL WE HEAR OTHERWISE.
HE'S STILL AT THE HOTEL?
YES. MOVED TO A DIFFERENT ROOM, BUT STILL THERE.

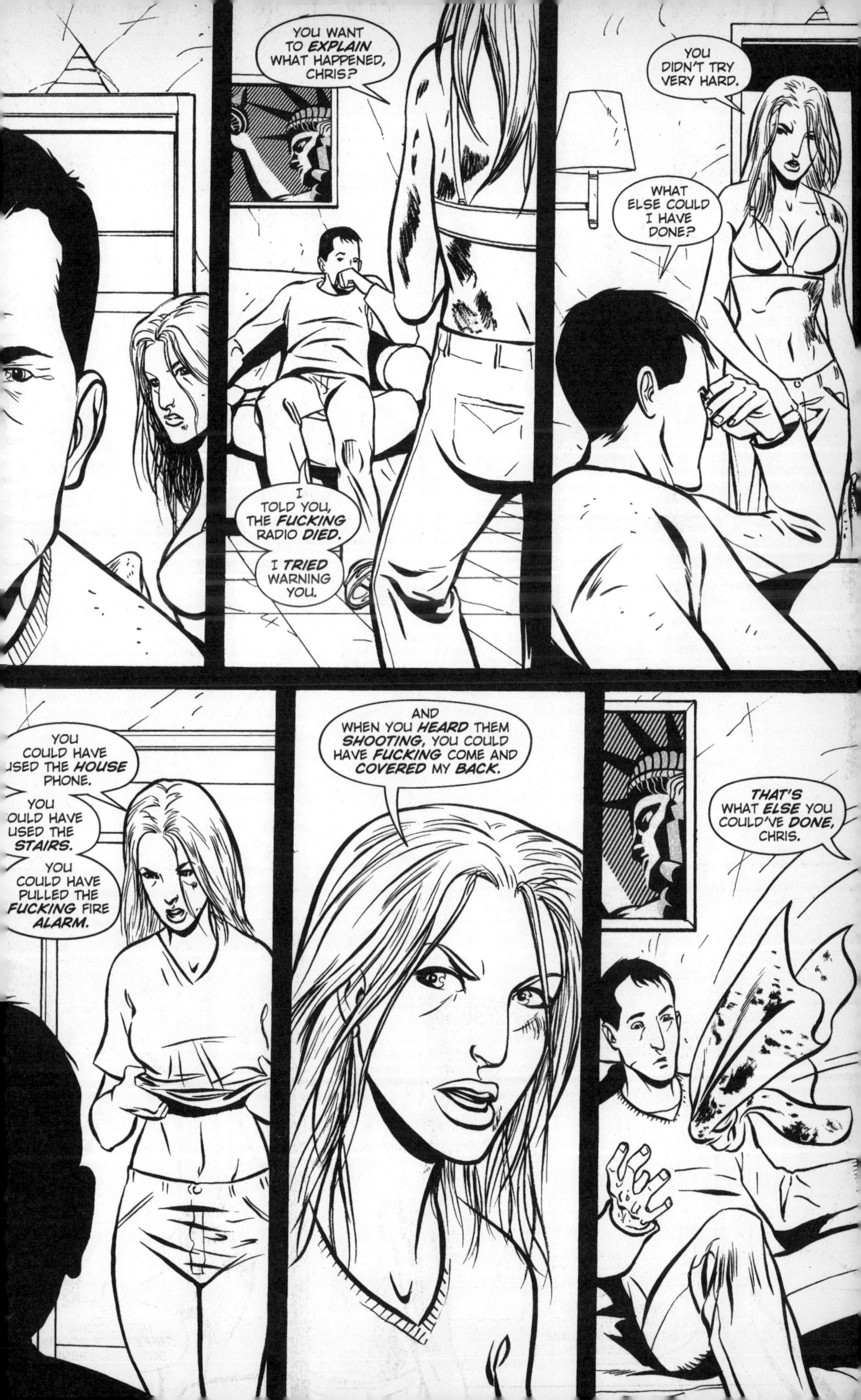

YOU WANT TO EXPLAIN WHAT HAPPENED, CHRIS?
I TOLD YOU, THE FUCKING RADIO DIED.
I TRIED WARNING YOU.
YOU DIDN'T TRY VERY HARD.
WHAT ELSE COULD I HAVE DONE?
YOU COULD HAVE USED THE HOUSE PHONE.
YOU COULD HAVE USED THE STAIRS.
YOU COULD HAVE PULLED THE FUCKING FIRE ALARM.
AND WHEN YOU HEARD THEM SHOOTING, YOU COULD HAVE FUCKING COME AND COVERED MY BACK.
THAT'S WHAT ELSE YOU COULD'VE DONE, CHRIS.

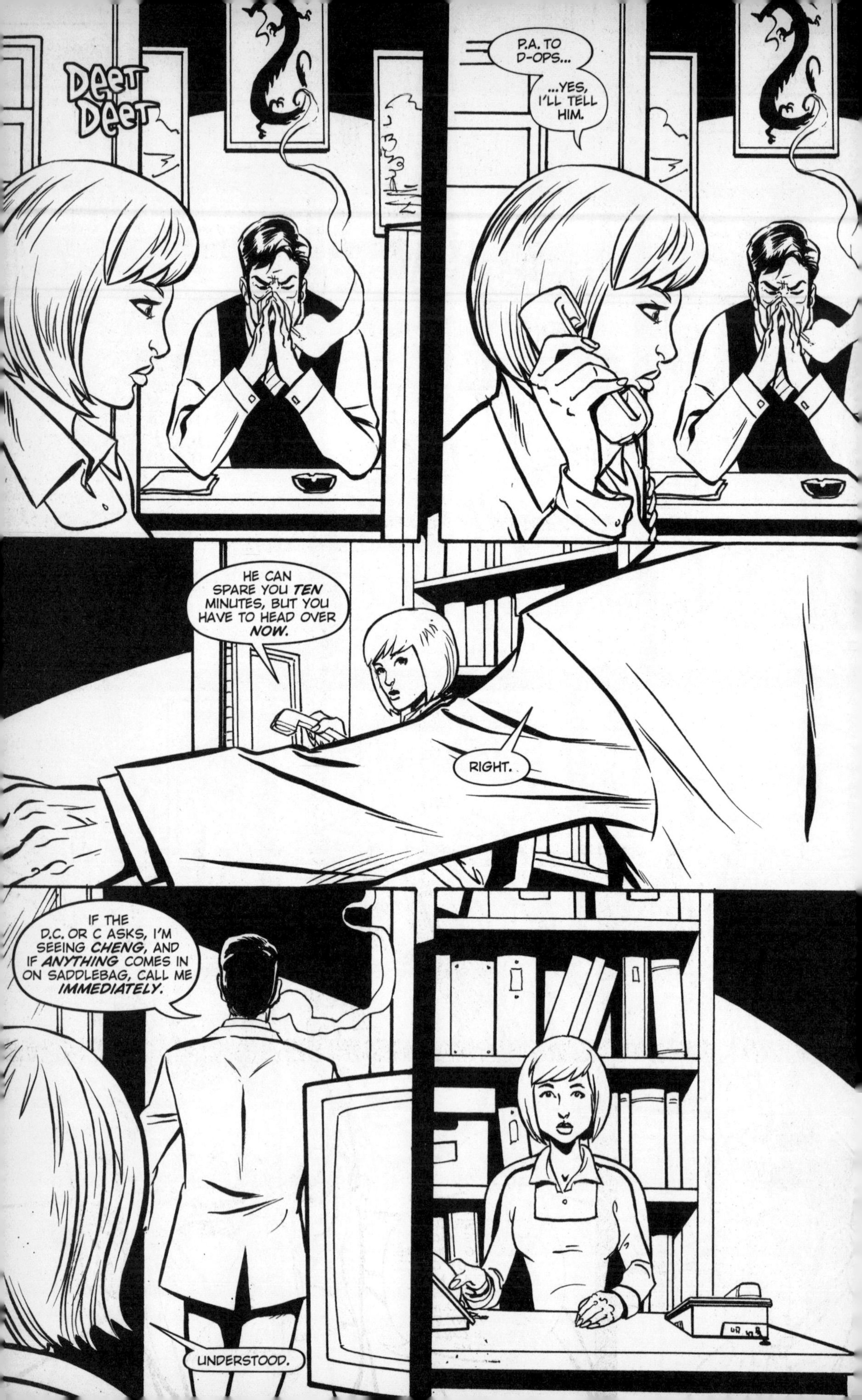
DEET DEET
P.A. TO D-OPS...
...YES, I'LL TELL HIM.
HE CAN SPARE YOU *TEN* MINUTES, BUT YOU HAVE TO HEAD OVER *NOW*.
RIGHT.
IF THE D.C. OR C ASKS, I'M SEEING *CHENG*, AND IF *ANYTHING* COMES IN ON SADDLEBAG, CALL ME *IMMEDIATELY*.
UNDERSTOOD.

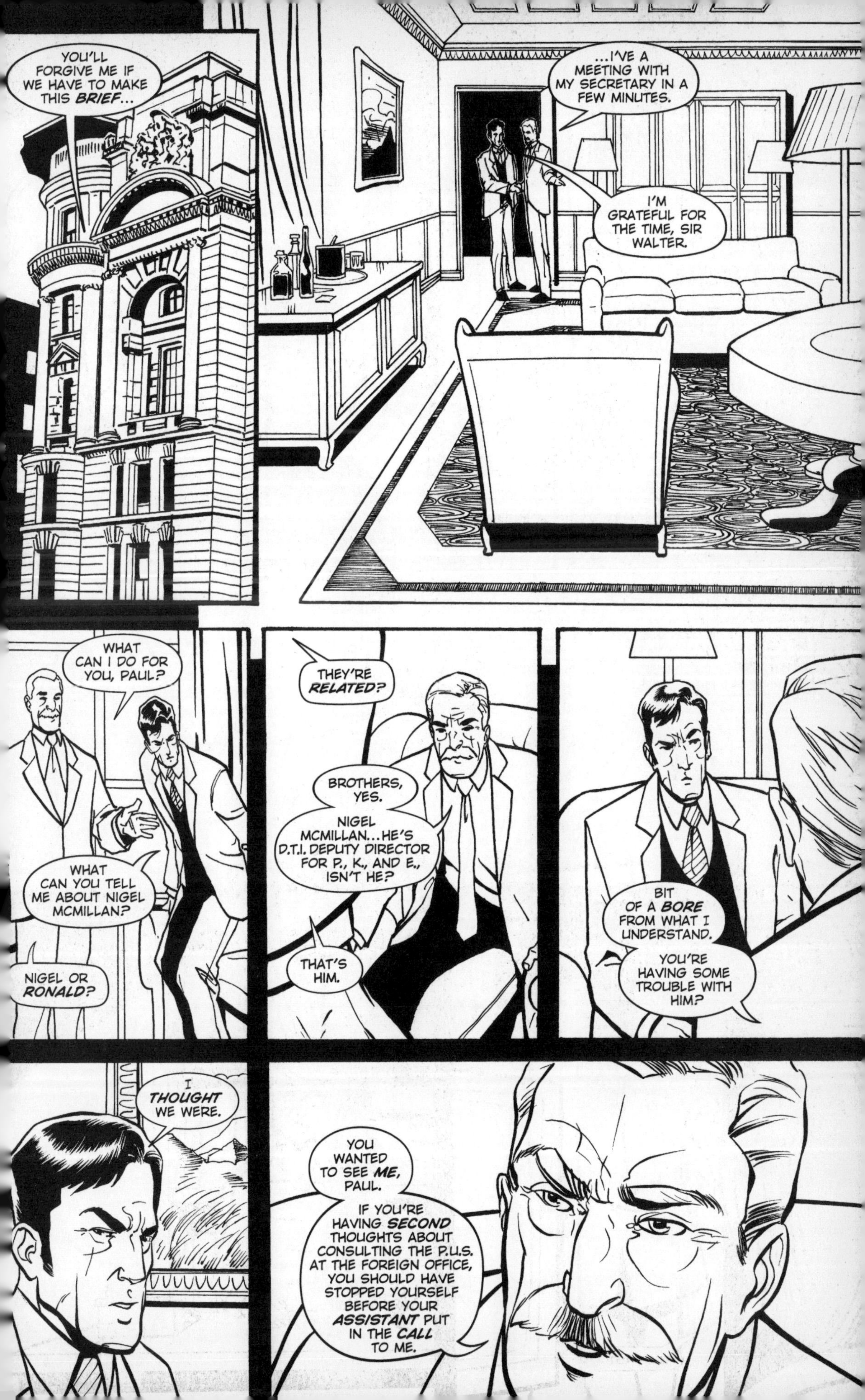
YOU'LL FORGIVE ME IF WE HAVE TO MAKE THIS BRIEF...
...I'VE A MEETING WITH MY SECRETARY IN A FEW MINUTES.
I'M GRATEFUL FOR THE TIME, SIR WALTER.
WHAT CAN I DO FOR YOU, PAUL?
WHAT CAN YOU TELL ME ABOUT NIGEL MCMILLAN?
NIGEL OR RONALD?
THEY'RE RELATED?
BROTHERS, YES.
NIGEL MCMILLAN...HE'S D.T.I. DEPUTY DIRECTOR FOR P., K., AND E., ISN'T HE?
THAT'S HIM.
BIT OF A BORE FROM WHAT I UNDERSTAND.
YOU'RE HAVING SOME TROUBLE WITH HIM?
I THOUGHT WE WERE.
YOU WANTED TO SEE ME, PAUL.
IF YOU'RE HAVING SECOND THOUGHTS ABOUT CONSULTING THE P.U.S. AT THE FOREIGN OFFICE, YOU SHOULD HAVE STOPPED YOURSELF BEFORE YOUR ASSISTANT PUT IN THE CALL TO ME.

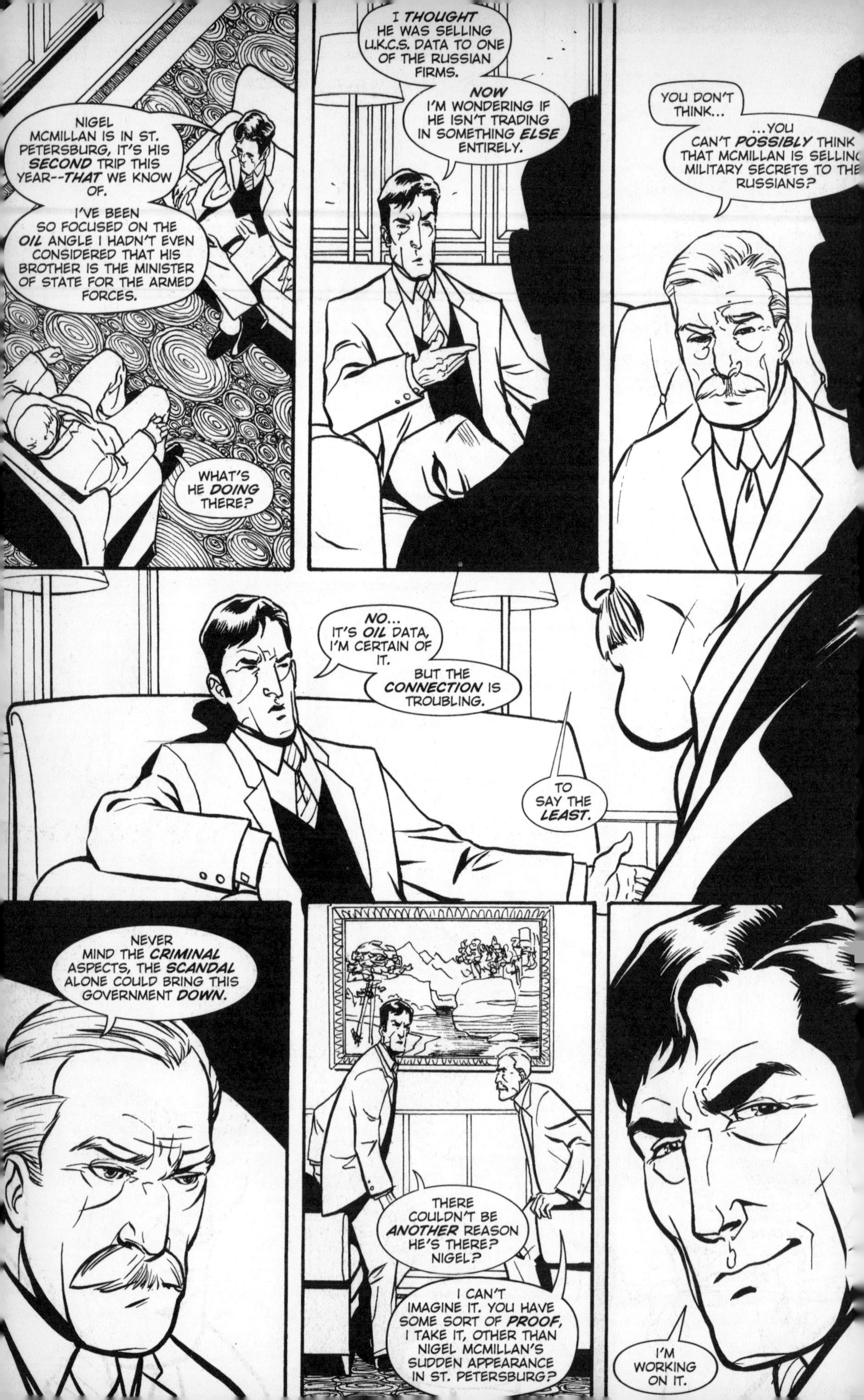
NIGEL MCMILLAN IS IN ST. PETERSBURG, IT'S HIS *SECOND* TRIP THIS YEAR--*THAT* WE KNOW OF.
I'VE BEEN SO FOCUSED ON THE *OIL* ANGLE I HADN'T EVEN CONSIDERED THAT HIS BROTHER IS THE MINISTER OF STATE FOR THE ARMED FORCES.
WHAT'S HE *DOING* THERE?
I *THOUGHT* HE WAS SELLING U.K.C.S. DATA TO ONE OF THE RUSSIAN FIRMS.
*NOW* I'M WONDERING IF HE ISN'T TRADING IN SOMETHING *ELSE* ENTIRELY.
YOU DON'T THINK...
...YOU CAN'T *POSSIBLY* THINK THAT MCMILLAN IS SELLING MILITARY SECRETS TO THE RUSSIANS?
*NO*... IT'S *OIL* DATA, I'M CERTAIN OF IT.
BUT THE *CONNECTION* IS TROUBLING.
TO SAY THE *LEAST*.
NEVER MIND THE *CRIMINAL* ASPECTS, THE *SCANDAL* ALONE COULD BRING THIS GOVERNMENT *DOWN*.
THERE COULDN'T BE *ANOTHER* REASON HE'S THERE? NIGEL?
I CAN'T IMAGINE IT. YOU HAVE SOME SORT OF *PROOF*, I TAKE IT, OTHER THAN NIGEL MCMILLAN'S SUDDEN APPEARANCE IN ST. PETERSBURG?
I'M WORKING ON IT.

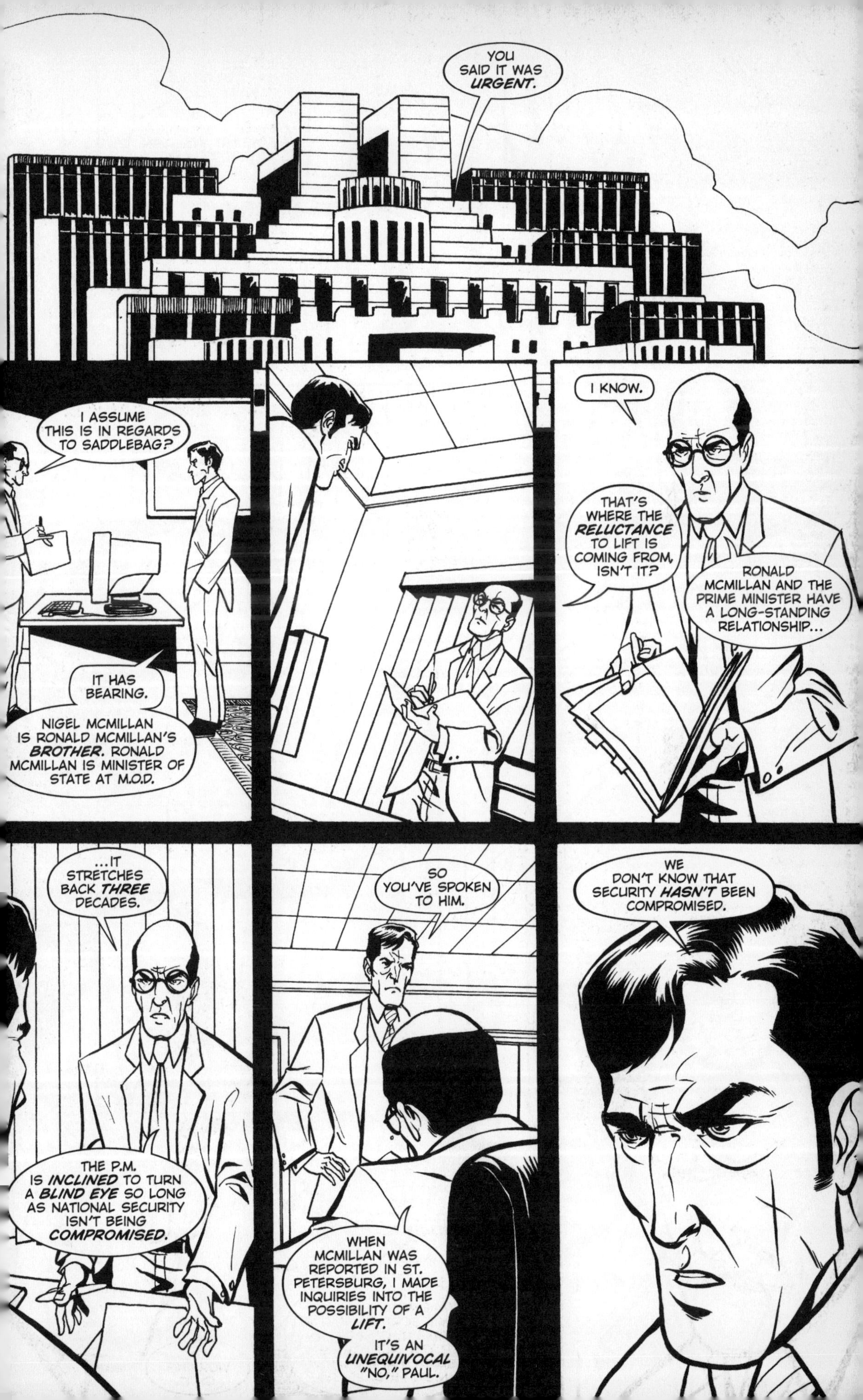

YOU SAID IT WAS *URGENT*.
I ASSUME THIS IS IN REGARDS TO SADDLEBAG?
IT HAS BEARING.
NIGEL MCMILLAN IS RONALD MCMILLAN'S *BROTHER*. RONALD MCMILLAN IS MINISTER OF STATE AT M.O.D.
I KNOW.
THAT'S WHERE THE *RELUCTANCE* TO LIFT IS COMING FROM, ISN'T IT?
RONALD MCMILLAN AND THE PRIME MINISTER HAVE A LONG-STANDING RELATIONSHIP...
...IT STRETCHES BACK *THREE* DECADES.
THE P.M. IS *INCLINED* TO TURN A *BLIND EYE* SO LONG AS NATIONAL SECURITY ISN'T BEING *COMPROMISED*.
SO YOU'VE SPOKEN TO HIM.
WHEN MCMILLAN WAS REPORTED IN ST. PETERSBURG, I MADE INQUIRIES INTO THE POSSIBILITY OF A *LIFT*.
IT'S AN *UNEQUIVOCAL* "NO," PAUL.
WE DON'T KNOW THAT SECURITY *HASN'T* BEEN COMPROMISED.

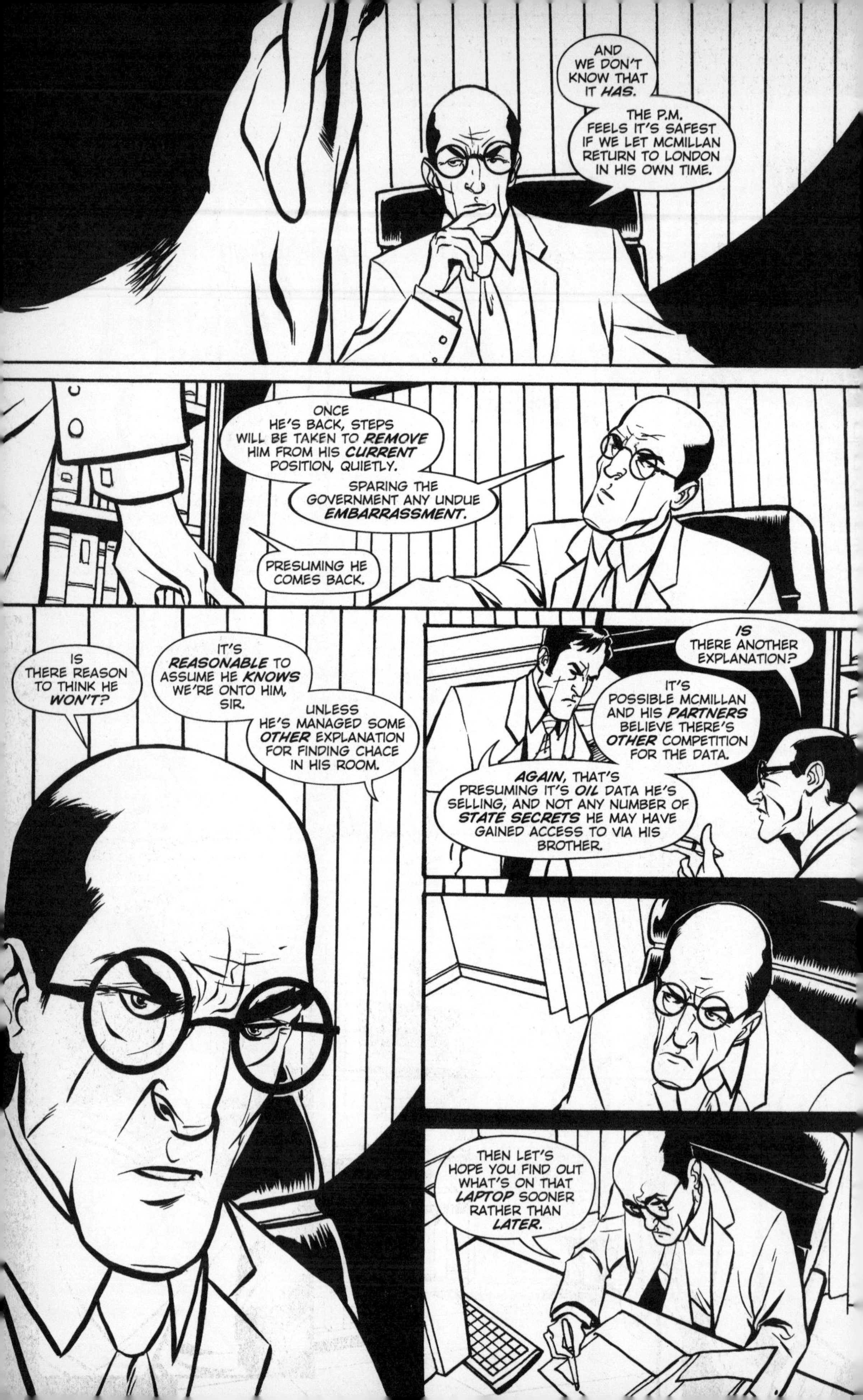
AND WE DON'T KNOW THAT IT HAS.
THE P.M. FEELS IT'S SAFEST IF WE LET MCMILLAN RETURN TO LONDON IN HIS OWN TIME.
ONCE HE'S BACK, STEPS WILL BE TAKEN TO REMOVE HIM FROM HIS CURRENT POSITION, QUIETLY.
SPARING THE GOVERNMENT ANY UNDUE EMBARRASSMENT.
PRESUMING HE COMES BACK.
IS THERE REASON TO THINK HE WON'T?
IT'S REASONABLE TO ASSUME HE KNOWS WE'RE ONTO HIM, SIR.
UNLESS HE'S MANAGED SOME OTHER EXPLANATION FOR FINDING CHACE IN HIS ROOM.
IS THERE ANOTHER EXPLANATION?
IT'S POSSIBLE MCMILLAN AND HIS PARTNERS BELIEVE THERE'S OTHER COMPETITION FOR THE DATA.
AGAIN, THAT'S PRESUMING IT'S OIL DATA HE'S SELLING, AND NOT ANY NUMBER OF STATE SECRETS HE MAY HAVE GAINED ACCESS TO VIA HIS BROTHER.
THEN LET'S HOPE YOU FIND OUT WHAT'S ON THAT LAPTOP SOONER RATHER THAN LATER.

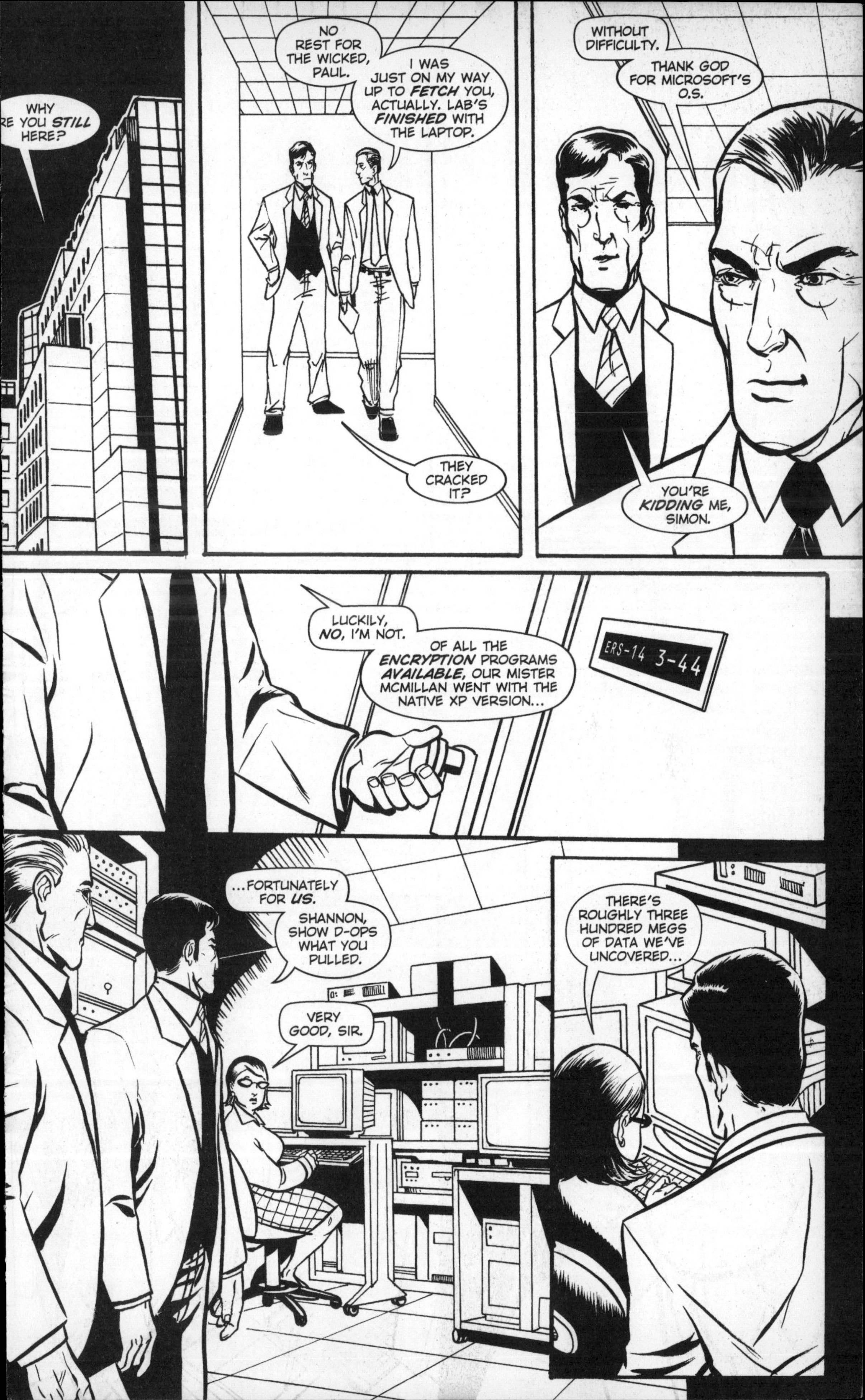
WHY
RE YOU STILL HERE?
NO REST FOR THE WICKED, PAUL.
I WAS JUST ON MY WAY UP TO FETCH YOU, ACTUALLY. LAB'S FINISHED WITH THE LAPTOP.
THEY CRACKED IT?
WITHOUT DIFFICULTY.
THANK GOD FOR MICROSOFT'S O.S.
YOU'RE KIDDING ME, SIMON.
LUCKILY, NO, I'M NOT.
OF ALL THE ENCRYPTION PROGRAMS AVAILABLE, OUR MISTER MCMILLAN WENT WITH THE NATIVE XP VERSION...
ERS-14 3-44
...FORTUNATELY FOR US.
SHANNON, SHOW D-OPS WHAT YOU PULLED.
VERY GOOD, SIR.
THERE'S ROUGHLY THREE HUNDRED MEGS OF DATA WE'VE UNCOVERED...

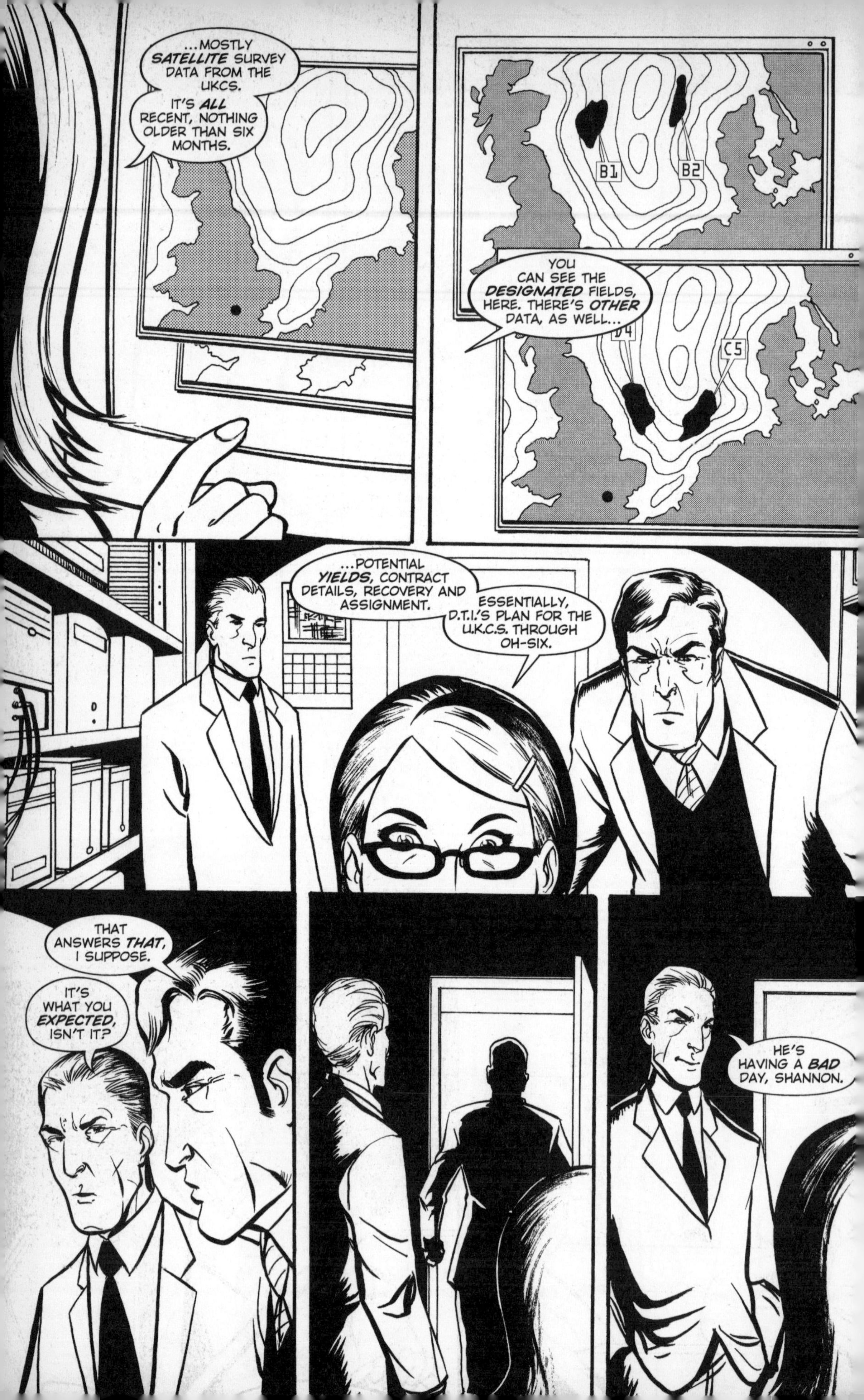
...MOSTLY SATELLITE SURVEY DATA FROM THE UKCS.
IT'S ALL RECENT, NOTHING OLDER THAN SIX MONTHS.
B1
B2
YOU CAN SEE THE DESIGNATED FIELDS, HERE. THERE'S OTHER DATA, AS WELL...
D4
C5
...POTENTIAL YIELDS, CONTRACT DETAILS, RECOVERY AND ASSIGNMENT.
ESSENTIALLY, D.T.I.'S PLAN FOR THE U.K.C.S. THROUGH OH-SIX.
THAT ANSWERS THAT, I SUPPOSE.
IT'S WHAT YOU EXPECTED, ISN'T IT?
HE'S HAVING A BAD DAY, SHANNON.

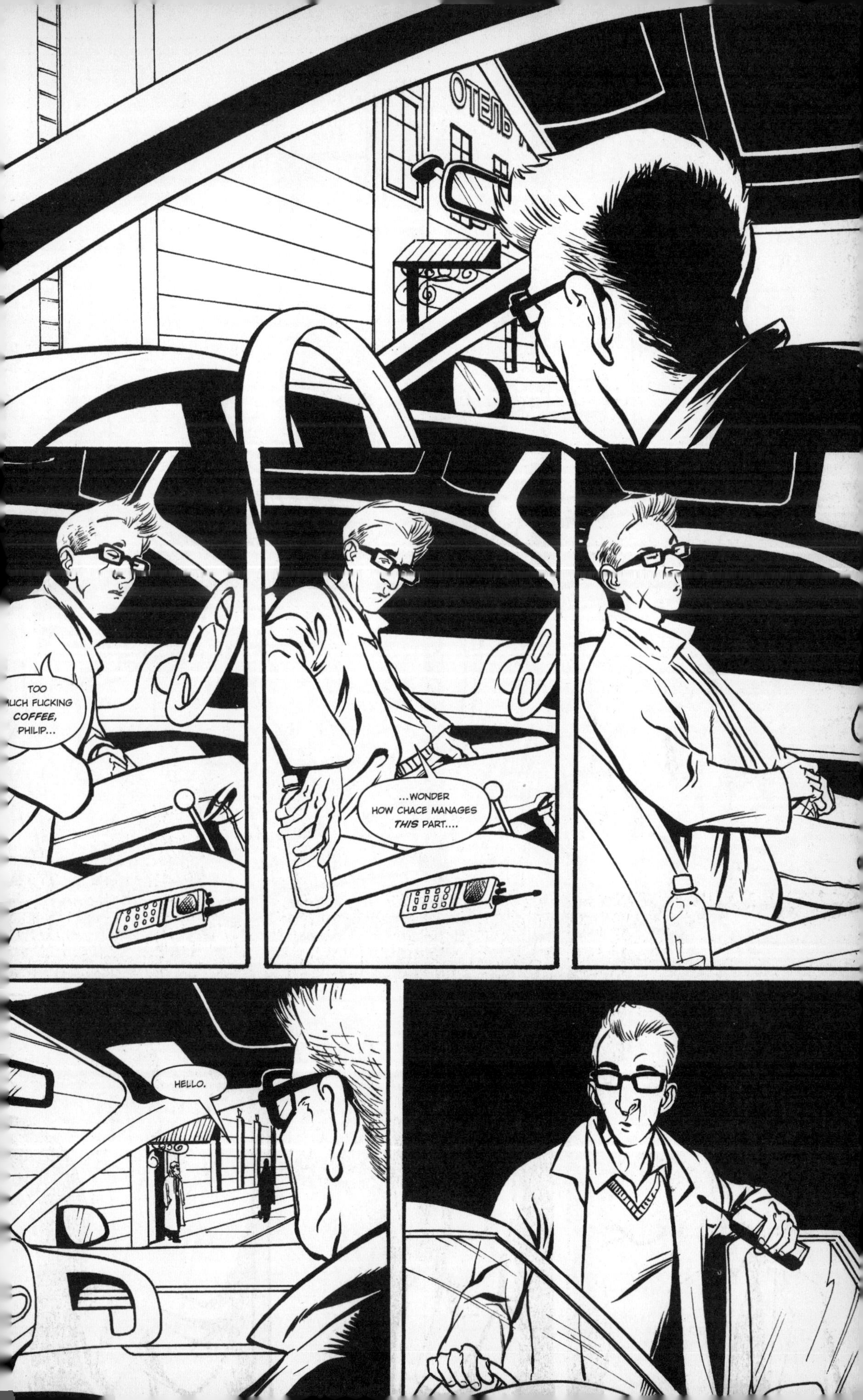
ОТЕЛЬ
TOO MUCH FUCKING *COFFEE*, PHILIP...
...WONDER HOW CHACE MANAGES *THIS* PART....
HELLO.

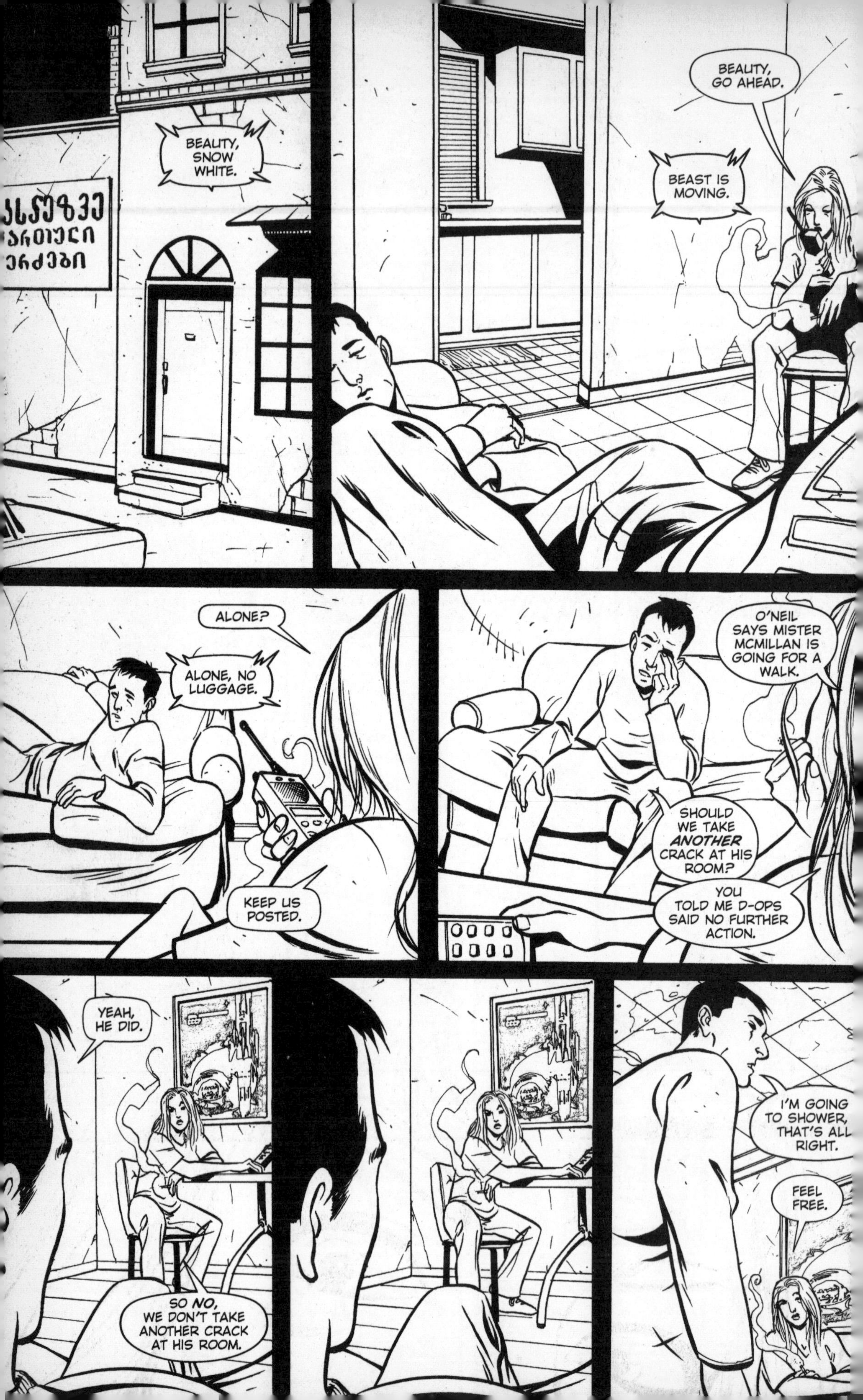

BEAUTY, SNOW WHITE.
BEAUTY, GO AHEAD.
BEAST IS MOVING.
ALONE?
ALONE, NO LUGGAGE.
KEEP US POSTED.
O'NEIL SAYS MISTER MCMILLAN IS GOING FOR A WALK.
SHOULD WE TAKE *ANOTHER* CRACK AT HIS ROOM?
YOU TOLD ME D-OPS SAID NO FURTHER ACTION.
YEAH, HE DID.
SO *NO*, WE DON'T TAKE ANOTHER CRACK AT HIS ROOM.
I'M GOING TO SHOWER, THAT'S ALL RIGHT.
FEEL FREE.

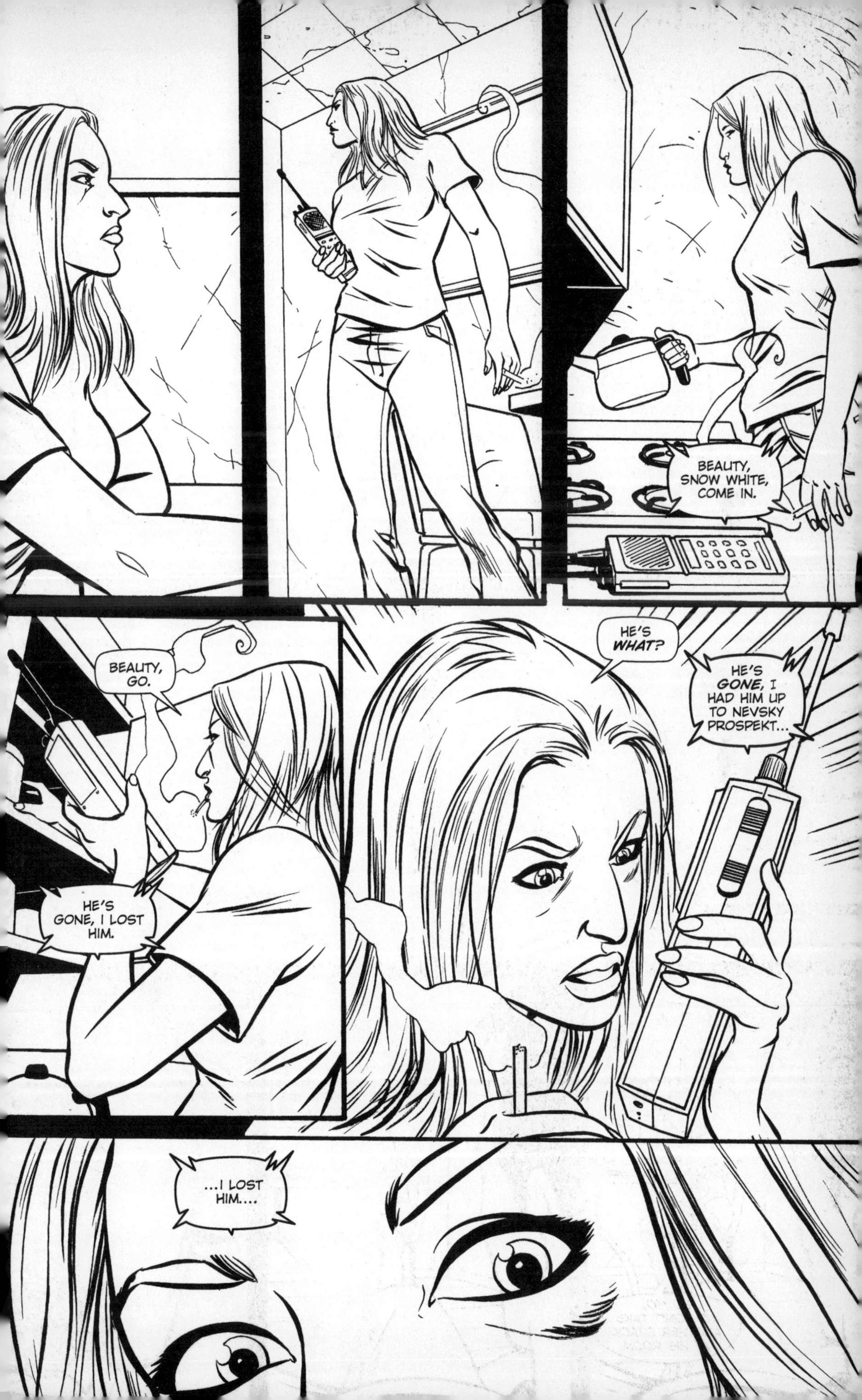
BEAUTY, SNOW WHITE, COME IN.
BEAUTY, GO.
HE'S GONE, I LOST HIM.
HE'S *WHAT?*
HE'S *GONE,* I HAD HIM UP TO NEVSKY PROSPEKT...
...I LOST HIM....

# CHAPTER 3

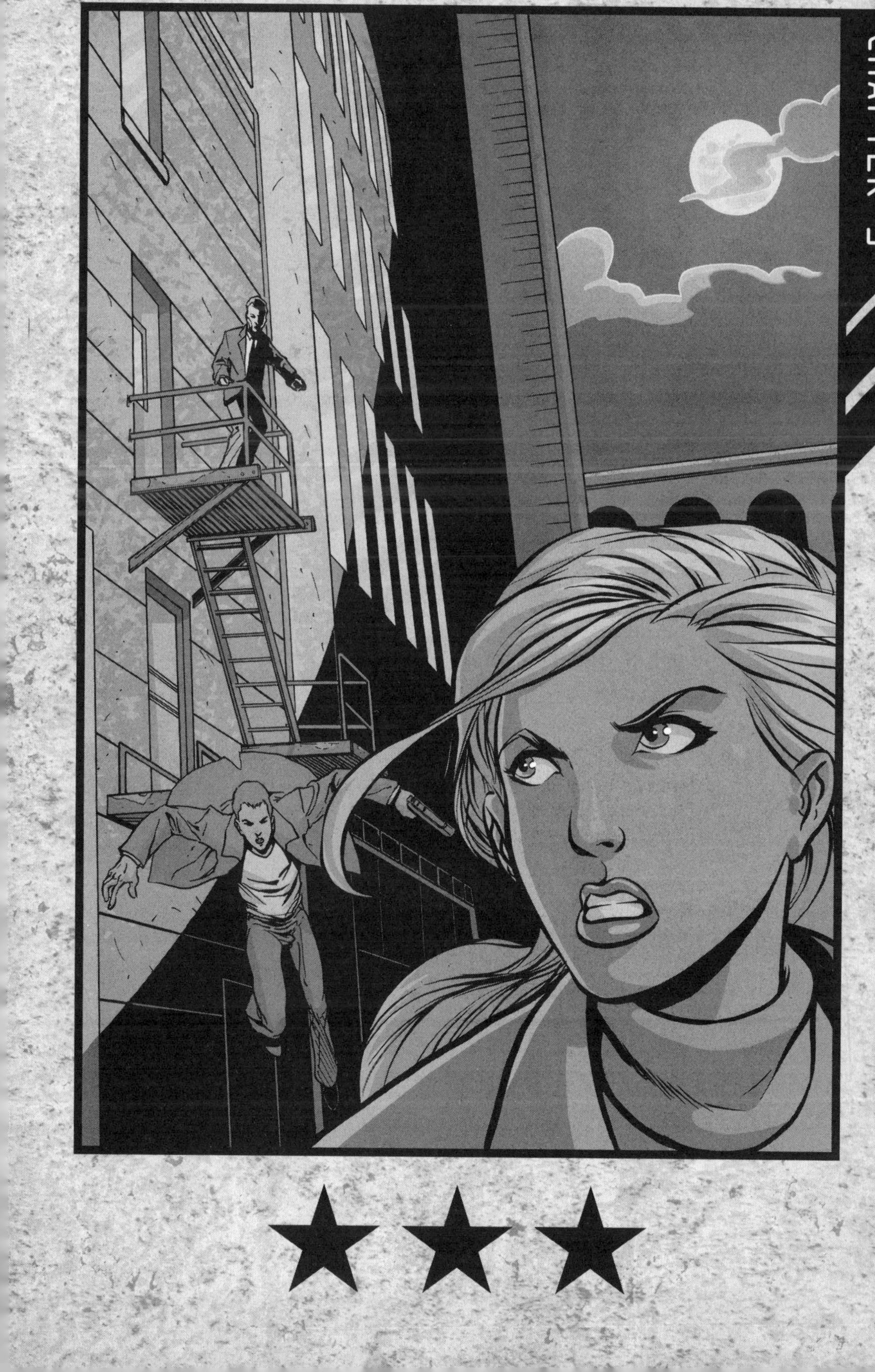

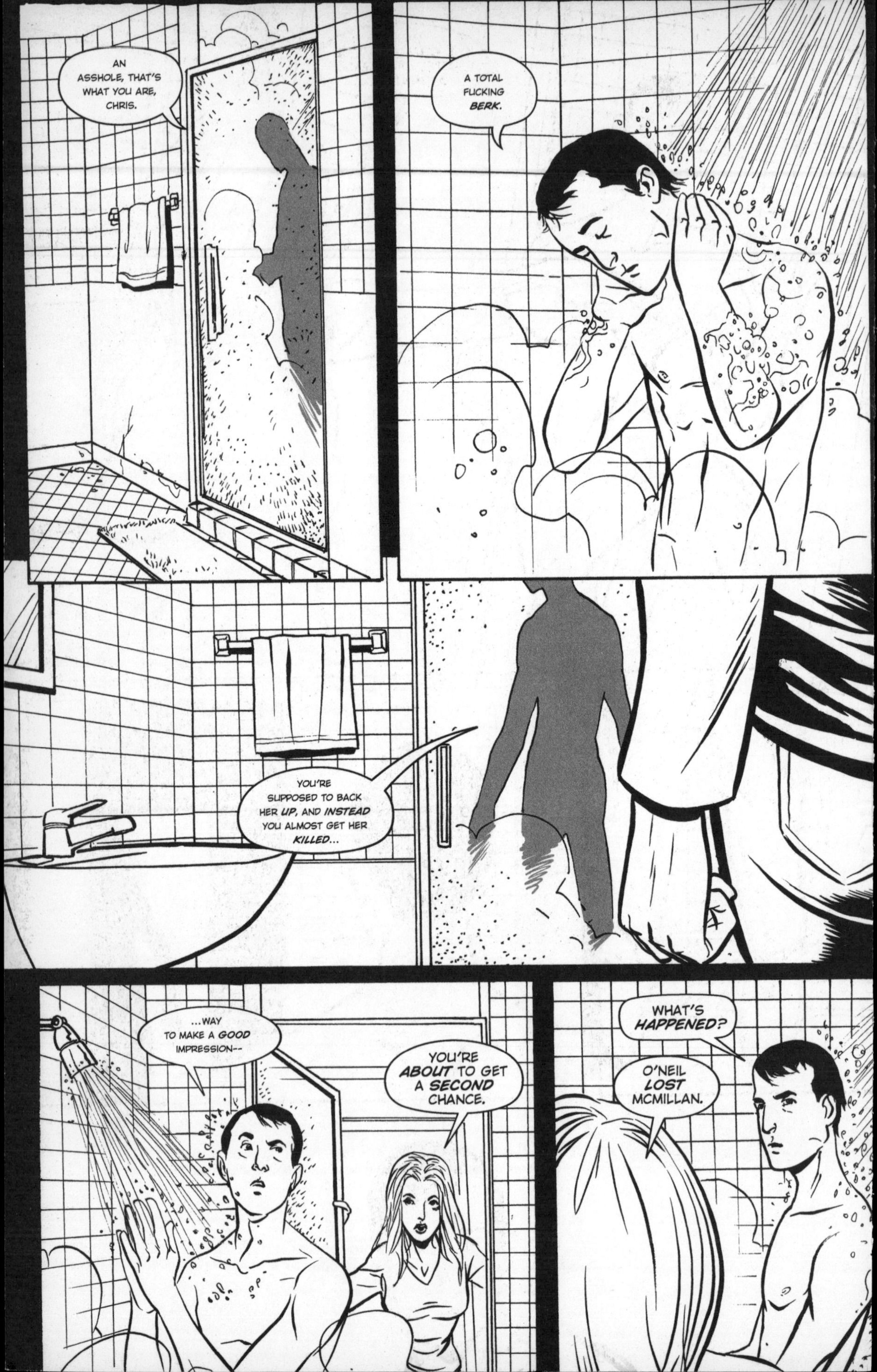
AN ASSHOLE, THAT'S WHAT YOU ARE, CHRIS.
A TOTAL FUCKING BERK.
YOU'RE SUPPOSED TO BACK HER UP, AND INSTEAD YOU ALMOST GET HER KILLED...
...WAY TO MAKE A GOOD IMPRESSION--
YOU'RE ABOUT TO GET A SECOND CHANCE.
WHAT'S HAPPENED?
O'NEIL LOST MCMILLAN.

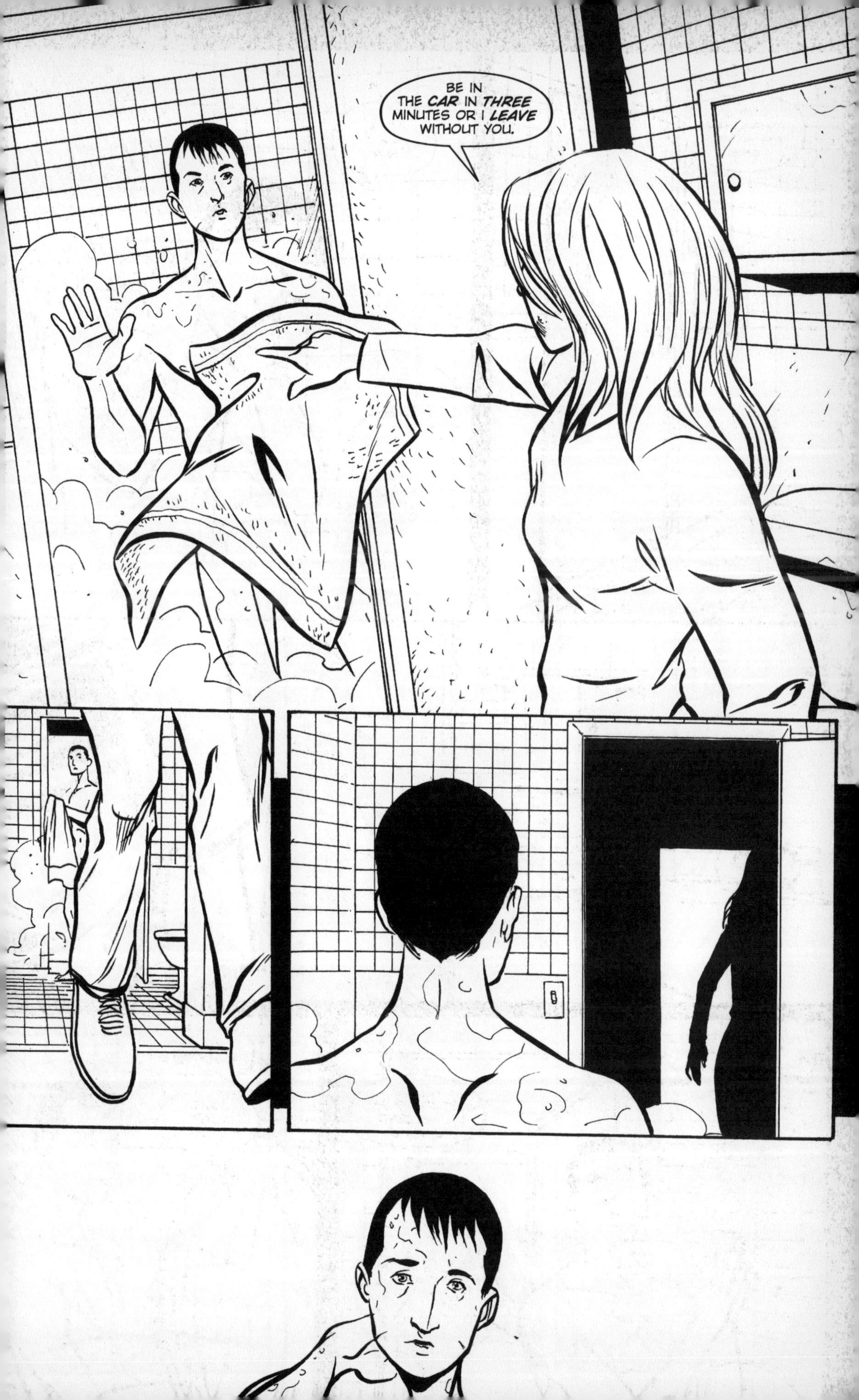
BE IN THE CAR IN THREE MINUTES OR I LEAVE WITHOUT YOU.

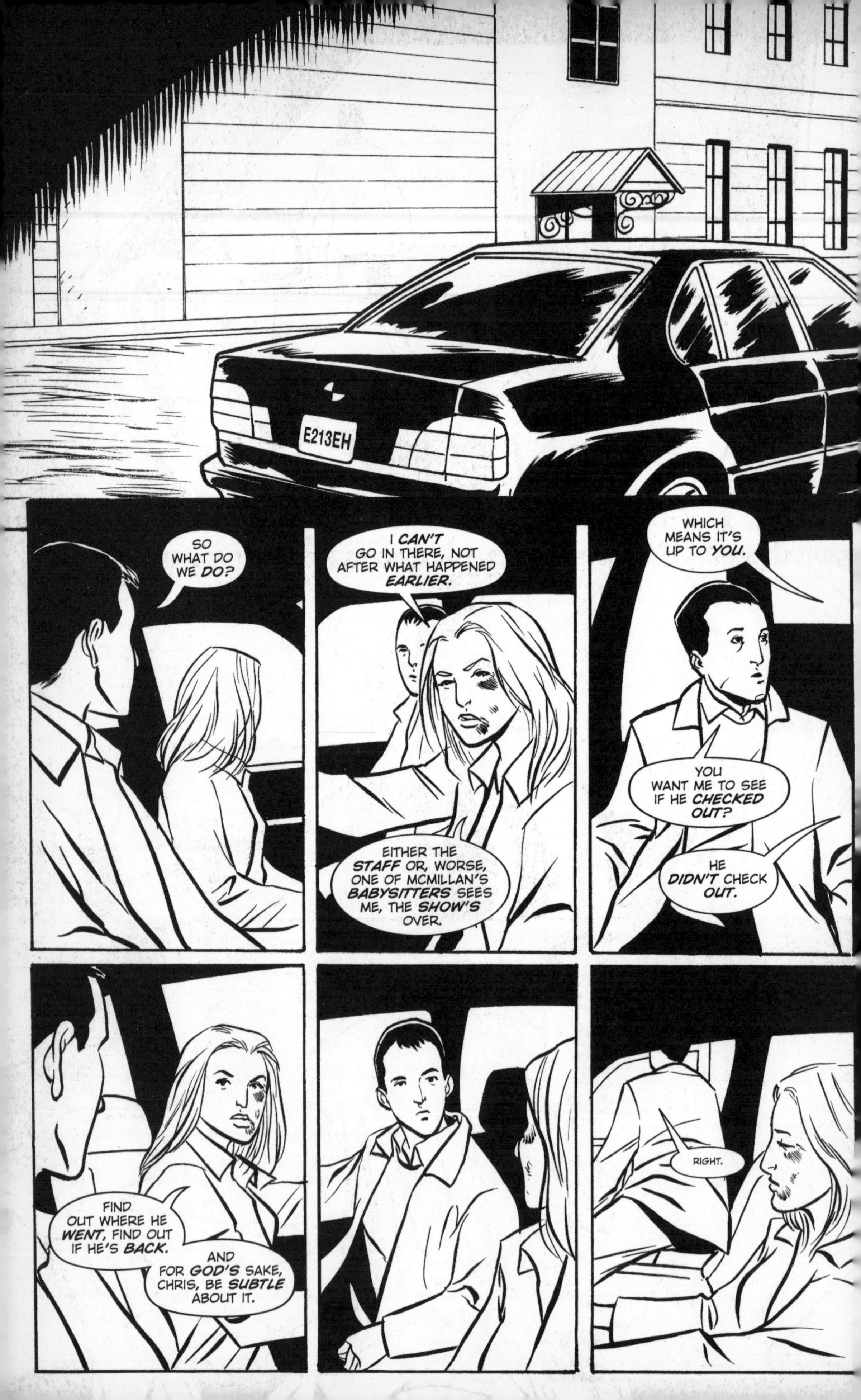
E213EH
SO WHAT DO WE DO?
I CAN'T GO IN THERE, NOT AFTER WHAT HAPPENED EARLIER.
EITHER THE STAFF OR, WORSE, ONE OF MCMILLAN'S BABYSITTERS SEES ME, THE SHOW'S OVER.
WHICH MEANS IT'S UP TO YOU.
YOU WANT ME TO SEE IF HE CHECKED OUT?
HE DIDN'T CHECK OUT.
FIND OUT WHERE HE WENT, FIND OUT IF HE'S BACK.
AND FOR GOD'S SAKE, CHRIS, BE SUBTLE ABOUT IT.
RIGHT.

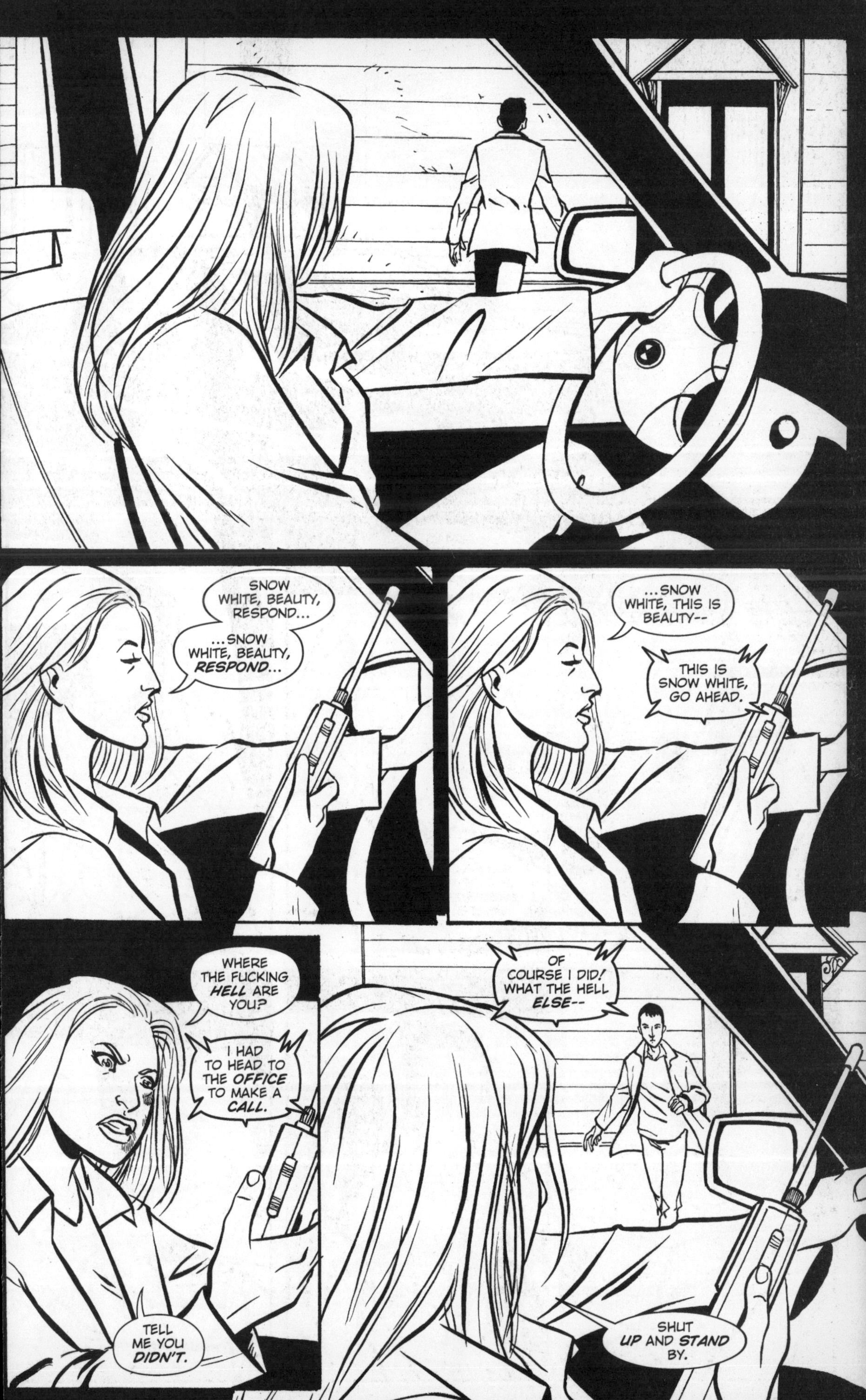
SNOW WHITE, BEAUTY, RESPOND...
...SNOW WHITE, BEAUTY, *RESPOND*...
...SNOW WHITE, THIS IS BEAUTY--
THIS IS SNOW WHITE, GO AHEAD.
WHERE THE FUCKING *HELL* ARE YOU?
I HAD TO HEAD TO THE *OFFICE* TO MAKE A *CALL*.
TELL ME YOU *DIDN'T*.
OF COURSE I DID! WHAT THE HELL *ELSE*--
SHUT *UP* AND *STAND* BY.

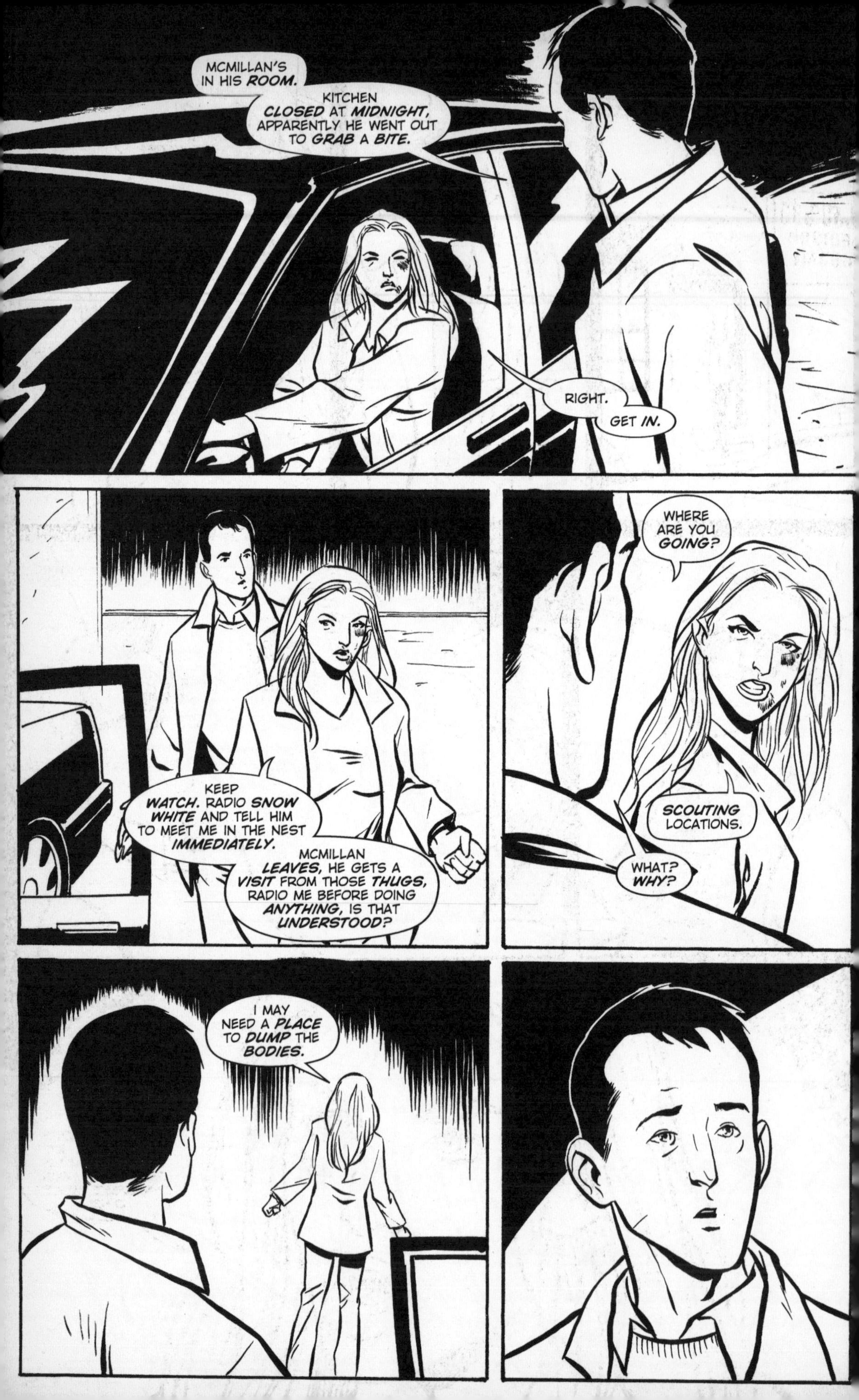
MCMILLAN'S IN HIS ROOM.
KITCHEN CLOSED AT MIDNIGHT, APPARENTLY HE WENT OUT TO GRAB A BITE.
RIGHT.
GET IN.
KEEP WATCH. RADIO SNOW WHITE AND TELL HIM TO MEET ME IN THE NEST IMMEDIATELY.
MCMILLAN LEAVES, HE GETS A VISIT FROM THOSE THUGS, RADIO ME BEFORE DOING ANYTHING, IS THAT UNDERSTOOD?
WHERE ARE YOU GOING?
SCOUTING LOCATIONS.
WHAT? WHY?
I MAY NEED A PLACE TO DUMP THE BODIES.

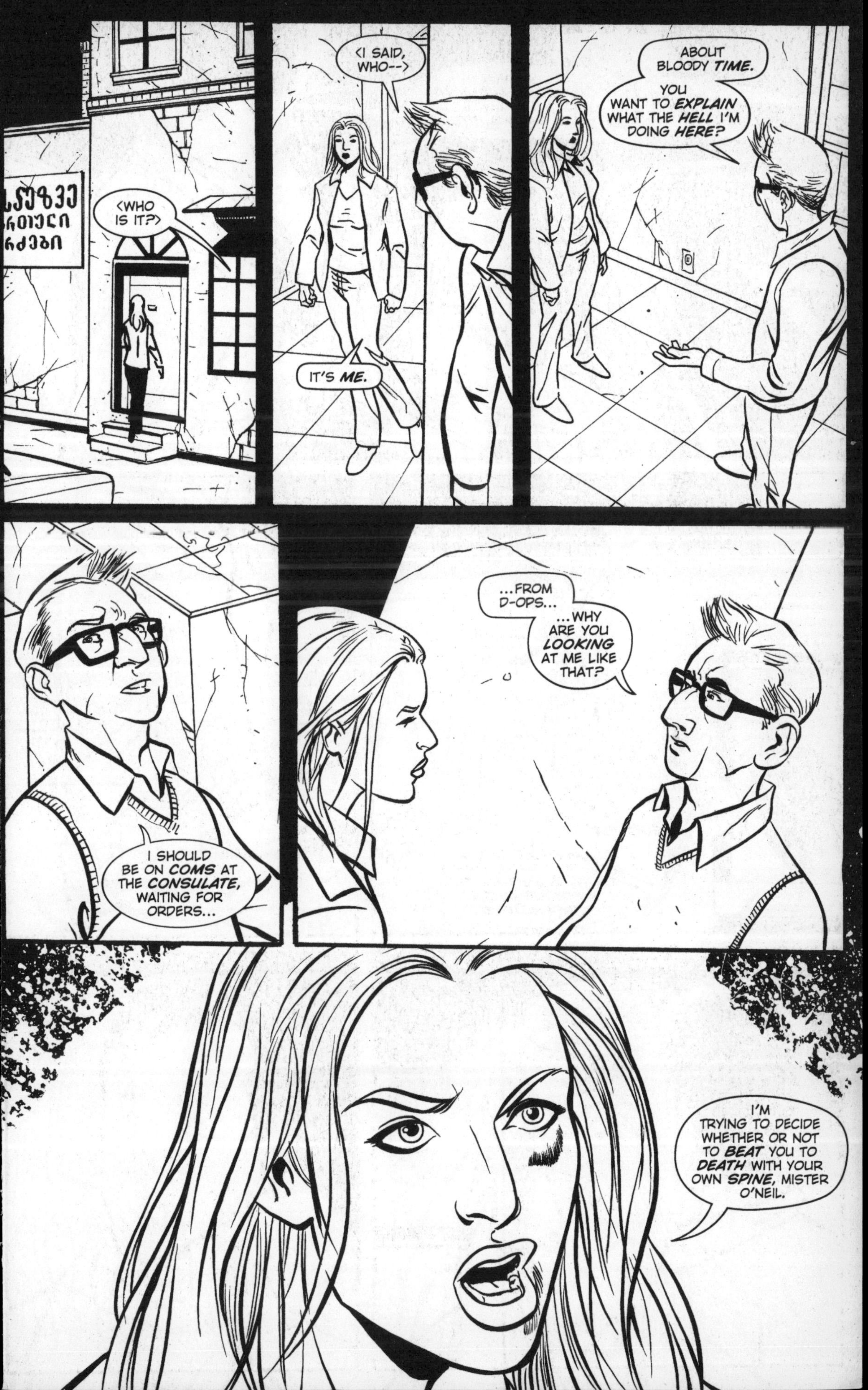
<WHO IS IT?>
<I SAID, WHO-->
IT'S *ME.*
ABOUT BLOODY *TIME.*
YOU WANT TO *EXPLAIN* WHAT THE *HELL* I'M DOING *HERE?*
I SHOULD BE ON *COMS* AT THE *CONSULATE,* WAITING FOR ORDERS...
...FROM D-OPS...
...WHY ARE YOU *LOOKING* AT ME LIKE THAT?
I'M TRYING TO DECIDE WHETHER OR NOT TO *BEAT* YOU TO *DEATH* WITH YOUR OWN *SPINE,* MISTER O'NEIL.

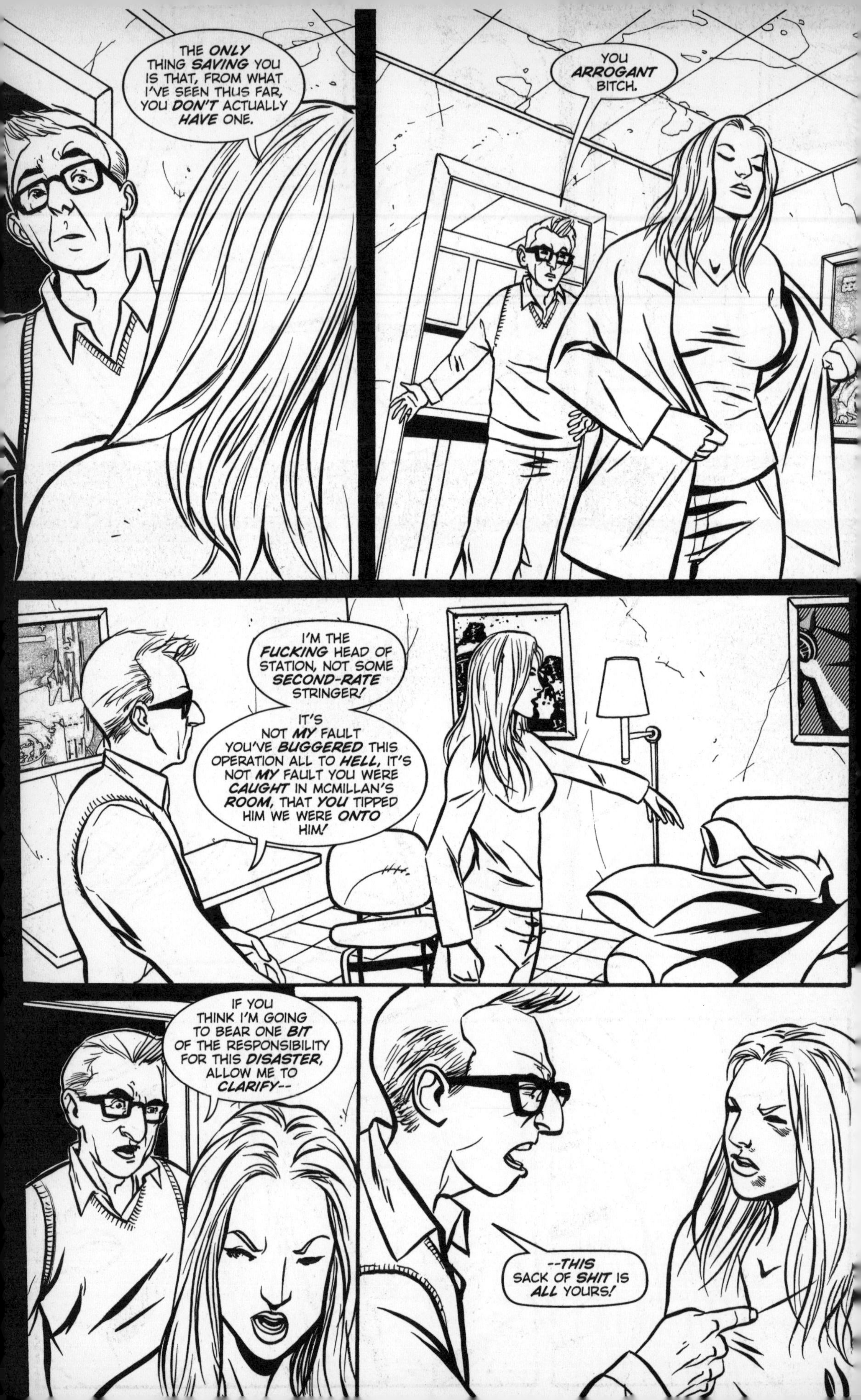
THE ONLY THING SAVING YOU IS THAT, FROM WHAT I'VE SEEN THUS FAR, YOU DON'T ACTUALLY HAVE ONE.
YOU ARROGANT BITCH.
I'M THE FUCKING HEAD OF STATION, NOT SOME SECOND-RATE STRINGER!
IT'S NOT MY FAULT YOU'VE BUGGERED THIS OPERATION ALL TO HELL, IT'S NOT MY FAULT YOU WERE CAUGHT IN MCMILLAN'S ROOM, THAT YOU TIPPED HIM WE WERE ONTO HIM!
IF YOU THINK I'M GOING TO BEAR ONE BIT OF THE RESPONSIBILITY FOR THIS DISASTER, ALLOW ME TO CLARIFY--
--THIS SACK OF SHIT IS ALL YOURS!

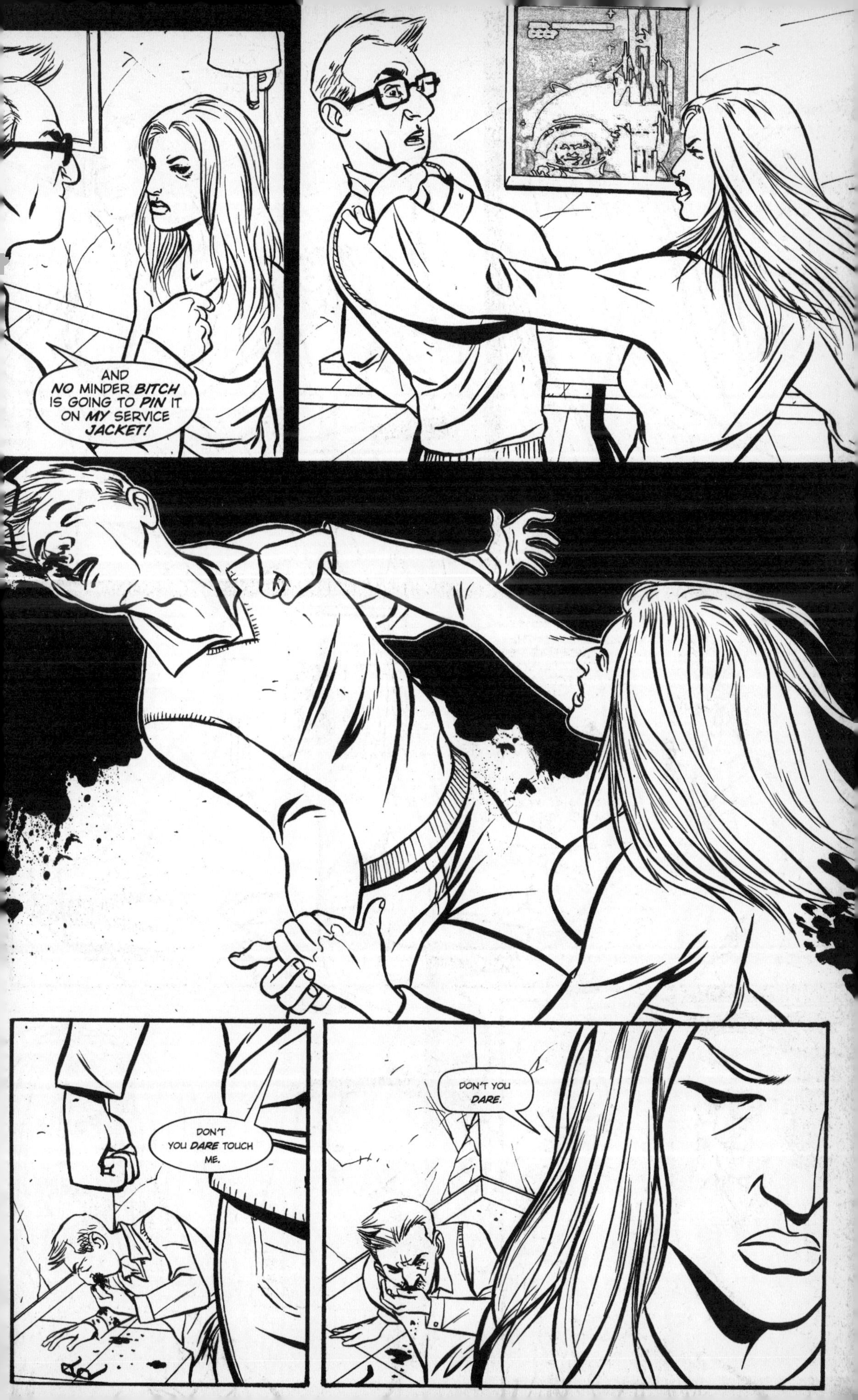
AND NO MINDER BITCH IS GOING TO PIN IT ON MY SERVICE JACKET!
DON'T YOU DARE TOUCH ME.
DON'T YOU DARE.

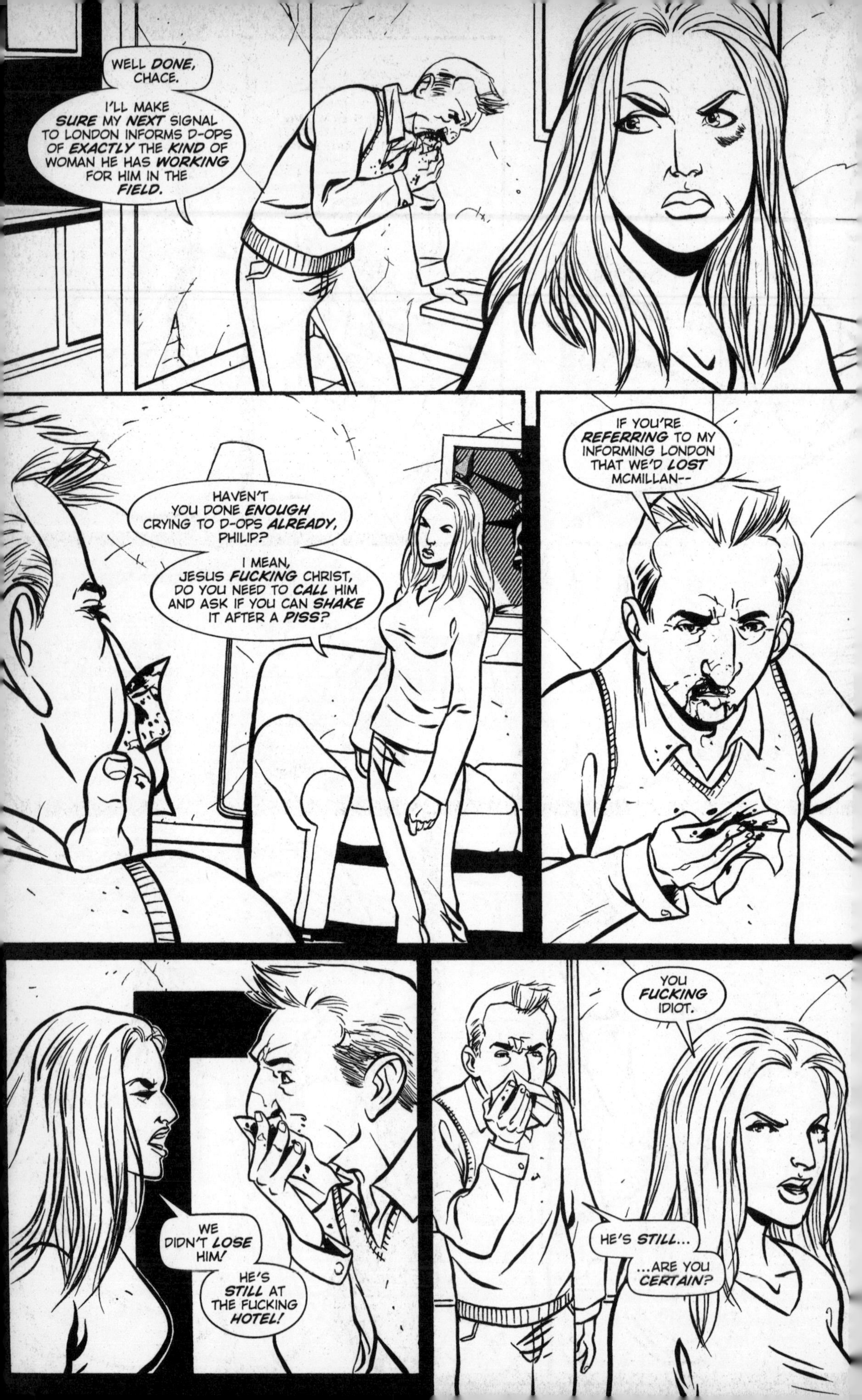
WELL *DONE,* CHACE.
I'LL MAKE *SURE* MY *NEXT* SIGNAL TO LONDON INFORMS D-OPS OF *EXACTLY* THE *KIND* OF WOMAN HE HAS *WORKING* FOR HIM IN THE *FIELD.*
HAVEN'T YOU DONE *ENOUGH* CRYING TO D-OPS *ALREADY,* PHILIP?
I MEAN, JESUS *FUCKING* CHRIST, DO YOU NEED TO *CALL* HIM AND ASK IF YOU CAN *SHAKE* IT AFTER A *PISS?*
IF YOU'RE *REFERRING* TO MY INFORMING LONDON THAT WE'D *LOST* MCMILLAN--
WE DIDN'T *LOSE* HIM!
HE'S *STILL* AT THE FUCKING *HOTEL!*
YOU *FUCKING* IDIOT.
HE'S *STILL*...
...ARE YOU *CERTAIN?*

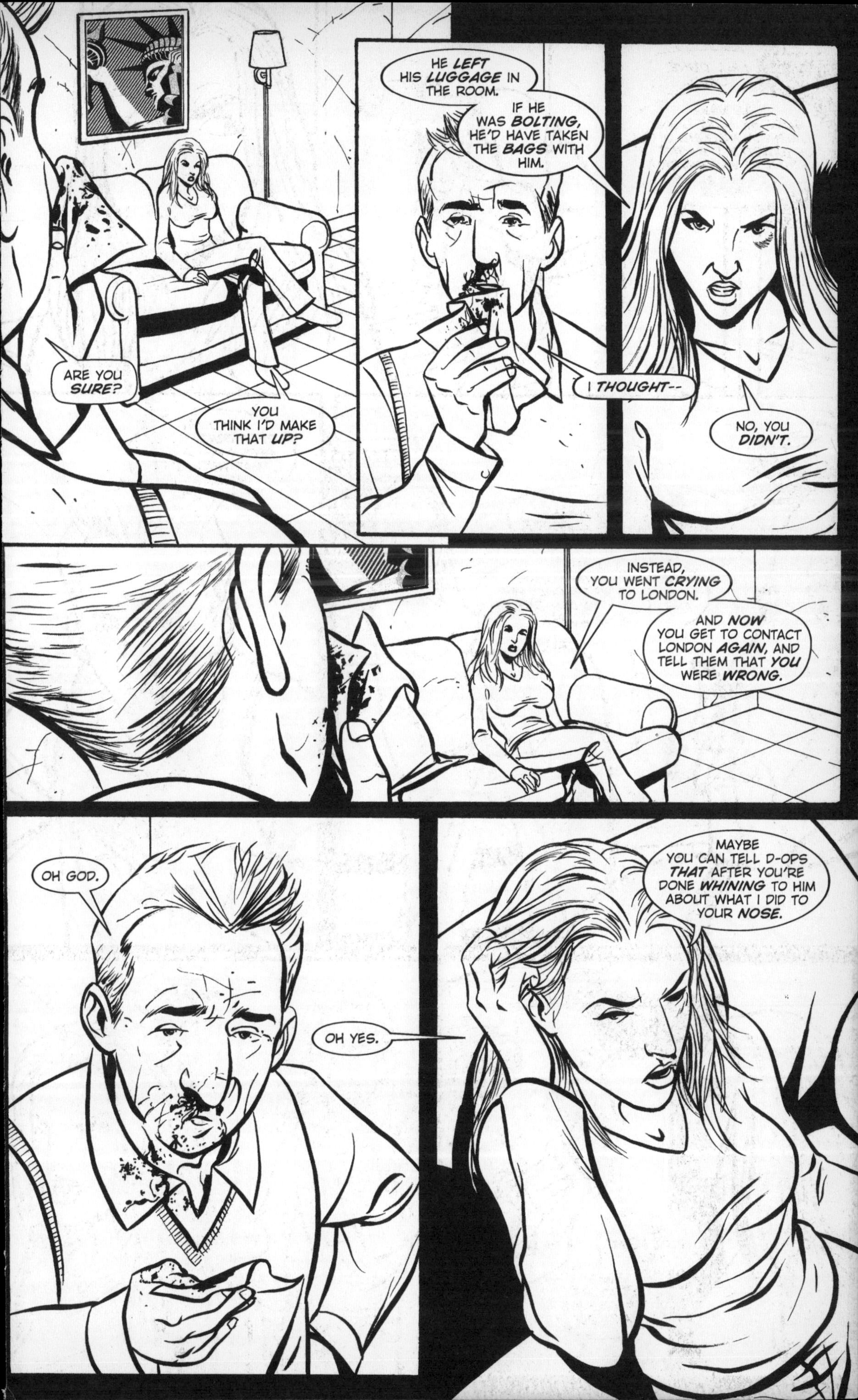
ARE YOU SURE?
YOU THINK I'D MAKE THAT UP?
HE LEFT HIS LUGGAGE IN THE ROOM.
IF HE WAS BOLTING, HE'D HAVE TAKEN THE BAGS WITH HIM.
I THOUGHT--
NO, YOU DIDN'T.
INSTEAD, YOU WENT CRYING TO LONDON.
AND NOW YOU GET TO CONTACT LONDON AGAIN, AND TELL THEM THAT YOU WERE WRONG.
OH GOD.
OH YES.
MAYBE YOU CAN TELL D-OPS THAT AFTER YOU'RE DONE WHINING TO HIM ABOUT WHAT I DID TO YOUR NOSE.

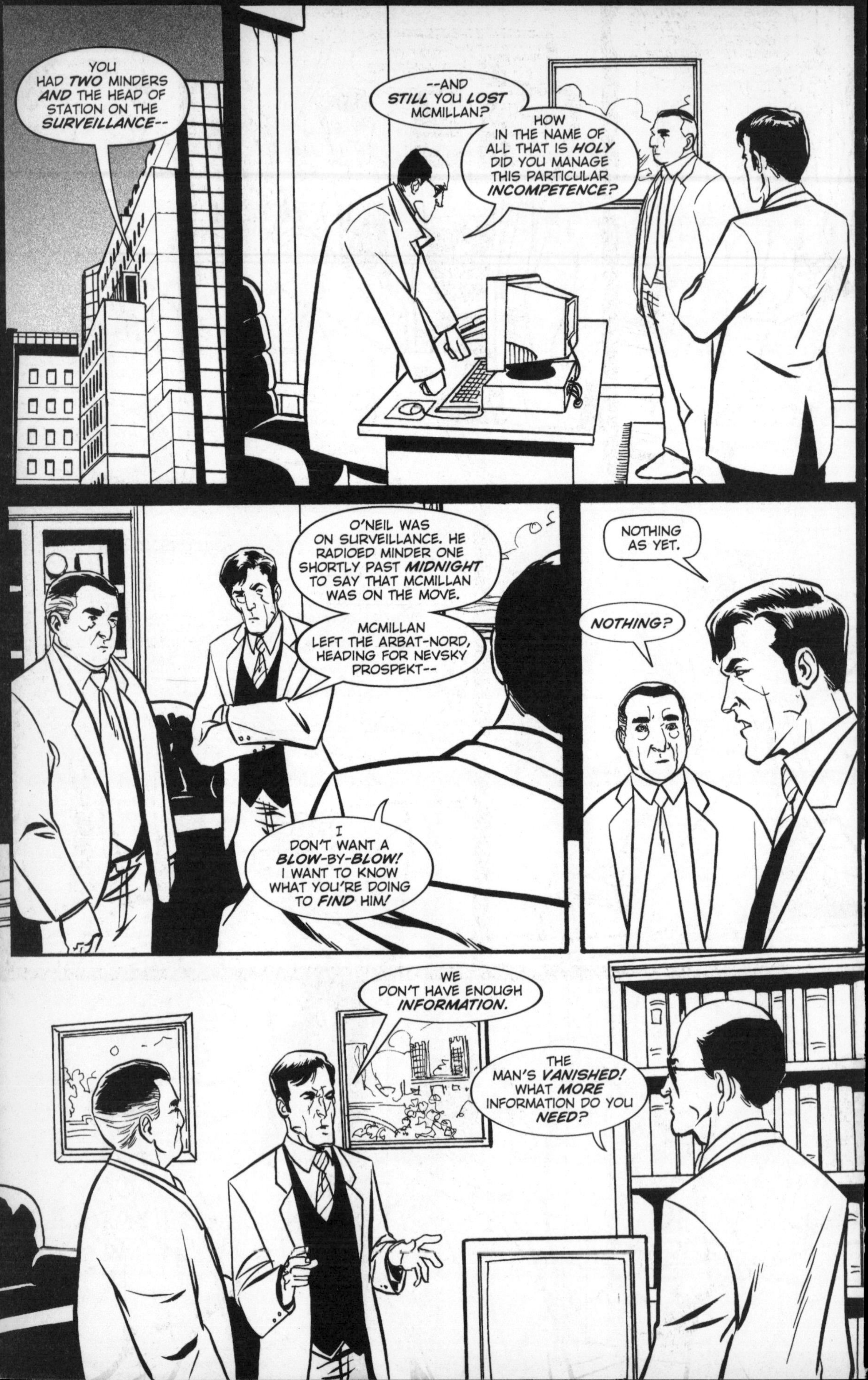
YOU HAD TWO MINDERS AND THE HEAD OF STATION ON THE SURVEILLANCE--
--AND STILL YOU LOST MCMILLAN?
HOW IN THE NAME OF ALL THAT IS HOLY DID YOU MANAGE THIS PARTICULAR INCOMPETENCE?
O'NEIL WAS ON SURVEILLANCE. HE RADIOED MINDER ONE SHORTLY PAST MIDNIGHT TO SAY THAT MCMILLAN WAS ON THE MOVE.
MCMILLAN LEFT THE ARBAT-NORD, HEADING FOR NEVSKY PROSPEKT--
I DON'T WANT A BLOW-BY-BLOW! I WANT TO KNOW WHAT YOU'RE DOING TO FIND HIM!
NOTHING AS YET.
NOTHING?
WE DON'T HAVE ENOUGH INFORMATION.
THE MAN'S VANISHED! WHAT MORE INFORMATION DO YOU NEED?

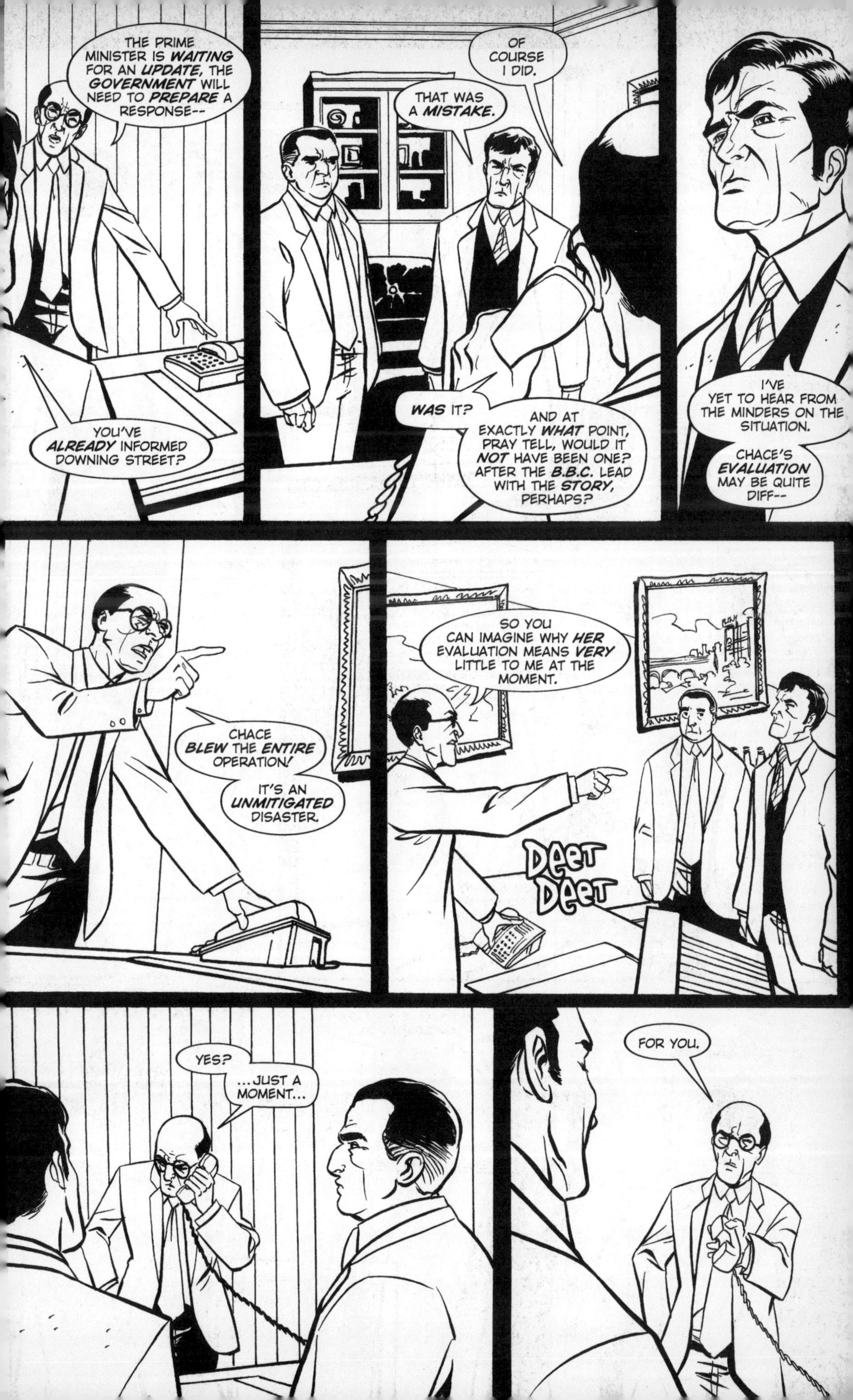
THE PRIME MINISTER IS WAITING FOR AN UPDATE, THE GOVERNMENT WILL NEED TO PREPARE A RESPONSE--
YOU'VE ALREADY INFORMED DOWNING STREET?
OF COURSE I DID.
THAT WAS A MISTAKE.
WAS IT?
AND AT EXACTLY WHAT POINT, PRAY TELL, WOULD IT NOT HAVE BEEN ONE? AFTER THE B.B.C. LEAD WITH THE STORY, PERHAPS?
I'VE YET TO HEAR FROM THE MINDERS ON THE SITUATION.
CHACE'S EVALUATION MAY BE QUITE DIFF--
CHACE BLEW THE ENTIRE OPERATION!
IT'S AN UNMITIGATED DISASTER.
SO YOU CAN IMAGINE WHY HER EVALUATION MEANS VERY LITTLE TO ME AT THE MOMENT.
DEET DEET
YES?
...JUST A MOMENT...
FOR YOU.

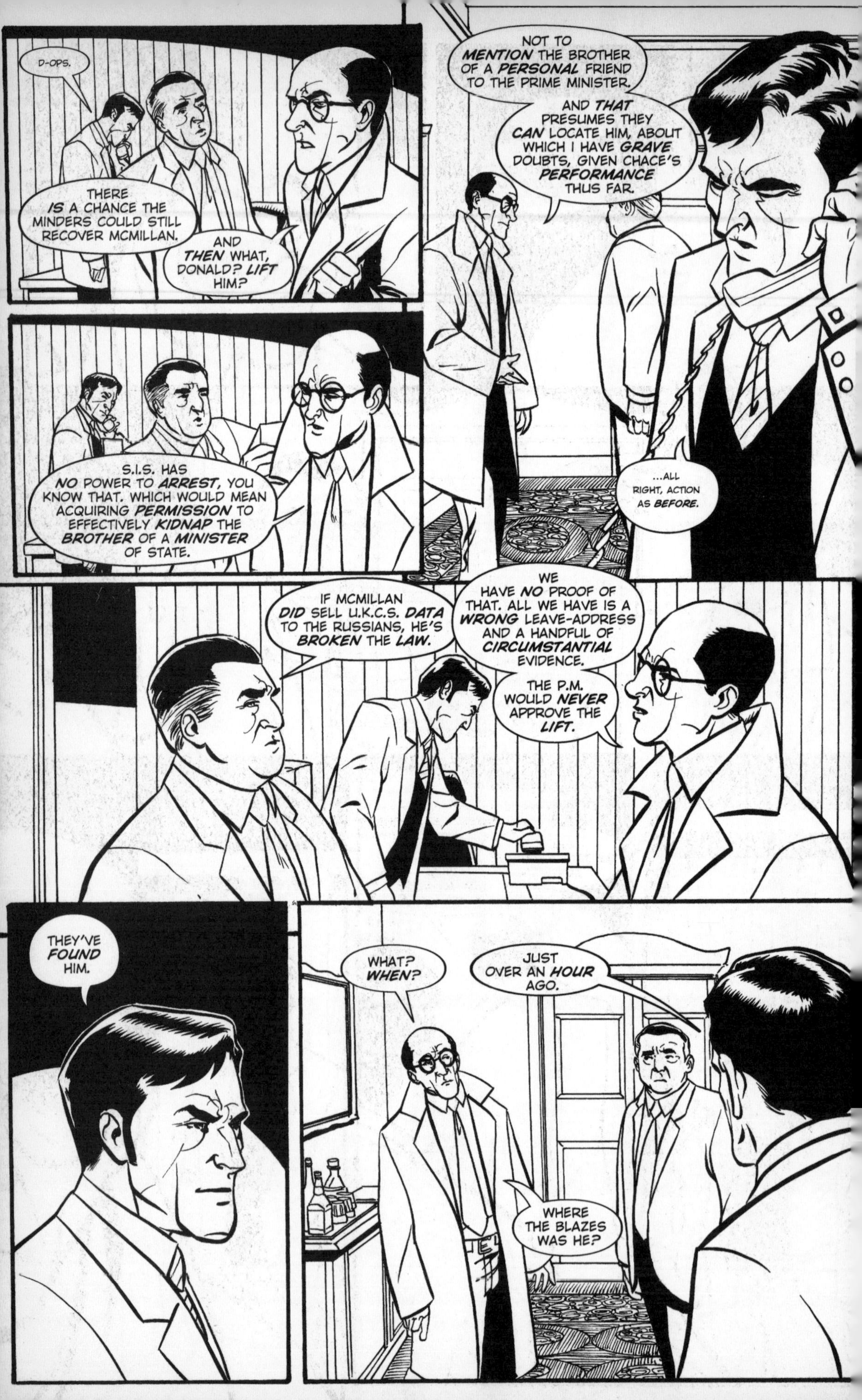
D-OPS.
THERE IS A CHANCE THE MINDERS COULD STILL RECOVER MCMILLAN.
AND THEN WHAT, DONALD? LIFT HIM?
NOT TO MENTION THE BROTHER OF A PERSONAL FRIEND TO THE PRIME MINISTER.
AND THAT PRESUMES THEY CAN LOCATE HIM, ABOUT WHICH I HAVE GRAVE DOUBTS, GIVEN CHACE'S PERFORMANCE THUS FAR.
S.I.S. HAS NO POWER TO ARREST, YOU KNOW THAT. WHICH WOULD MEAN ACQUIRING PERMISSION TO EFFECTIVELY KIDNAP THE BROTHER OF A MINISTER OF STATE.
...ALL RIGHT, ACTION AS BEFORE.
IF MCMILLAN DID SELL U.K.C.S. DATA TO THE RUSSIANS, HE'S BROKEN THE LAW.
WE HAVE NO PROOF OF THAT. ALL WE HAVE IS A WRONG LEAVE-ADDRESS AND A HANDFUL OF CIRCUMSTANTIAL EVIDENCE.
THE P.M. WOULD NEVER APPROVE THE LIFT.
THEY'VE FOUND HIM.
WHAT? WHEN?
JUST OVER AN HOUR AGO.
WHERE THE BLAZES WAS HE?

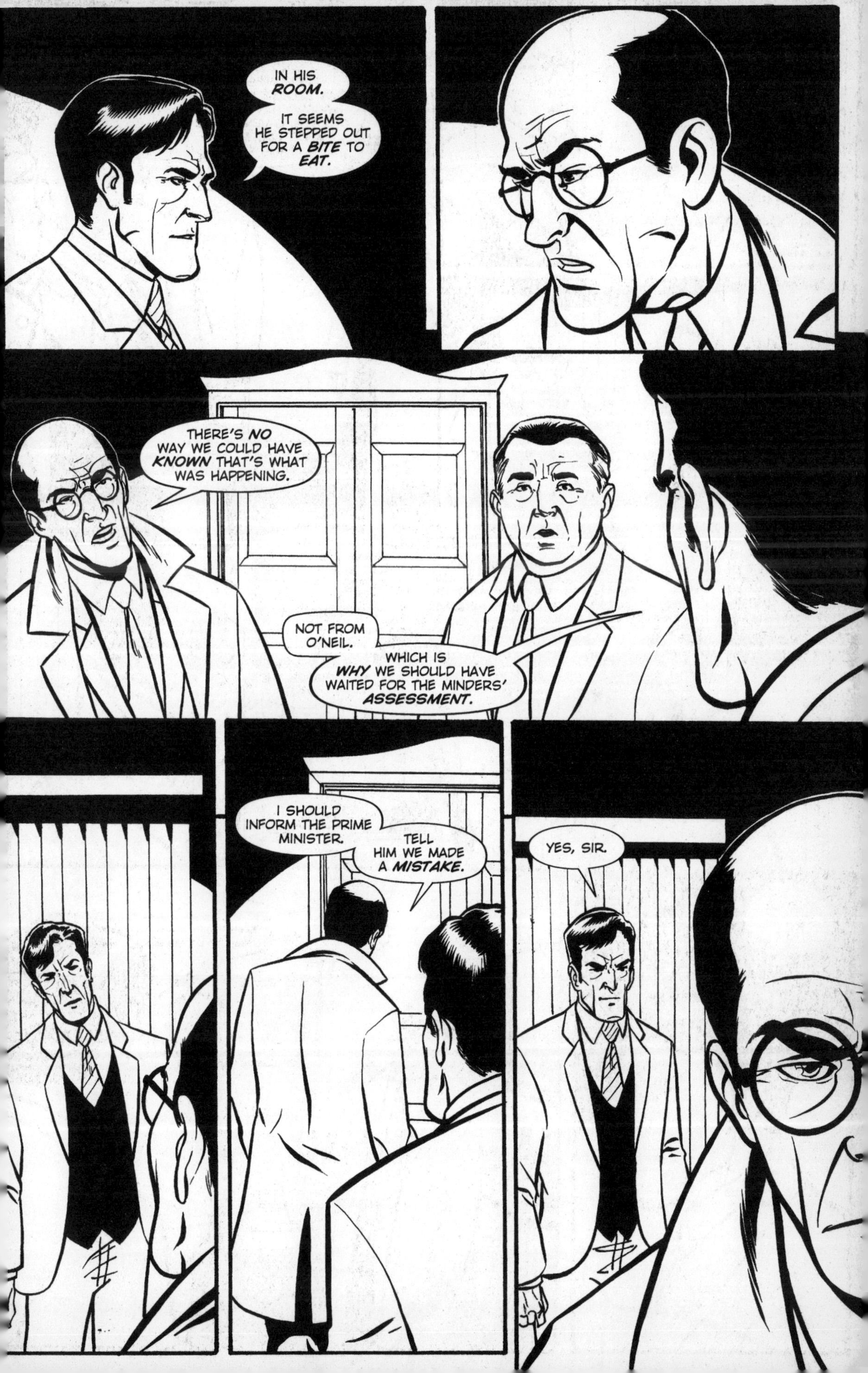
IN HIS ROOM.
IT SEEMS HE STEPPED OUT FOR A BITE TO EAT.
THERE'S NO WAY WE COULD HAVE KNOWN THAT'S WHAT WAS HAPPENING.
NOT FROM O'NEIL.
WHICH IS WHY WE SHOULD HAVE WAITED FOR THE MINDERS' ASSESSMENT.
I SHOULD INFORM THE PRIME MINISTER.
TELL HIM WE MADE A MISTAKE.
YES, SIR.

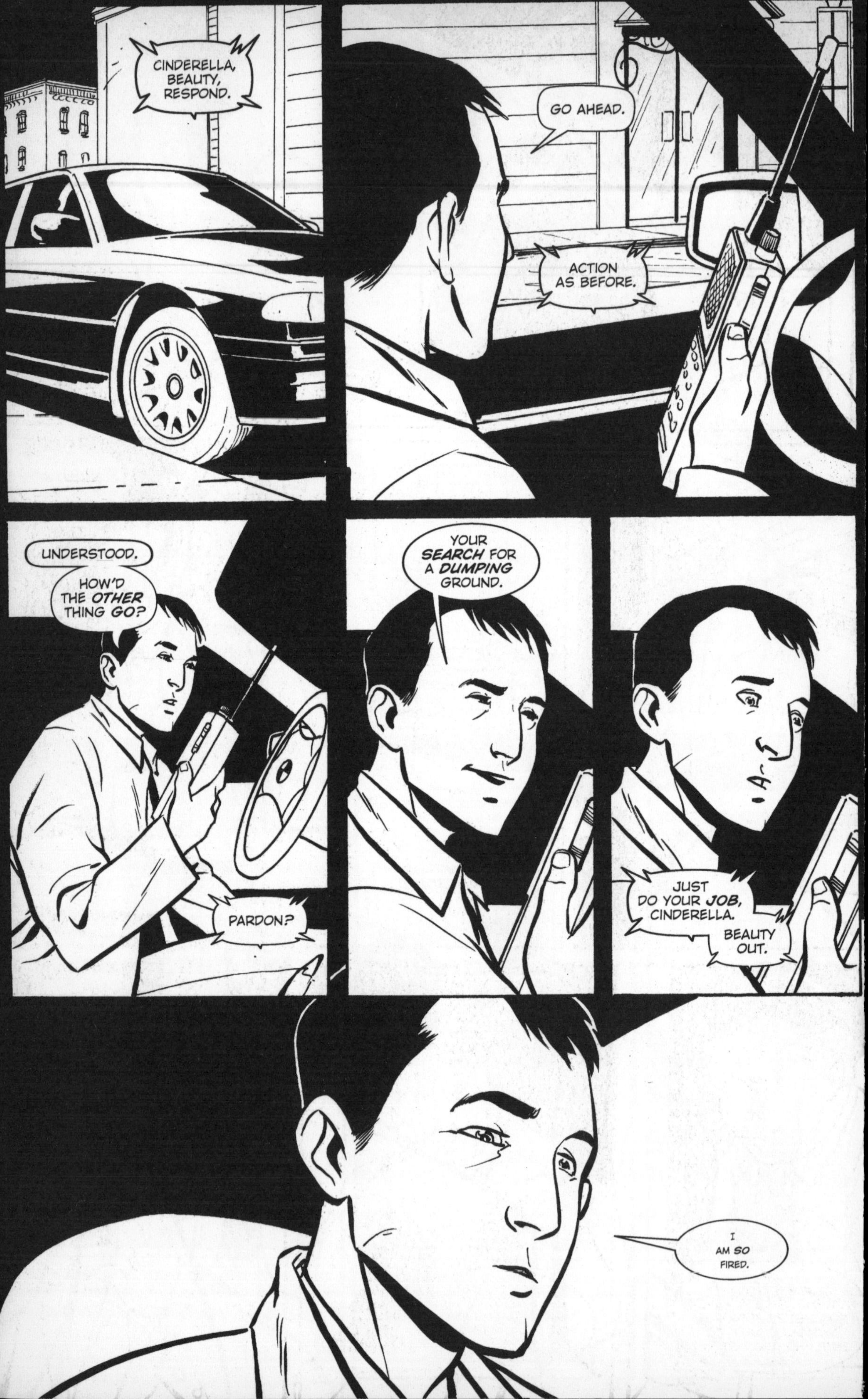
CINDERELLA, BEAUTY, RESPOND.
GO AHEAD.
ACTION AS BEFORE.
UNDERSTOOD.
HOW'D THE OTHER THING GO?
PARDON?
YOUR SEARCH FOR A DUMPING GROUND.
JUST DO YOUR JOB, CINDERELLA.
BEAUTY OUT.
I AM SO FIRED.

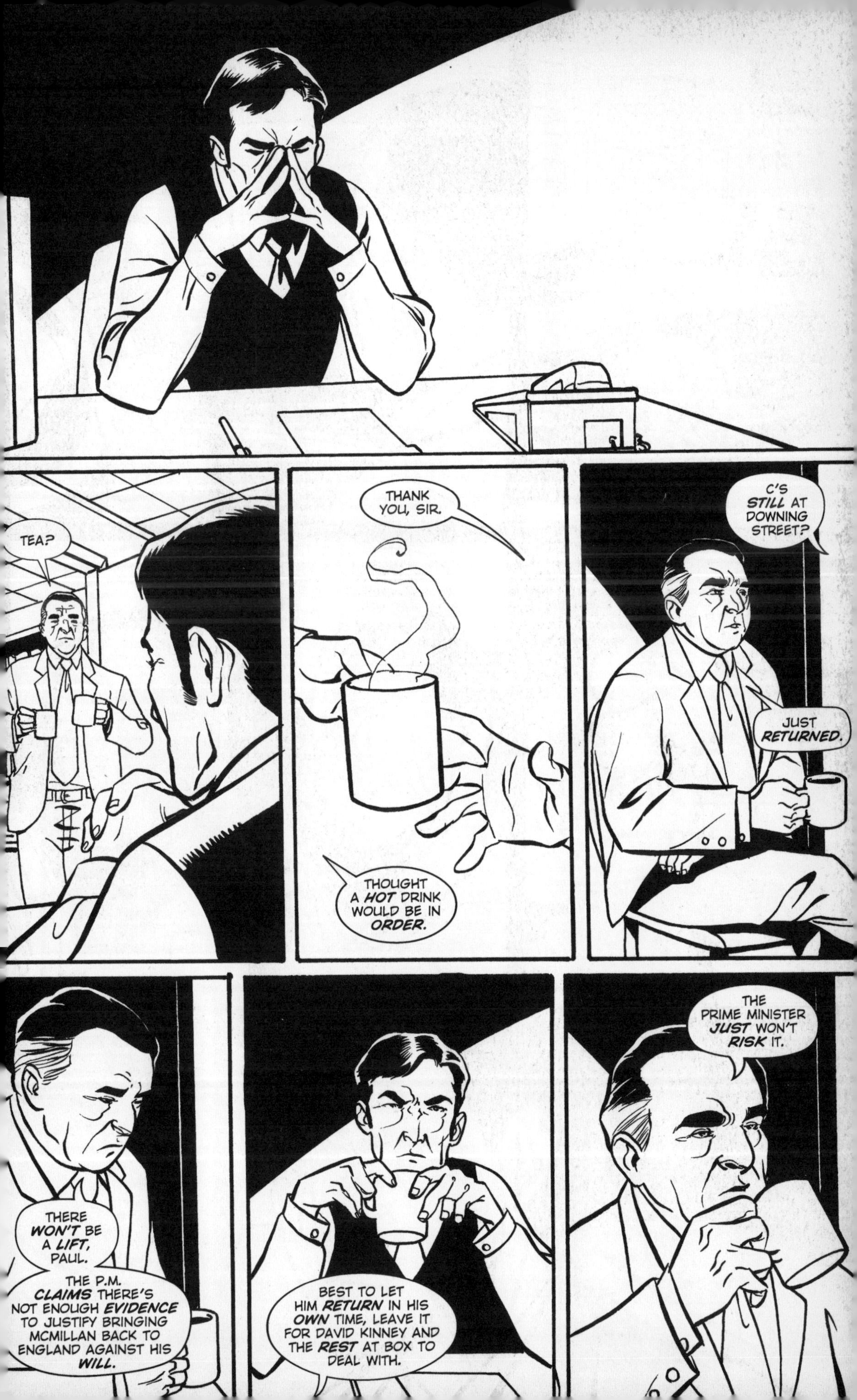
TEA?
THANK YOU, SIR.
THOUGHT A HOT DRINK WOULD BE IN ORDER.
C'S STILL AT DOWNING STREET?
JUST RETURNED.
THERE WON'T BE A LIFT, PAUL.
THE P.M. CLAIMS THERE'S NOT ENOUGH EVIDENCE TO JUSTIFY BRINGING MCMILLAN BACK TO ENGLAND AGAINST HIS WILL.
BEST TO LET HIM RETURN IN HIS OWN TIME, LEAVE IT FOR DAVID KINNEY AND THE REST AT BOX TO DEAL WITH.
THE PRIME MINISTER JUST WON'T RISK IT.

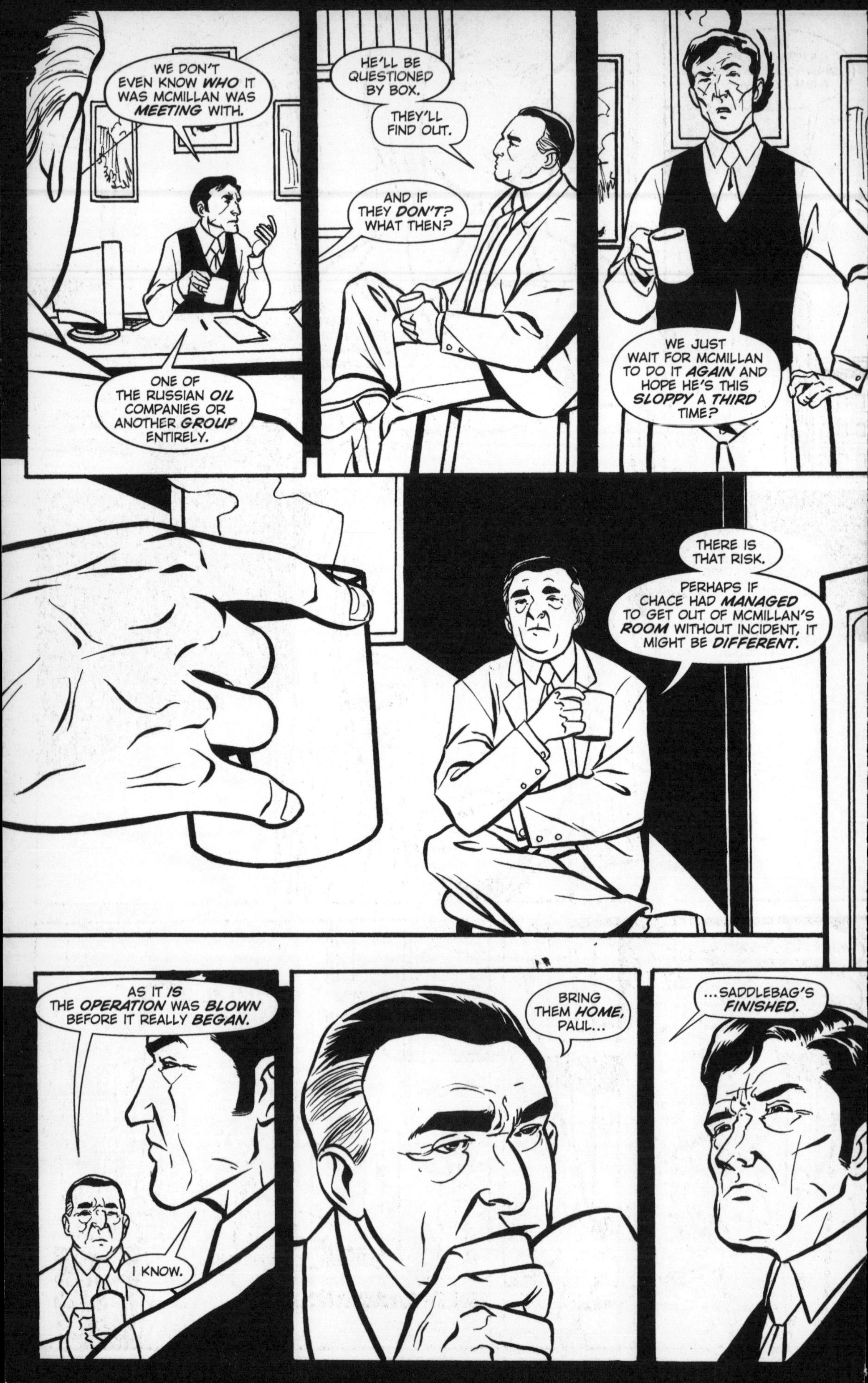
WE DON'T EVEN KNOW WHO IT WAS MCMILLAN WAS MEETING WITH.
ONE OF THE RUSSIAN OIL COMPANIES OR ANOTHER GROUP ENTIRELY.
HE'LL BE QUESTIONED BY BOX.
THEY'LL FIND OUT.
AND IF THEY DON'T? WHAT THEN?
WE JUST WAIT FOR MCMILLAN TO DO IT AGAIN AND HOPE HE'S THIS SLOPPY A THIRD TIME?
THERE IS THAT RISK.
PERHAPS IF CHACE HAD MANAGED TO GET OUT OF MCMILLAN'S ROOM WITHOUT INCIDENT, IT MIGHT BE DIFFERENT.
AS IT IS THE OPERATION WAS BLOWN BEFORE IT REALLY BEGAN.
I KNOW.
BRING THEM HOME, PAUL...
...SADDLEBAG'S FINISHED.

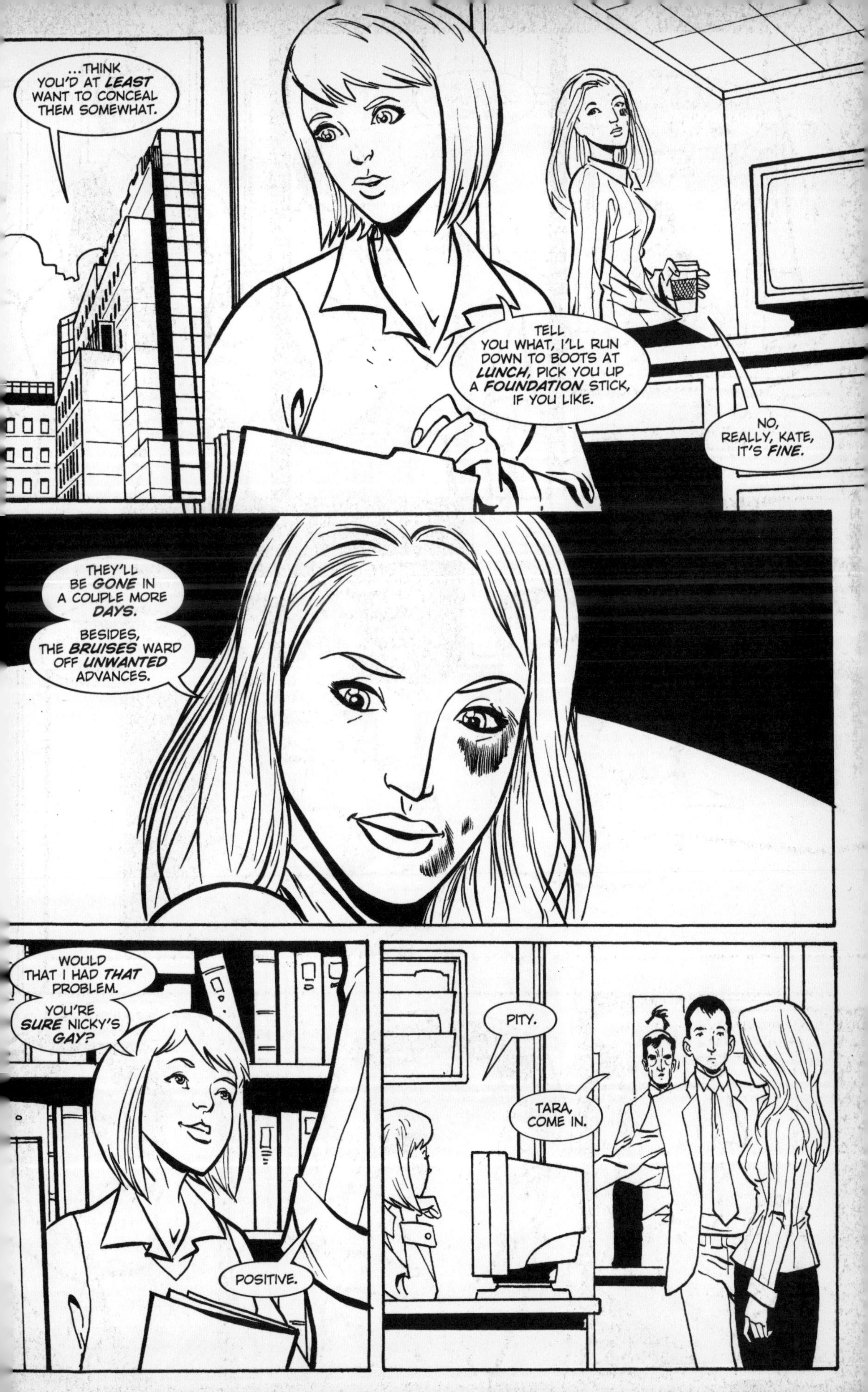
...THINK YOU'D AT LEAST WANT TO CONCEAL THEM SOMEWHAT.
TELL YOU WHAT, I'LL RUN DOWN TO BOOTS AT LUNCH, PICK YOU UP A FOUNDATION STICK, IF YOU LIKE.
NO, REALLY, KATE, IT'S FINE.
THEY'LL BE GONE IN A COUPLE MORE DAYS.
BESIDES, THE BRUISES WARD OFF UNWANTED ADVANCES.
WOULD THAT I HAD THAT PROBLEM.
YOU'RE SURE NICKY'S GAY?
POSITIVE.
PITY.
TARA, COME IN.

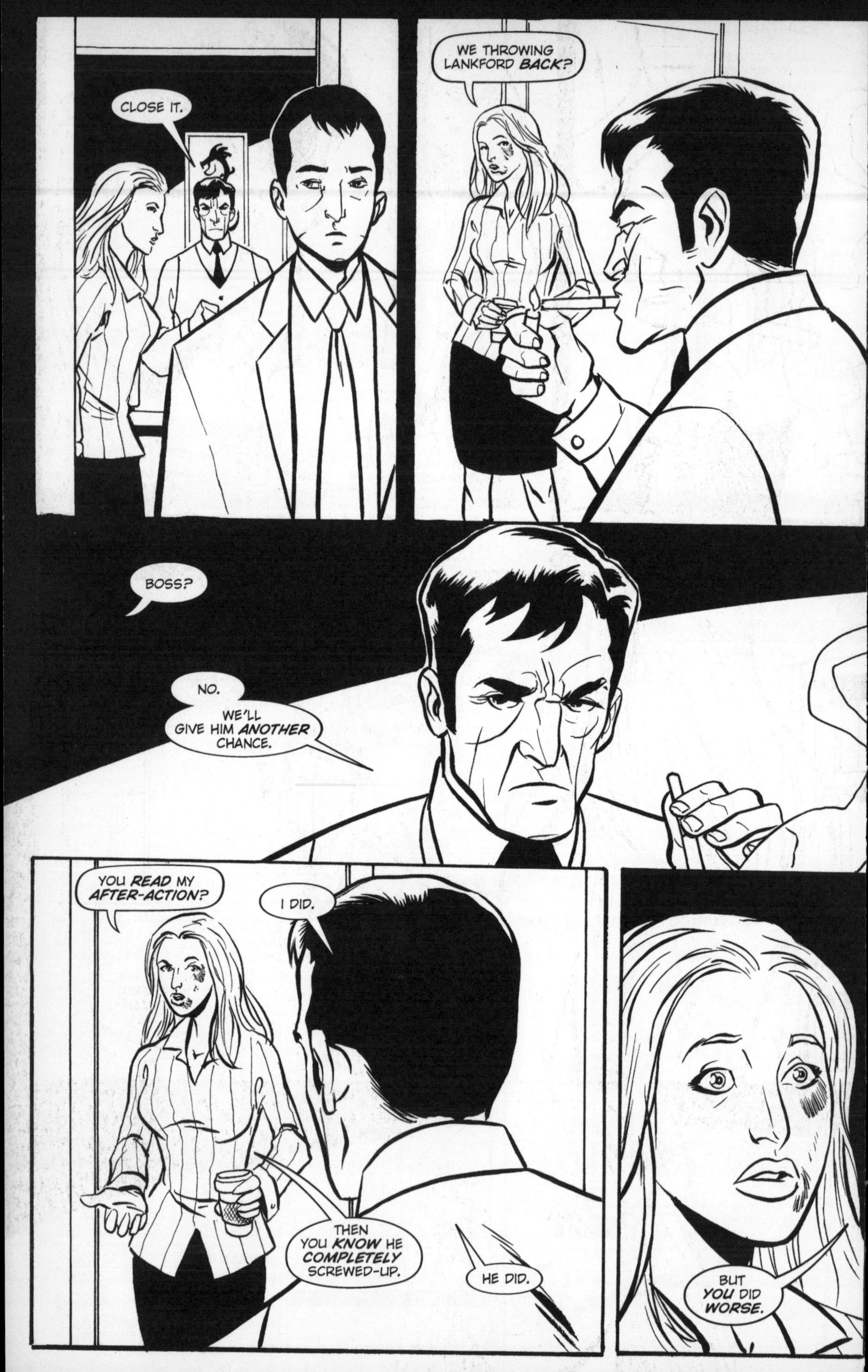
CLOSE IT.
WE THROWING LANKFORD BACK?
BOSS?
NO.
WE'LL GIVE HIM ANOTHER CHANCE.
YOU READ MY AFTER-ACTION?
I DID.
THEN YOU KNOW HE COMPLETELY SCREWED-UP.
HE DID.
BUT YOU DID WORSE.

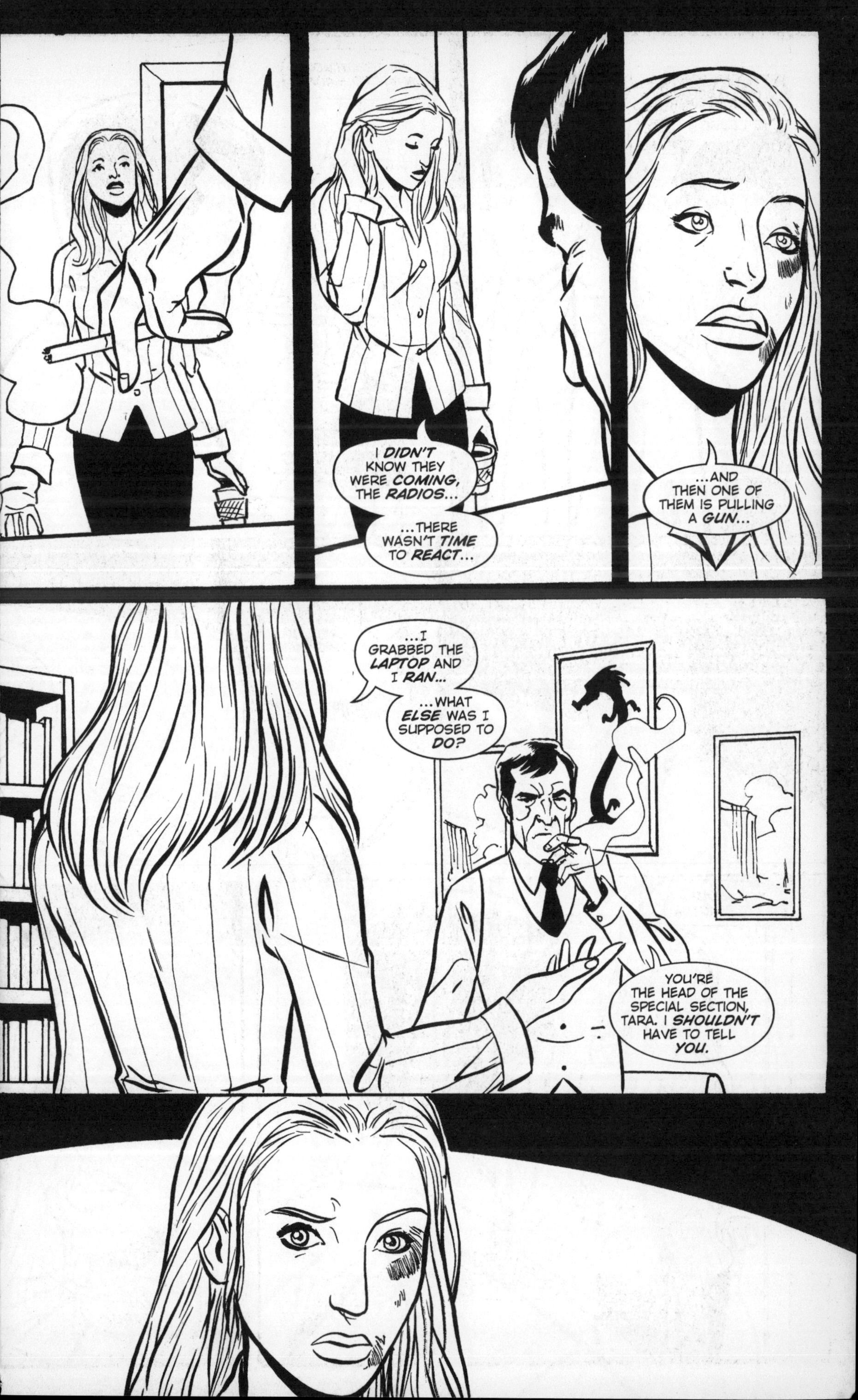
I *DIDN'T* KNOW THEY WERE *COMING,* THE *RADIOS...*
...THERE WASN'T *TIME* TO *REACT...*
...AND THEN ONE OF THEM IS PULLING A *GUN...*
...I GRABBED THE *LAPTOP* AND I *RAN...*
...WHAT *ELSE* WAS I SUPPOSED TO *DO?*
YOU'RE THE HEAD OF THE SPECIAL SECTION, TARA. I *SHOULDN'T* HAVE TO TELL *YOU.*

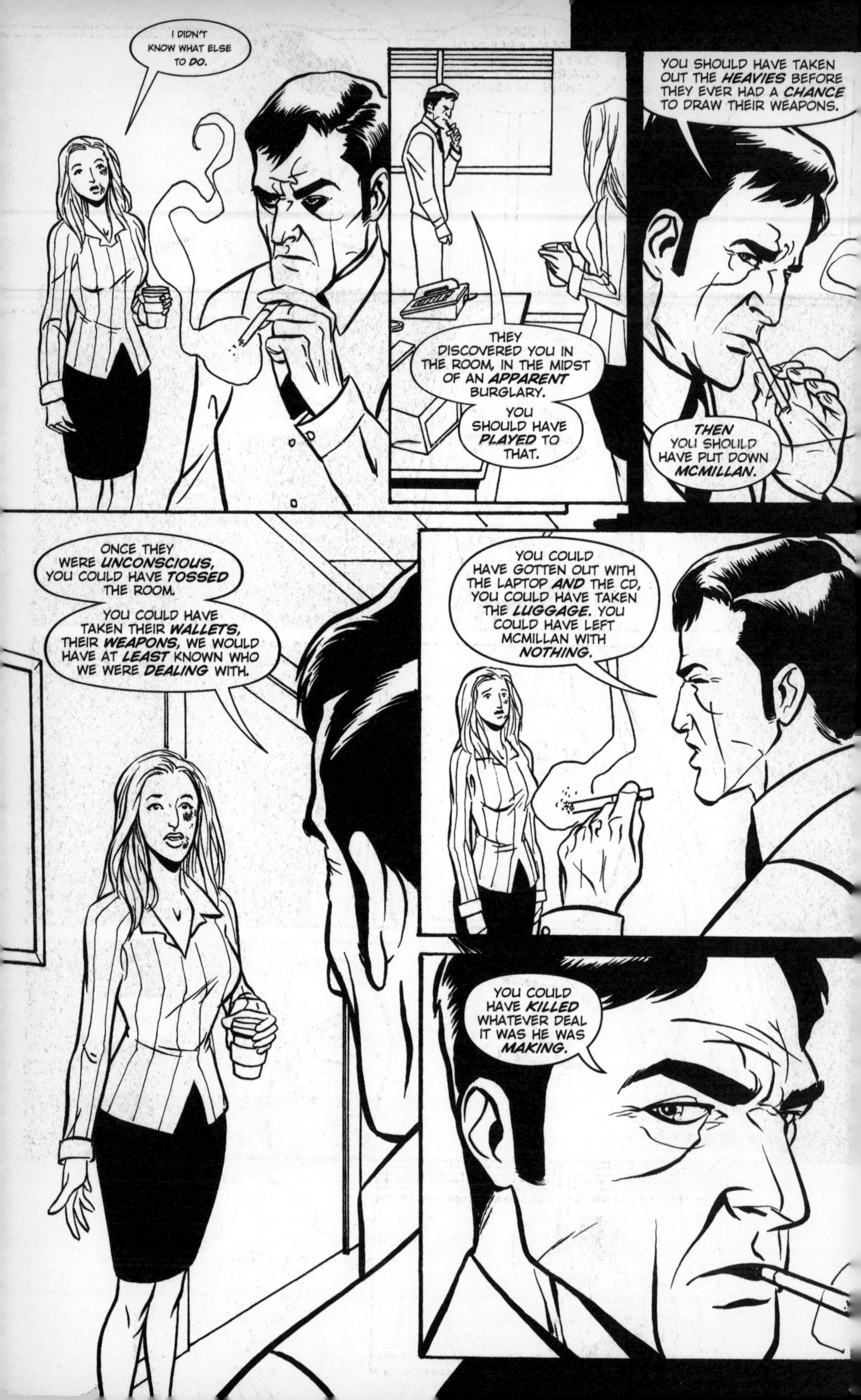
I DIDN'T KNOW WHAT ELSE TO DO.
THEY DISCOVERED YOU IN THE ROOM, IN THE MIDST OF AN APPARENT BURGLARY.
YOU SHOULD HAVE PLAYED TO THAT.
YOU SHOULD HAVE TAKEN OUT THE HEAVIES BEFORE THEY EVER HAD A CHANCE TO DRAW THEIR WEAPONS.
THEN YOU SHOULD HAVE PUT DOWN MCMILLAN.
ONCE THEY WERE UNCONSCIOUS, YOU COULD HAVE TOSSED THE ROOM.
YOU COULD HAVE TAKEN THEIR WALLETS, THEIR WEAPONS, WE WOULD HAVE AT LEAST KNOWN WHO WE WERE DEALING WITH.
YOU COULD HAVE GOTTEN OUT WITH THE LAPTOP AND THE CD, YOU COULD HAVE TAKEN THE LUGGAGE. YOU COULD HAVE LEFT MCMILLAN WITH NOTHING.
YOU COULD HAVE KILLED WHATEVER DEAL IT WAS HE WAS MAKING.

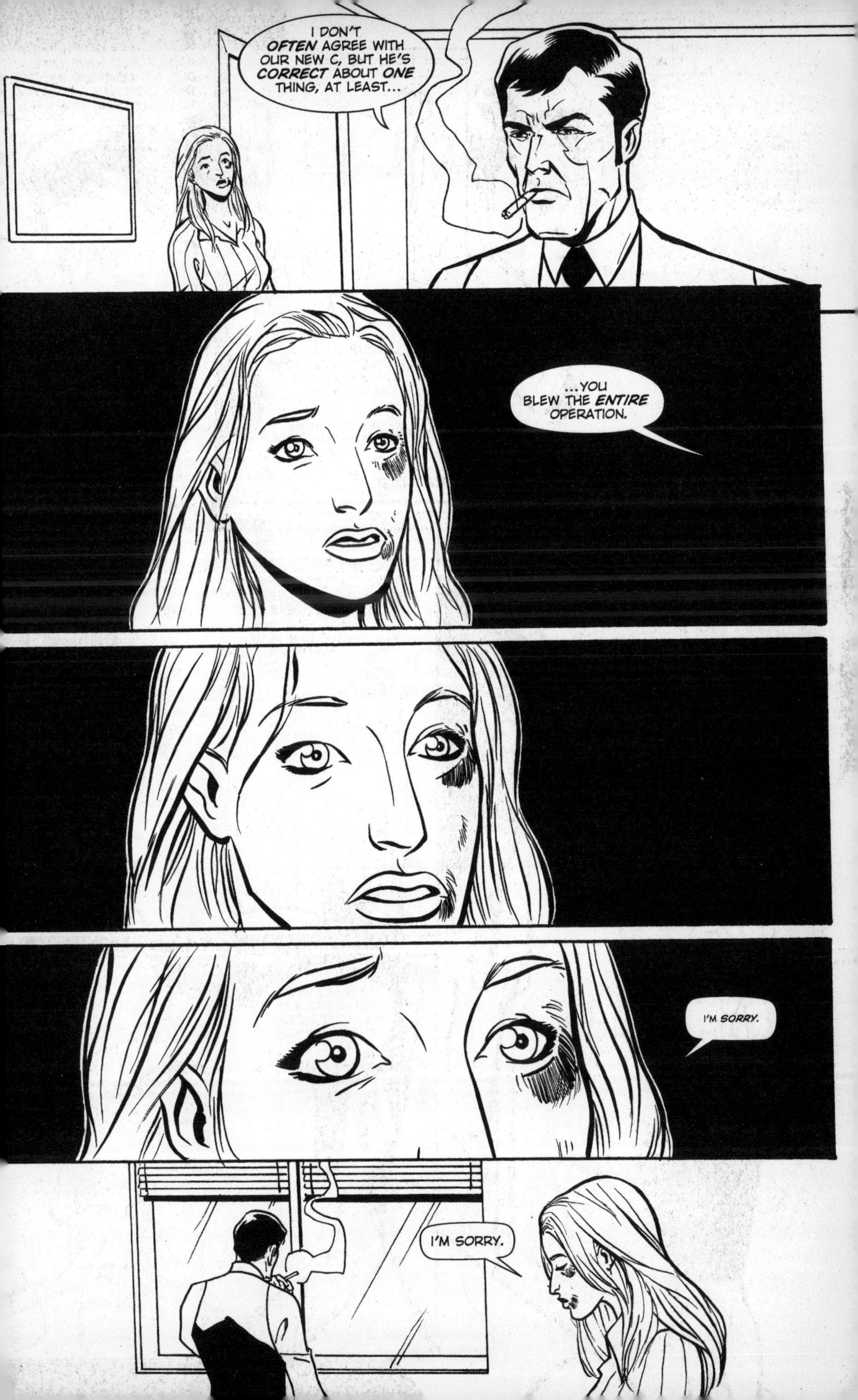
I DON'T OFTEN AGREE WITH OUR NEW C, BUT HE'S CORRECT ABOUT ONE THING, AT LEAST...
...YOU BLEW THE ENTIRE OPERATION.
I'M SORRY.
I'M SORRY.

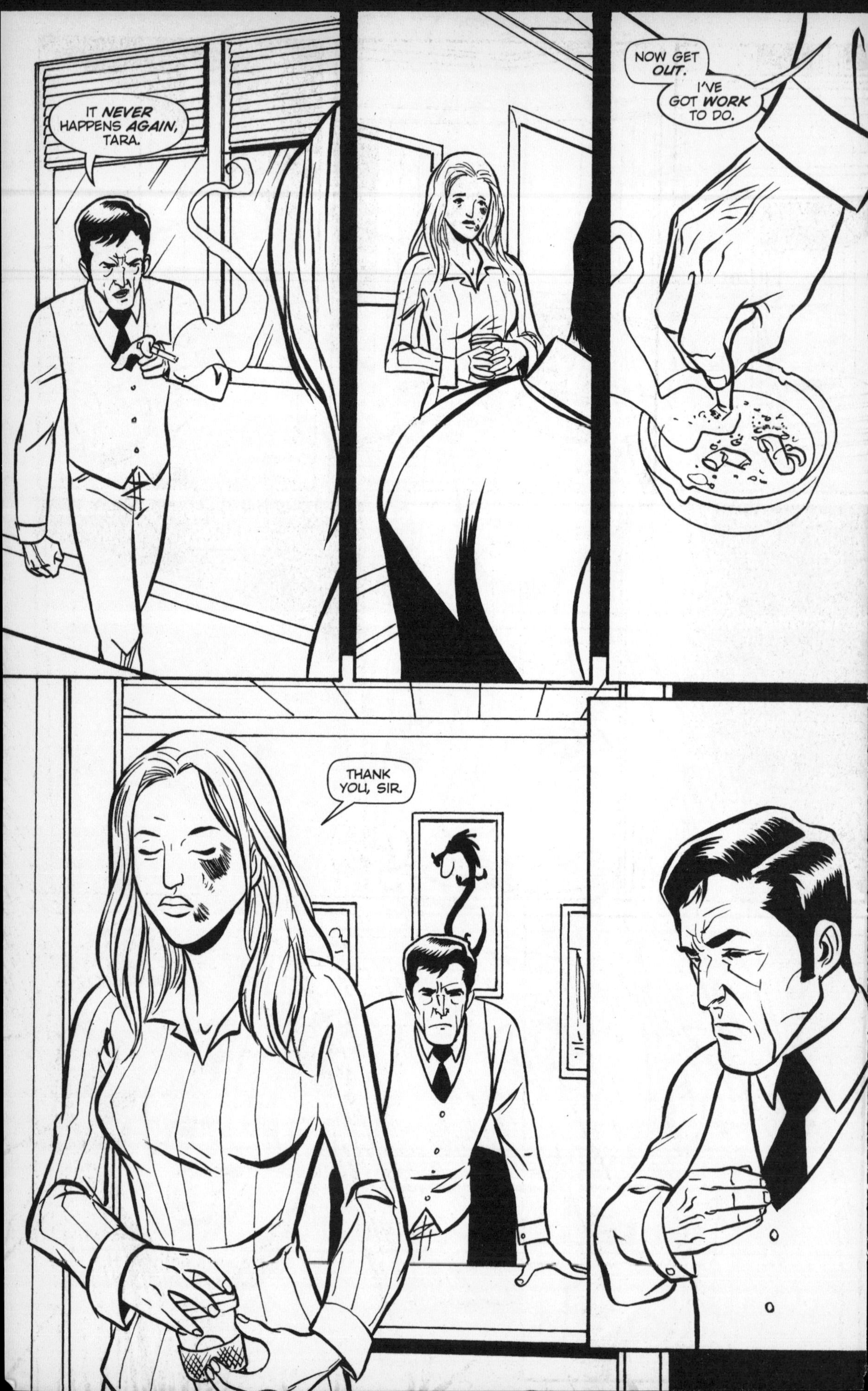
IT NEVER HAPPENS AGAIN, TARA.
NOW GET OUT.
I'VE GOT WORK TO DO.
THANK YOU, SIR.

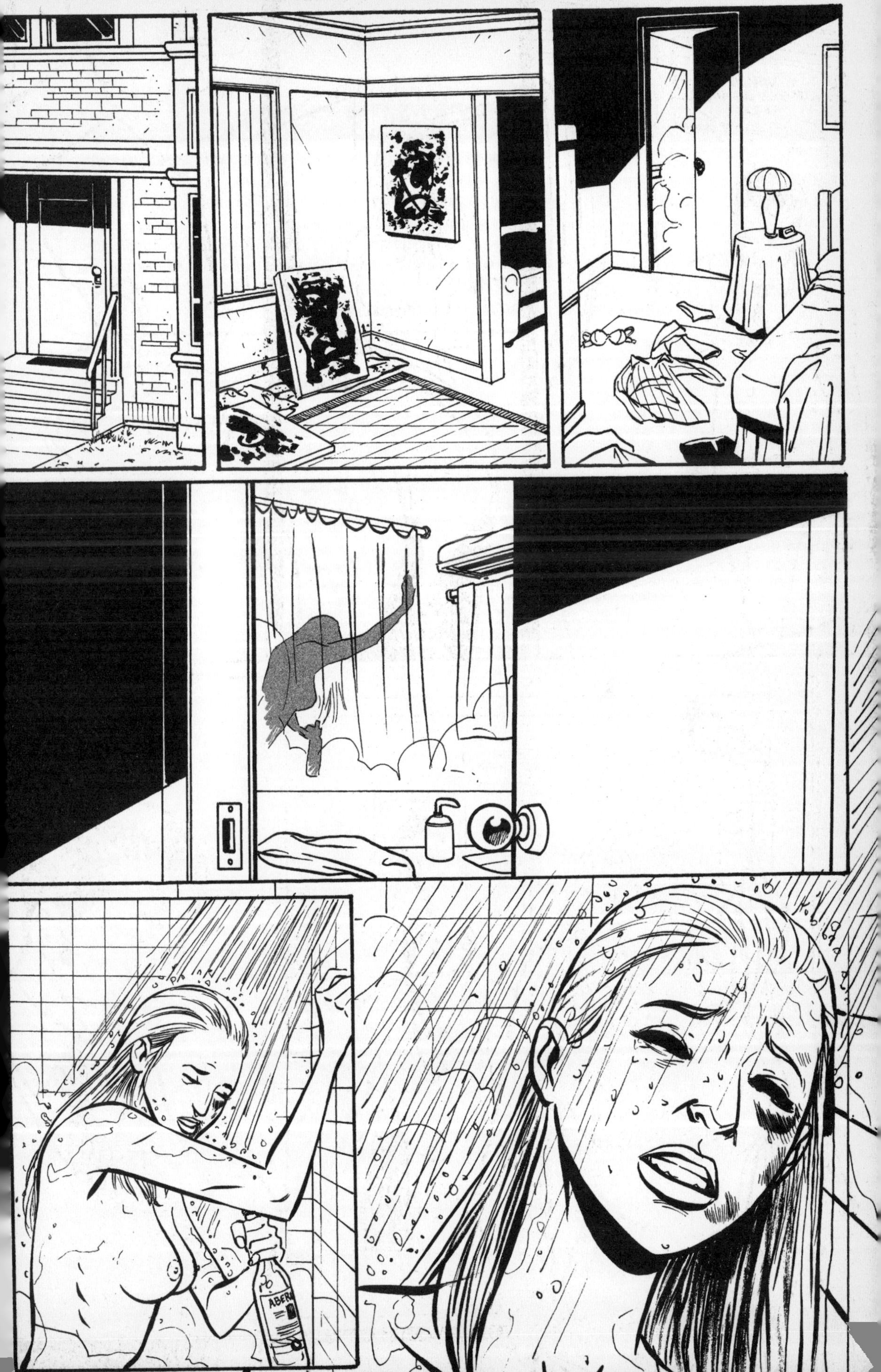

## SPECIAL SECTION:

Though Mike Norton was the seventh artist to collaborate with Mr. Rucka on *Q&C*, he was actually the first artist to submit samples after the book premiered. We immediately knew Mike was going to have to draw an arc for us, but scheduling conflicts prevented him joining the team until *Operation: Saddlebags*. Presented here are Mike's original sketches for the cast of the Special Section—drawn almost three years before he would actually draw them in the comics.

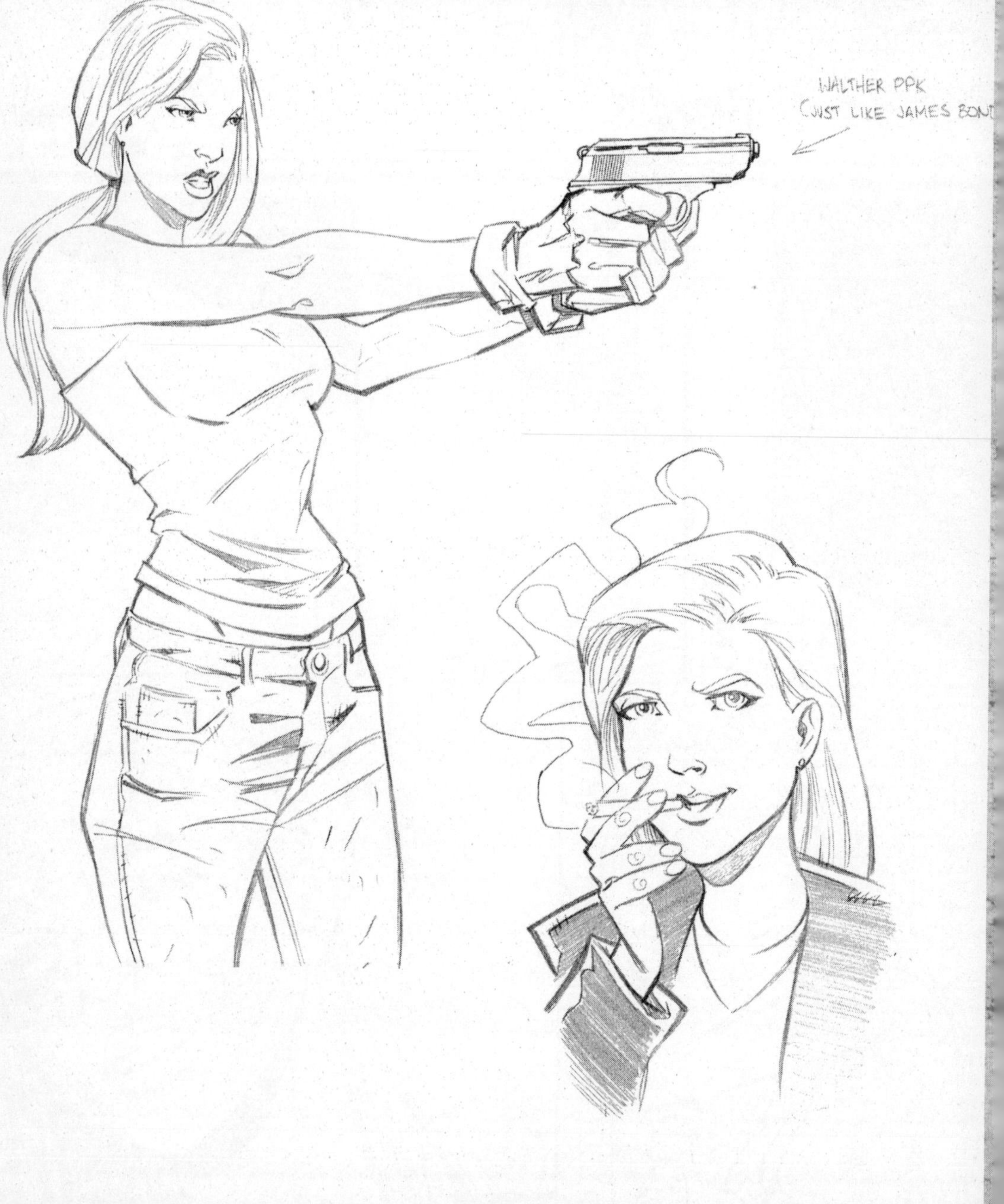
WALTHER PPK
(JUST LIKE JAMES BOND

DAVID
KINNEY

EDWARD
KITTERING

KATE

DONALD
WELDON

TOM
WALLACE

ANGELA
CHENG

PAUL CROCKER

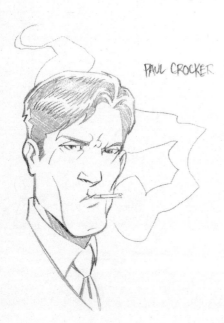

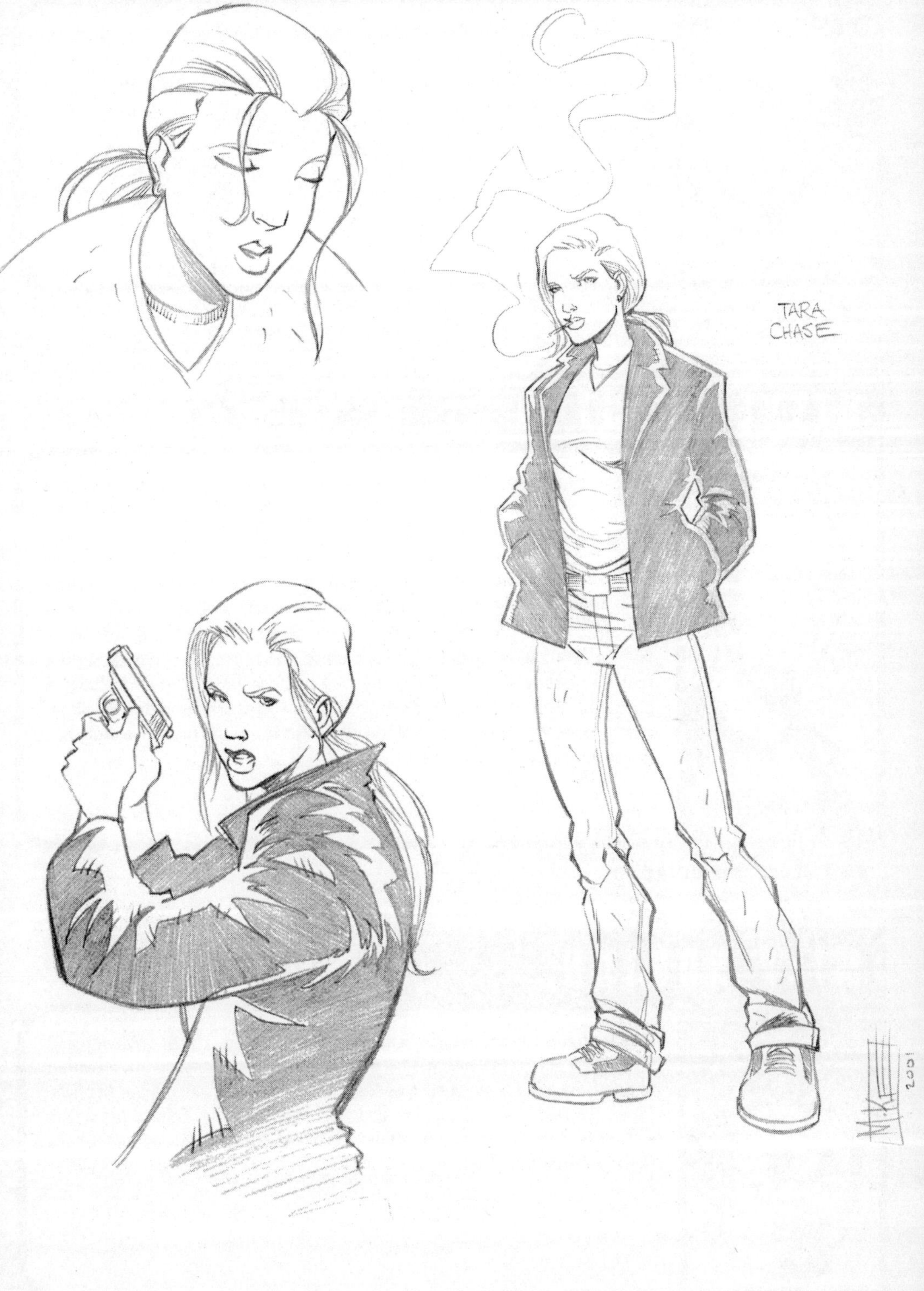
TARA
CHASE
2001

# GREG RUCKA

Born in San Francisco, Greg Rucka was raised on the Monterey Peninsula. He is the author of several novels, including one featuring characters from this very series, as well as several comic books, for which he has won three Eisner Awards. He resides in Portland, Oregon, with his wife, Jennifer, and their children, Elliot and Dashiell.

www.gregrucka.com

# STEVE ROLSTON

Born in Vancouver, BC, Canada, Steve was raised a little further north in a small town called Pender Harbour. After high school he moved to Vancouver to study classical animation at Capilano College. Upon graduating, he spent a couple years drawing storyboards for various cartoon shows. Seeking greater artistic satisfaction, Steve took a departure from animation work to pursue a career in the field of comic books. While honing his skills, he created two animated webcomics starring his own characters Jack Spade & Tony Two-Fist. In 2000, Steve landed his first professional comic gig—illustrating the first four issues of *Queen & Country*. His comic work since then includes a portion of Paul Dini's *Jingle Belle Jubilee* and all the artwork for *Pounded*, a miniseries written by Brian Wood. *Pounded* is a punk rock love story set in Vancouver, where Steve still lives.

www.steverolston.com

# MIKE NORTON

Mike Norton is the second man named "Mike" to work on *Queen & Country* and his skill and enthusiasm matches his predecessor's pound for pound. His attention to detail and grasp of storytelling as blessed such comics as *Jason & the Argobots*, *Closer*, *The Waiting Place*, *G.I. Joe*, and most recently Image Comics' *Night Club* with writer Mike Baron. Norton resides in Chicago, IL and is happy to not have to write his own bio.

www.ihatemike.com

# A GENTLEMAN'S GAME

A QUEEN AND COUNTRY NOVEL

# GREG RUCKA

The story of Tara Chace continues in *A Gentleman's Game: A Queen & Country Novel*!
Available now from Bantam Books and a bookseller near you!

# Other books from Greg Rucka and Oni Press

**"Greg Rucka is not a lesser writer. As an author, he thrives in political, moral and emotional complexity."**

**– Warren Ellis, creator of Transmetropolitan *and* Global Frequency**

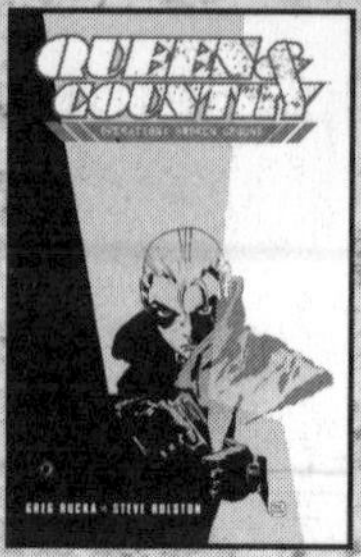
QUEEN & COUNTRY

*Queen & Country™ Vol. 1*
***Operation: Broken Ground***
by Greg Rucka, Steve Rolston & Stan Sakai
128 pages • black-and-white interiors
$11.95 US • ISBN 1-929998-21-X

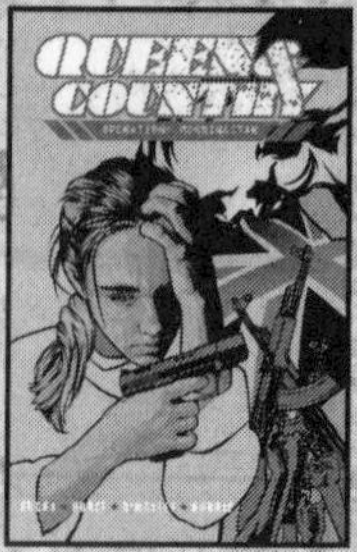
QUEEN & COUNTRY

*Queen & Country™ Vol. 2*
***Operation: Morningstar***
by Greg Rucka, Brian Hurtt, Bryan O'Malley, and Christine Norrie
88 pages • black-and-white interiors
$8.95 US • ISBN 1-929998-35-X

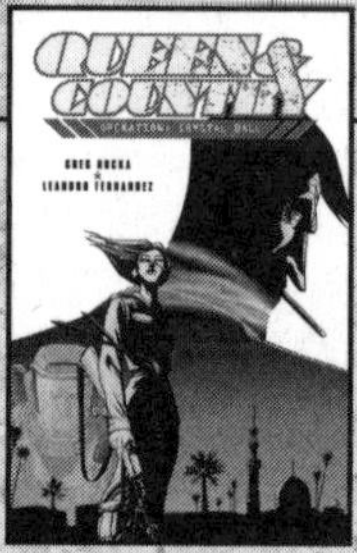
QUEEN & COUNTRY

*Queen & Country™ Vol. 3*
***Operation: Crystal Ball***
by Greg Rucka & Leandro Fernandez
144 pages • black-and-white interiors
$14.95 US • ISBN 1-929998-49-X

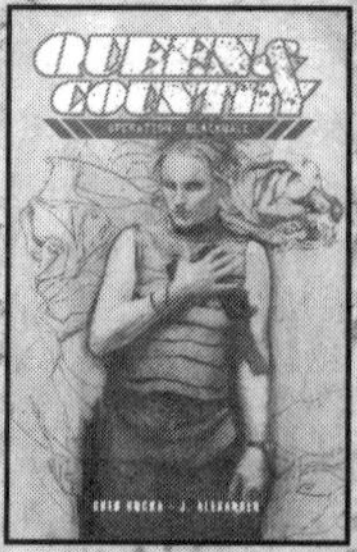
QUEEN & COUNTRY

*Queen & Country™ Vol. 4*
***Operation: Blackwall***
by Greg Rucka & J. Alexander
88 pages • black-and-white interiors
$9.95 US • ISBN 1-929998-68-6

**"Whiteout's *well researched, well written and expertly rendered. Don't buy it for those reasons, though. Buy it because Carrie Stetko's mouthy, freckled and cool...*"**

***– Kelly Sue DeConnick, artbomb.net***

**For a comics store near you, call 1-888-COMIC-BOOK or visit www.the-master-list.com.**

**For more information on more Oni Press books go to: www.onipress.com**

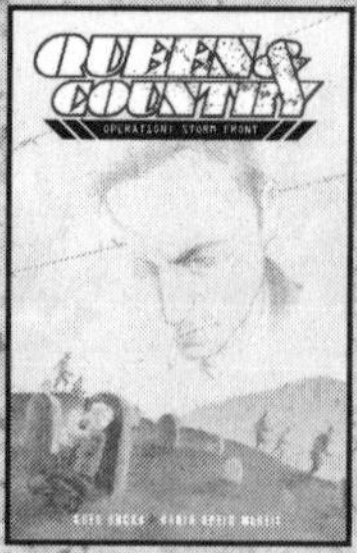
QUEEN & COUNTRY

*Queen & Country™ Vol. 5*
***Operation: Storm Front***
by Greg Rucka & Carla Speed McNeil
152 pages • black-and-white interiors
$14.95 US • ISBN 1-929998-84-8

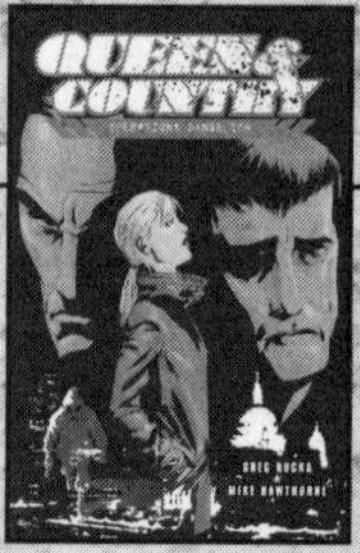
QUEEN & COUNTRY

*Queen & Country™ Vol. 6*
***Operation: Dandelion***
by Greg Rucka & Mike Hawthorne
120 pages • black-and-white interiors
$11.95 US • 1-929998-99-0

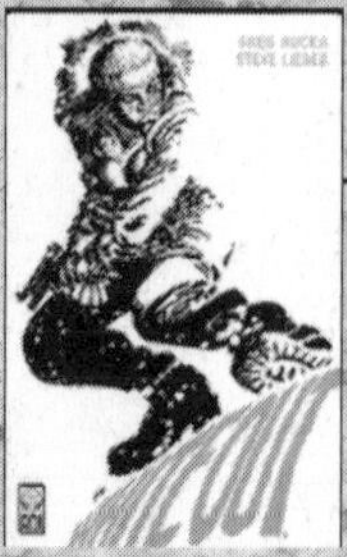
GREG RUCKA
STEVE LIEBER
WHITEOUT

***Whiteout™***
by Greg Rucka & Steve Lieber
128 pages • black-and-white interiors
$11.95 US • ISBN 0-9667127-1-4

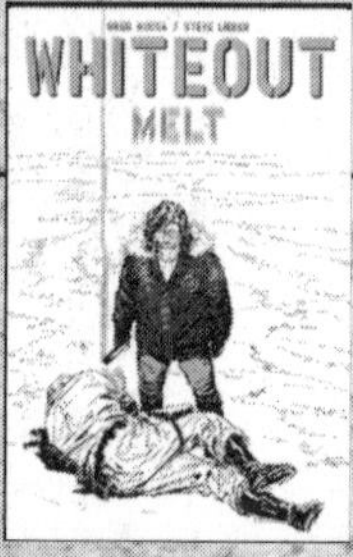
GREG RUCKA / STEVE LIEBER
WHITEOUT
MELT

***Whiteout: Melt™***
by Greg Rucka & Steve Lieber
128 pages • black-and-white interiors
$11.95 US • ISBN 1-929998-03-1

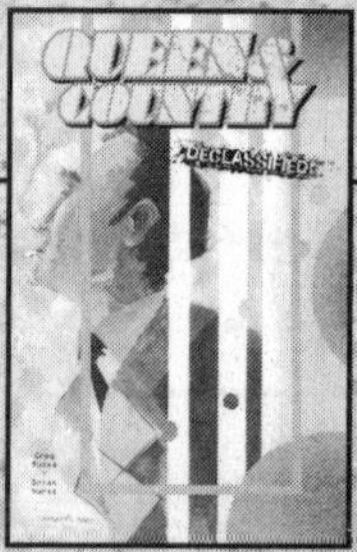
QUEEN & COUNTRY
DECLASSIFIED

***Queen & Country™***
***Declassified Vol. 1***
by Greg Rucka & Brian Hurtt
96 pages • black-and-white interiors
$8.95 US • ISBN 1-929998-58-9